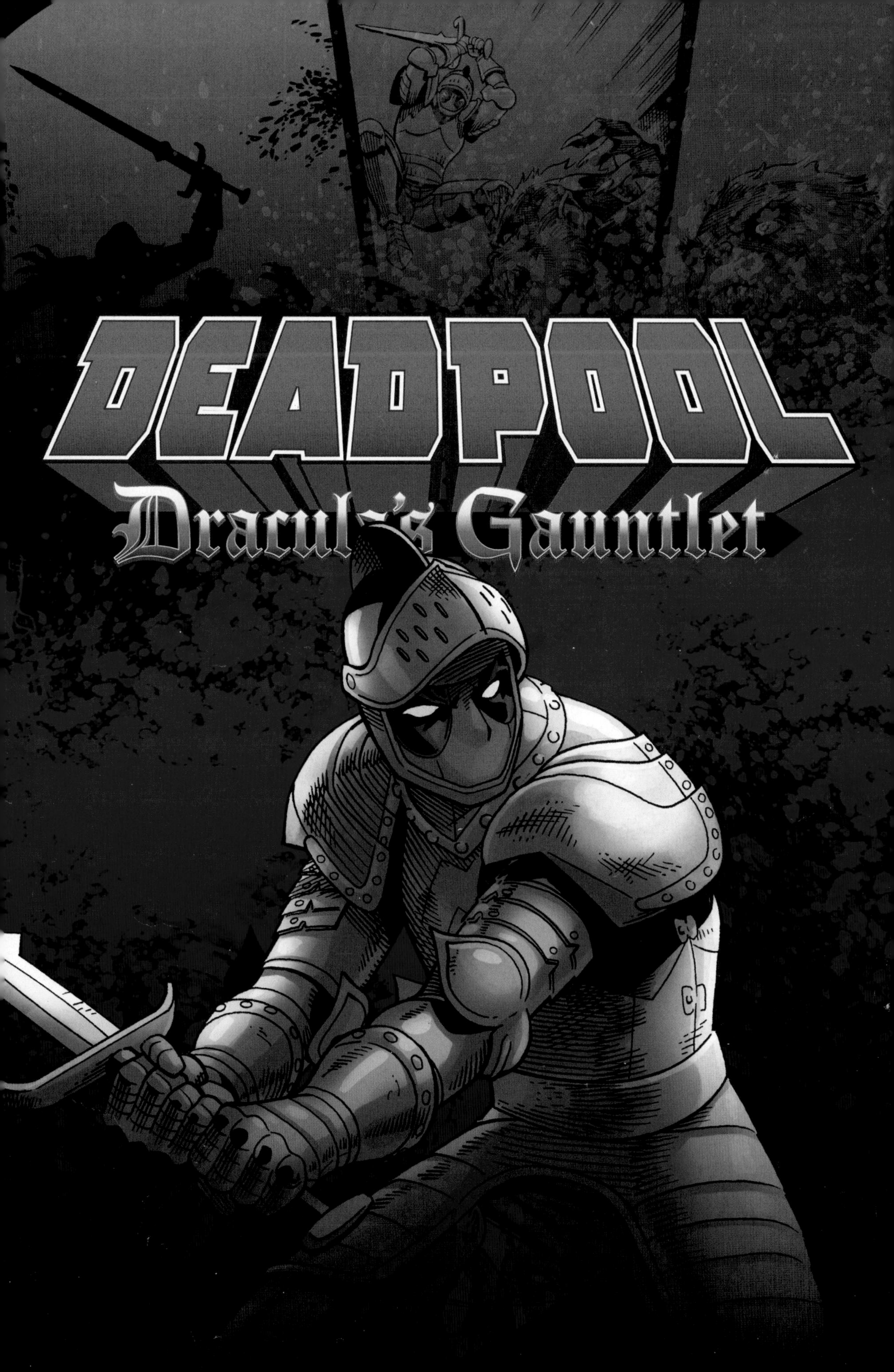
DEADPOOL
Dracula's Gauntlet

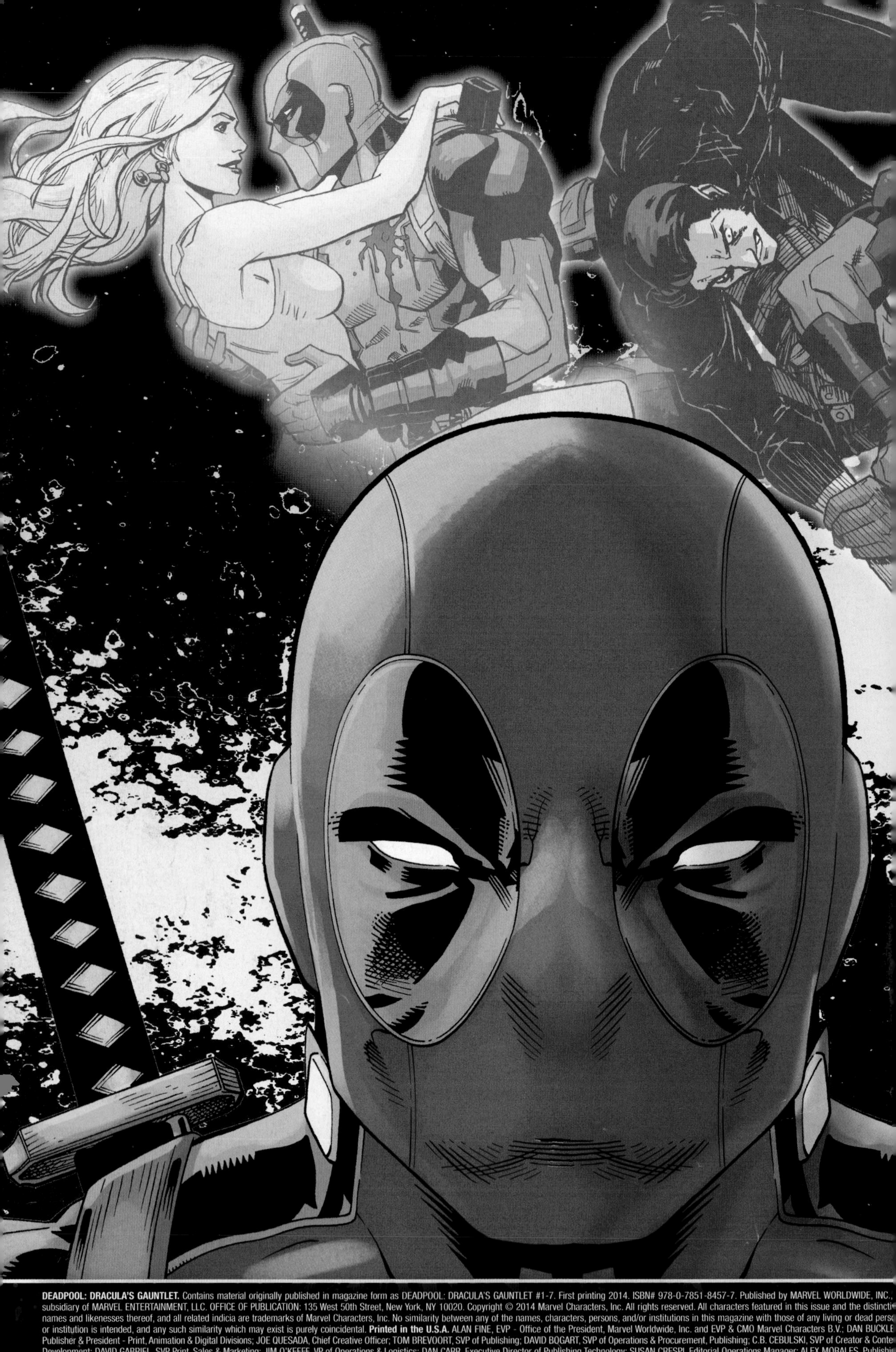

DEADPOOL: DRACULA'S GAUNTLET. Contains material originally published in magazine form as DEADPOOL: DRACULA'S GAUNTLET #1-7. First printing 2014. ISBN# 978-0-7851-8457-7. Published by MARVEL WORLDWIDE, INC., a subsidiary of MARVEL ENTERTAINMENT, LLC. OFFICE OF PUBLICATION: 135 West 50th Street, New York, NY 10020. **Printed in the U.S.A.** ALAN FINE, EVP - Office of the President, Marvel Worldwide, Inc. and EVP & CMO Marvel Characters B.V.; DAN BUCKLE Publisher & President - Print, Animation & Digital Divisions; JOE QUESADA, Chief Creative Officer; TOM BREVOORT, SVP of Publishing; DAVID BOGART, SVP of Operations & Procurement, Publishing; C.B. CEBULSKI, SVP of Creator & Conte Development; DAVID GABRIEL, SVP Print, Sales & Marketing; JIM O'KEEFE, VP of Operations & Logistics; DAN CARR, Executive Director of Publishing Technology; SUSAN CRESPI, Editorial Operations Manager; ALEX MORALES, Publishi Operations Manager; STAN LEE, Chairman Emeritus. For information regarding advertising in Marvel Comics or on Marvel.com, please contact Niza Disla, Director of Marvel Partnerships, at ndisla@marvel.com. For Marvel subscripti

DEADPOOL
Dracula's Gauntlet

STORY **BRIAN POSEHN
& GERRY DUGGAN**

WRITER **GERRY DUGGAN**

STORYBOARDS **REILLY BROWN**
PENCILERS **REILLY BROWN** (Chapters 1-8, 10-14)
WITH **KHARY RANDOLPH** (9) & **SCOTT KOBLISH** (11-13)
INKERS **REILLY BROWN** (1-4),
NELSON DECASTRO (5-7, 10, 12-14),
TERRY PALLOT (7-8, 11-13), **KHARY RANDOLPH** (9)
& **SCOTT KOBLISH** (11-13)

COLORISTS **JIM CHARALAMPIDIS** (1-5, 7, 9, 12-13) &
JIM CAMPBELL (6, 8, 10-11, 14)
LETTERERS **VC'S JOE SABINO**
WITH **CHRIS ELIOPOULOS** (11)
COVER ARTISTS **REILLY BROWN** &
JIM CHARALAMPIDIS

ASSISTANT EDITORS **FRANKIE JOHNSON** & **XANDER JAROWEY**
EDITOR **JORDAN D. WHITE**

COLLECTION EDITOR **ALEX STARBUCK**
ASSISTANT EDITOR **SARAH BRUNSTAD**
EDITORS, SPECIAL PROJECTS **JENNIFER GRÜNWALD & MARK D. BEAZLEY**
SENIOR EDITOR, SPECIAL PROJECTS **JEFF YOUNGQUIST**
SVP PRINT, SALES & MARKETING **DAVID GABRIEL**
BOOK DESIGNER **NELSON RIBEIRO**

EDITOR IN CHIEF **AXEL ALONSO**
CHIEF CREATIVE OFFICER **JOE QUESADA**
PUBLISHER **DAN BUCKLEY**
EXECUTIVE PRODUCER **ALAN FINE**

DEADPOOL CREATED BY **ROB LIEFELD & FABIAN NICIEZA**

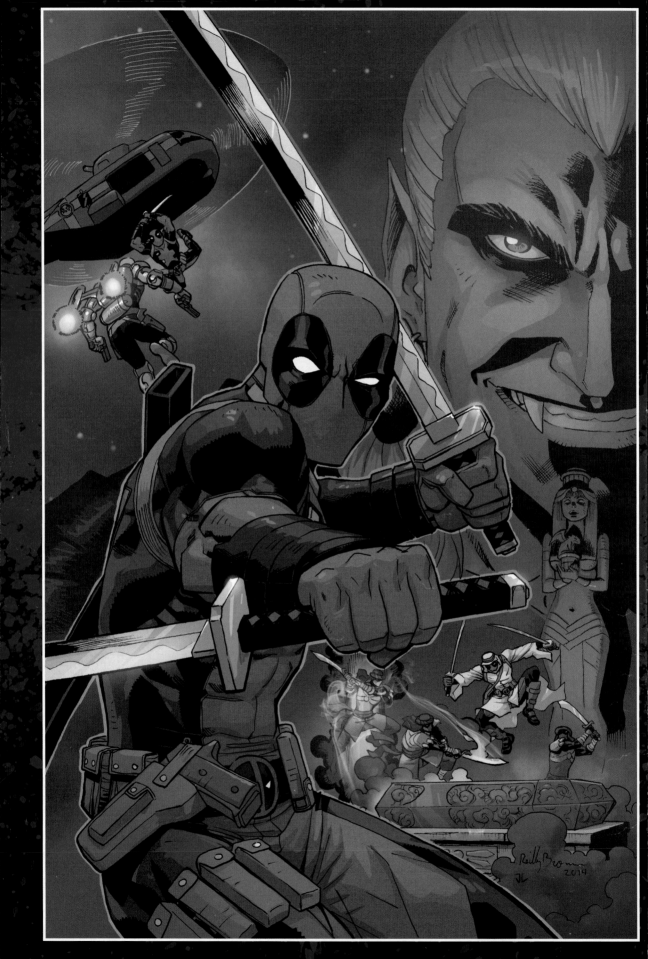

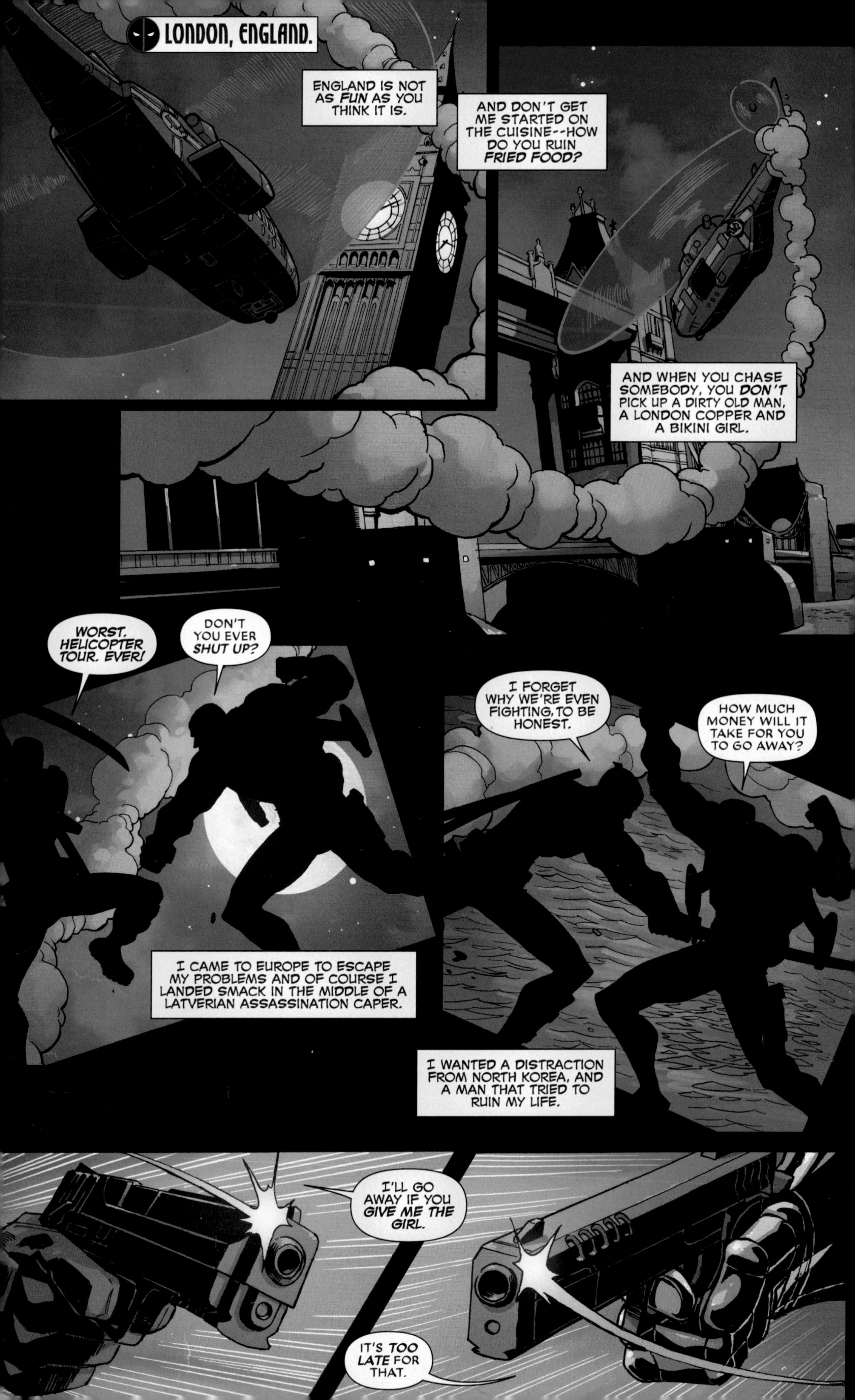
LONDON, ENGLAND.
ENGLAND IS NOT AS FUN AS YOU THINK IT IS.
AND DON'T GET ME STARTED ON THE CUISINE--HOW DO YOU RUIN FRIED FOOD?
AND WHEN YOU CHASE SOMEBODY, YOU DON'T PICK UP A DIRTY OLD MAN, A LONDON COPPER AND A BIKINI GIRL.
WORST. HELICOPTER TOUR. EVER!
DON'T YOU EVER SHUT UP?
I CAME TO EUROPE TO ESCAPE MY PROBLEMS AND OF COURSE I LANDED SMACK IN THE MIDDLE OF A LATVERIAN ASSASSINATION CAPER.
I FORGET WHY WE'RE EVEN FIGHTING, TO BE HONEST.
HOW MUCH MONEY WILL IT TAKE FOR YOU TO GO AWAY?
I WANTED A DISTRACTION FROM NORTH KOREA, AND A MAN THAT TRIED TO RUIN MY LIFE.
I'LL GO AWAY IF YOU GIVE ME THE GIRL.
IT'S TOO LATE FOR THAT.

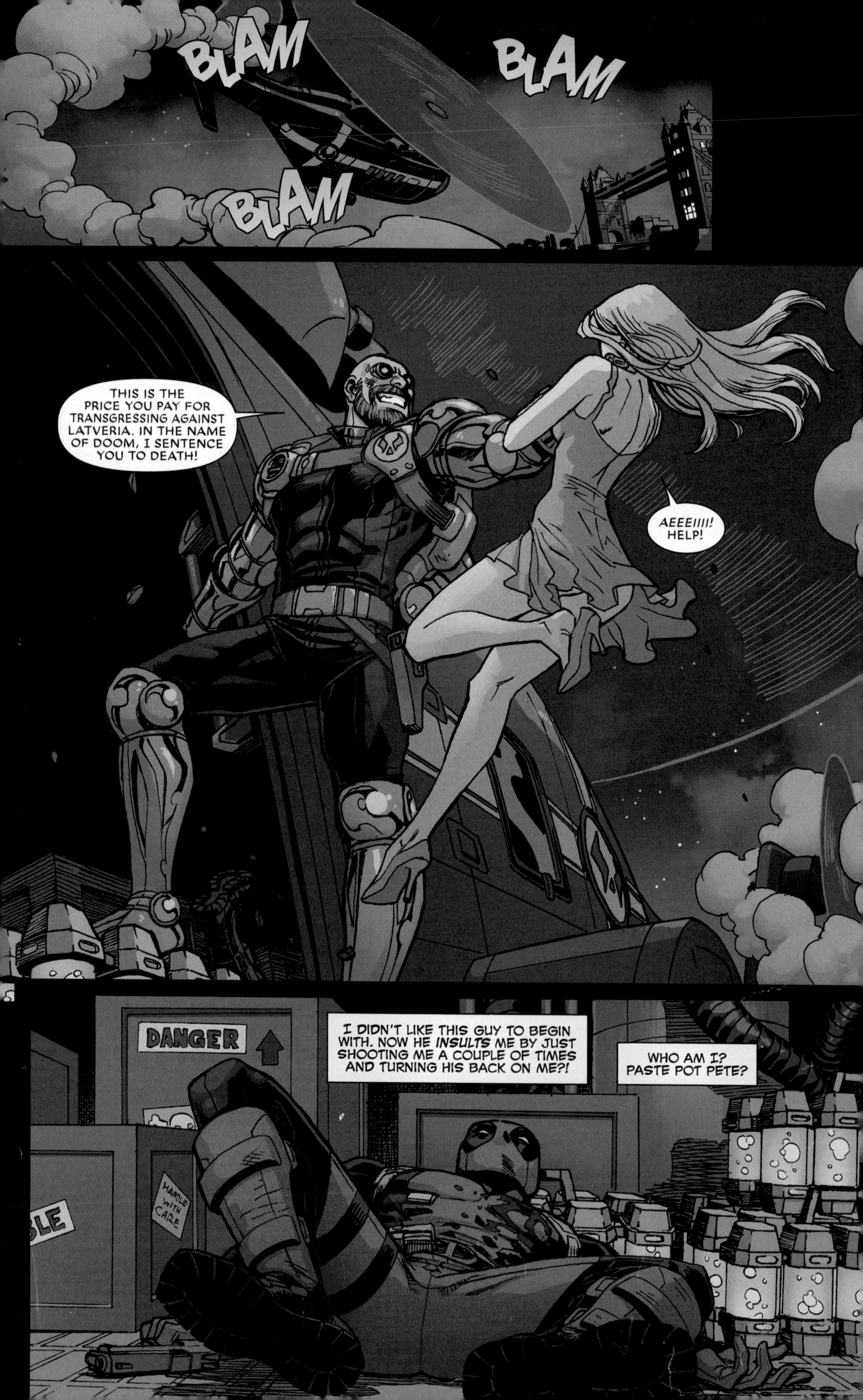

BLAM
BLAM
BLAM
THIS IS THE PRICE YOU PAY FOR TRANSGRESSING AGAINST LATVERIA. IN THE NAME OF DOOM, I SENTENCE YOU TO DEATH!
AEEEIIII! HELP!
DANGER
I DIDN'T LIKE THIS GUY TO BEGIN WITH. NOW HE *INSULTS* ME BY JUST SHOOTING ME A COUPLE OF TIMES AND TURNING HIS BACK ON ME?!
WHO AM I? PASTE POT PETE?
HANDLE WITH CARE

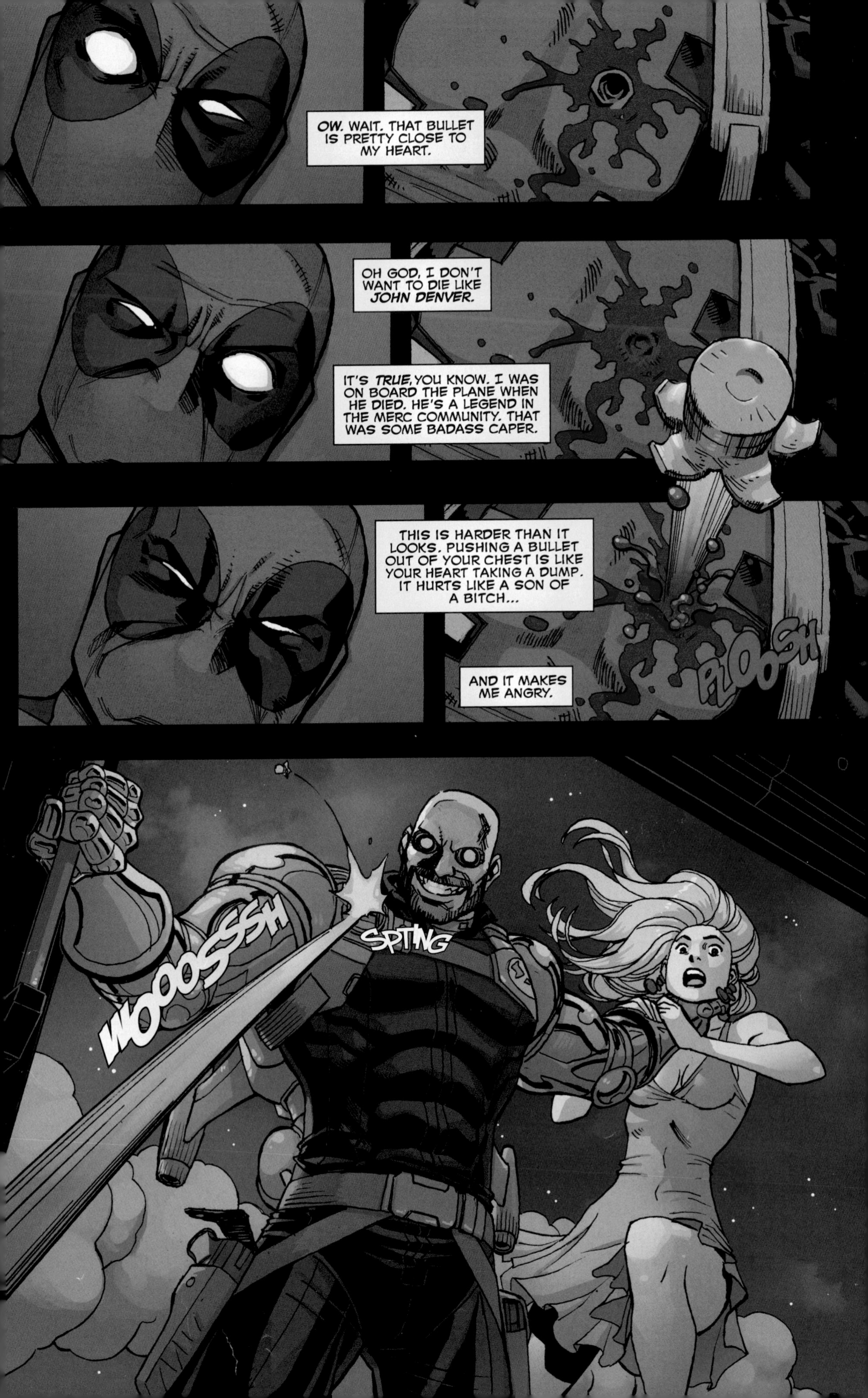
OW. WAIT. THAT BULLET IS PRETTY CLOSE TO MY HEART.
OH GOD, I DON'T WANT TO DIE LIKE JOHN DENVER.
IT'S TRUE, YOU KNOW. I WAS ON BOARD THE PLANE WHEN HE DIED. HE'S A LEGEND IN THE MERC COMMUNITY. THAT WAS SOME BADASS CAPER.
THIS IS HARDER THAN IT LOOKS. PUSHING A BULLET OUT OF YOUR CHEST IS LIKE YOUR HEART TAKING A DUMP. IT HURTS LIKE A SON OF A BITCH...
PLOOSH
AND IT MAKES ME ANGRY.
WOOOSSSH
SPTING

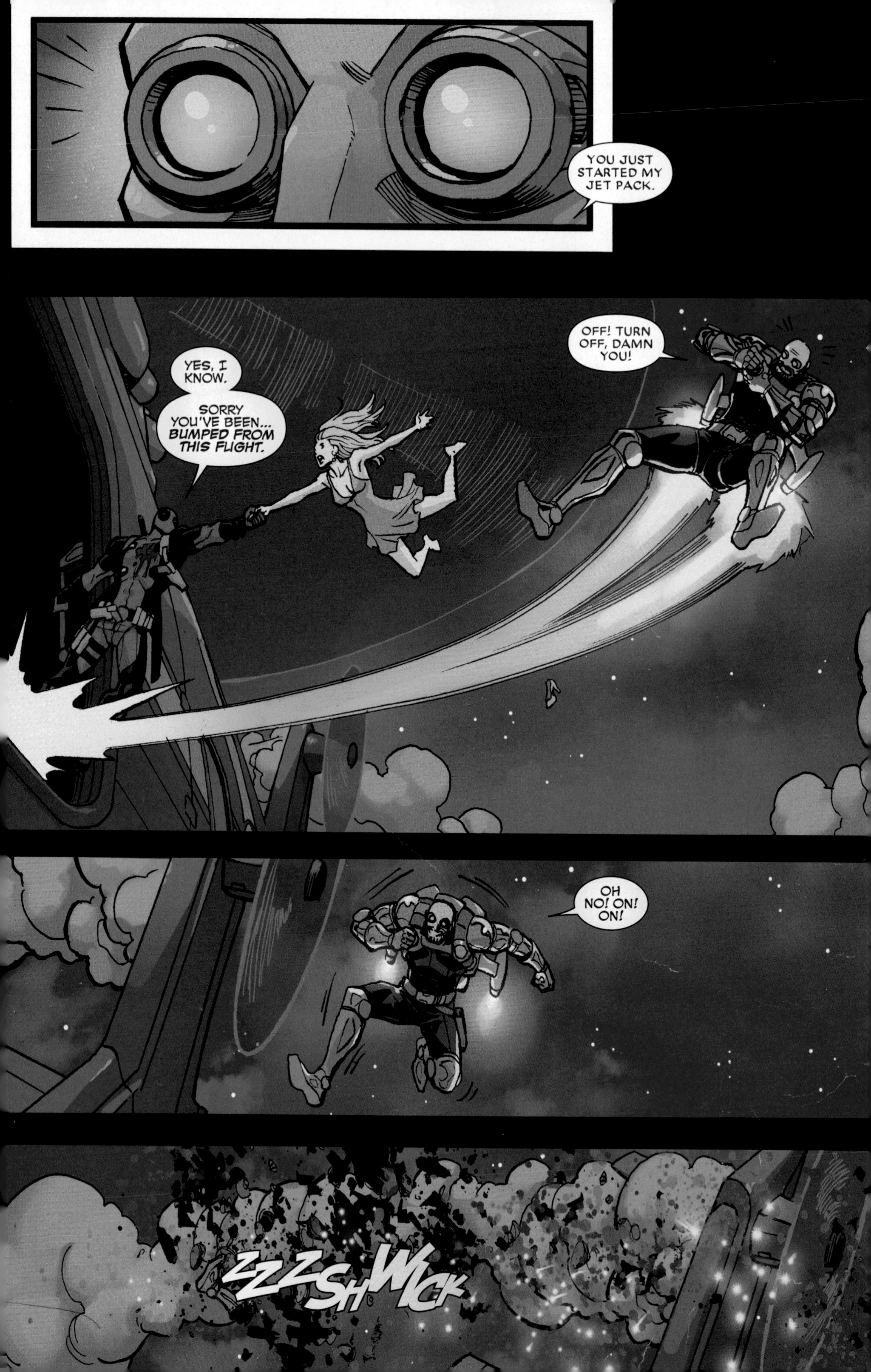
YOU JUST STARTED MY JET PACK.
YES, I KNOW.
SORRY YOU'VE BEEN... BUMPED FROM THIS FLIGHT.
OFF! TURN OFF, DAMN YOU!
OH NO! ON! ON!
ZZZZSHWICK

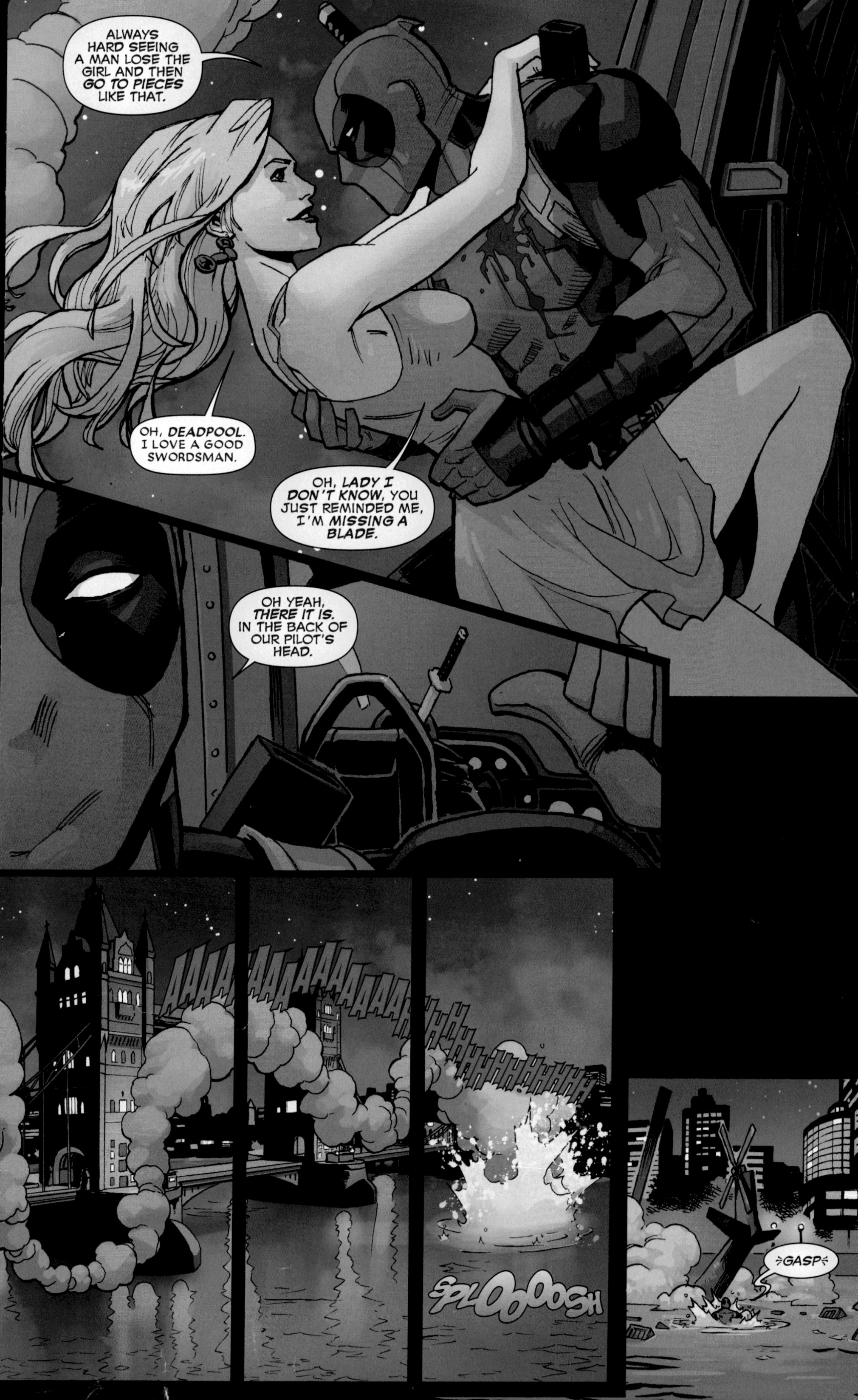
ALWAYS HARD SEEING A MAN LOSE THE GIRL AND THEN GO TO PIECES LIKE THAT.
OH, DEADPOOL. I LOVE A GOOD SWORDSMAN.
OH, LADY I DON'T KNOW, YOU JUST REMINDED ME, I'M MISSING A BLADE.
OH YEAH, THERE IT IS. IN THE BACK OF OUR PILOT'S HEAD.
SPLOOOOOSH
GASP

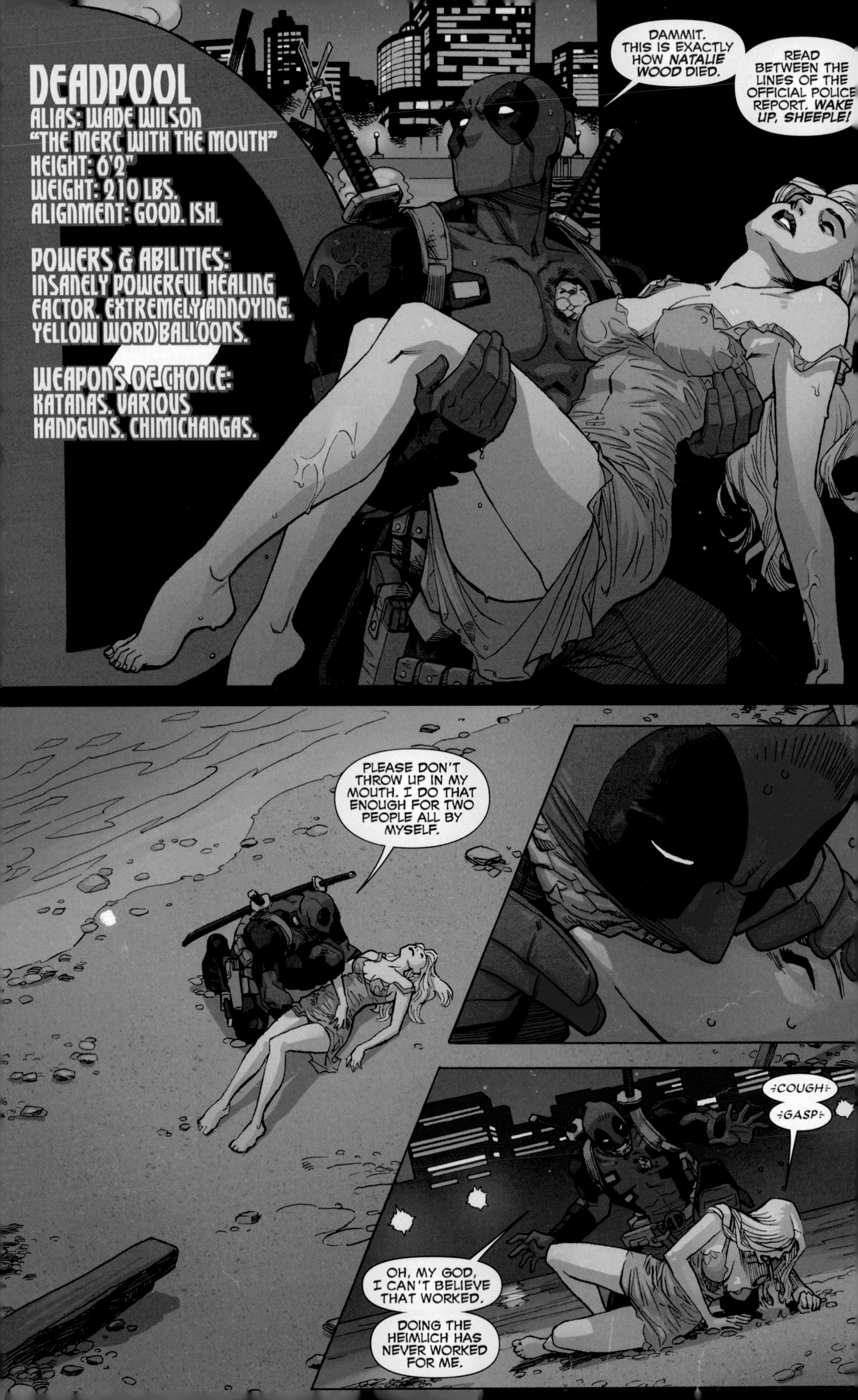
DEADPOOL
ALIAS: WADE WILSON
"THE MERC WITH THE MOUTH"
HEIGHT: 6'2"
WEIGHT: 210 LBS.
ALIGNMENT: GOOD. ISH.
POWERS & ABILITIES:
INSANELY POWERFUL HEALING FACTOR. EXTREMELY ANNOYING. YELLOW WORD BALLOONS.
WEAPONS OF CHOICE:
KATANAS. VARIOUS HANDGUNS. CHIMICHANGAS.
DAMMIT. THIS IS EXACTLY HOW NATALIE WOOD DIED.
READ BETWEEN THE LINES OF THE OFFICIAL POLICE REPORT. WAKE UP, SHEEPLE!
PLEASE DON'T THROW UP IN MY MOUTH. I DO THAT ENOUGH FOR TWO PEOPLE ALL BY MYSELF.
COUGH
GASP
OH, MY GOD, I CAN'T BELIEVE THAT WORKED.
DOING THE HEIMLICH HAS NEVER WORKED FOR ME.

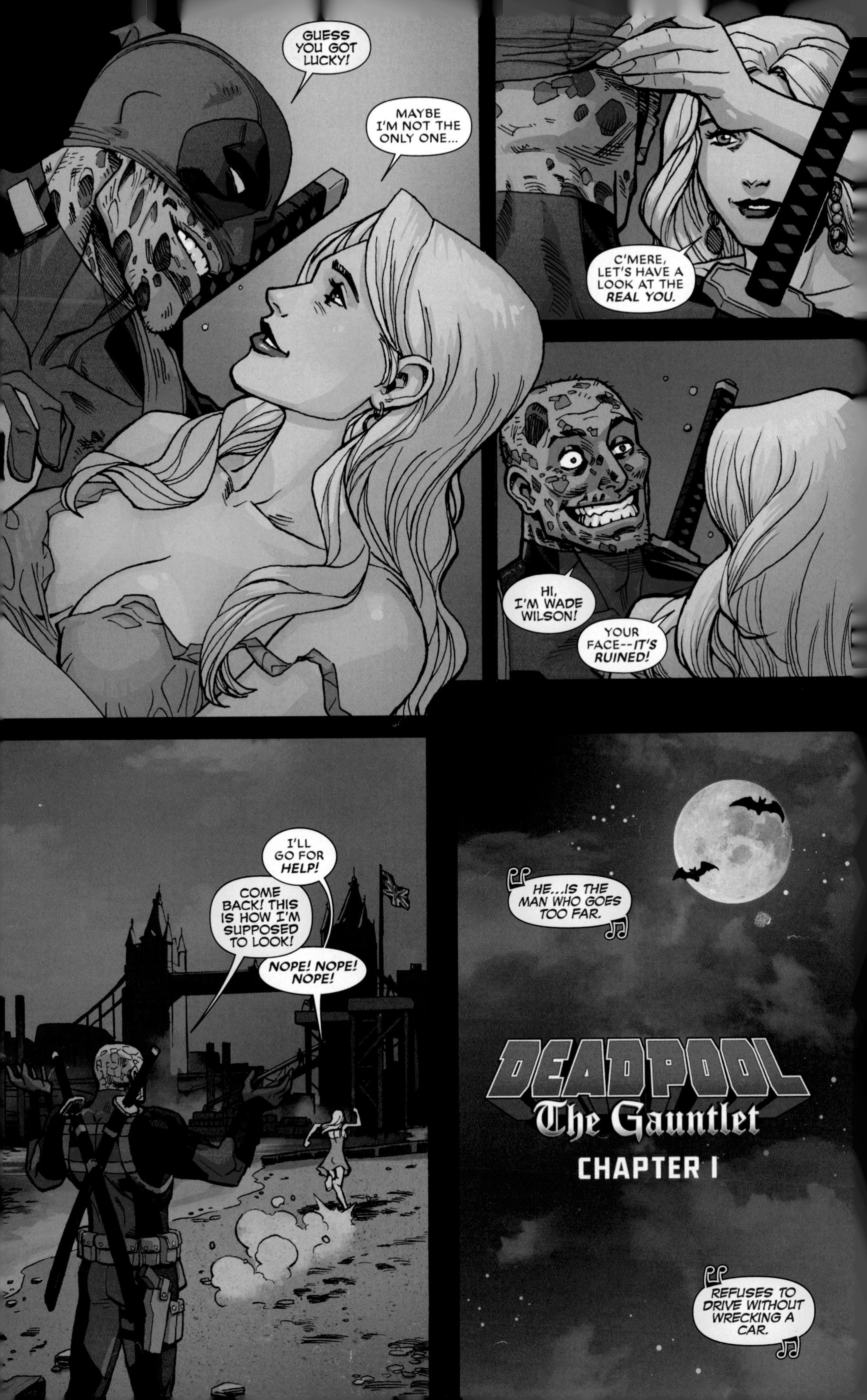

GUESS YOU GOT LUCKY!
MAYBE I'M NOT THE ONLY ONE...
C'MERE, LET'S HAVE A LOOK AT THE REAL YOU.
HI, I'M WADE WILSON!
YOUR FACE--IT'S RUINED!
I'LL GO FOR HELP!
COME BACK! THIS IS HOW I'M SUPPOSED TO LOOK!
NOPE! NOPE! NOPE!
HE...IS THE MAN WHO GOES TOO FAR.
DEADPOOL
The Gauntlet
CHAPTER 1
REFUSES TO DRIVE WITHOUT WRECKING A CAR.

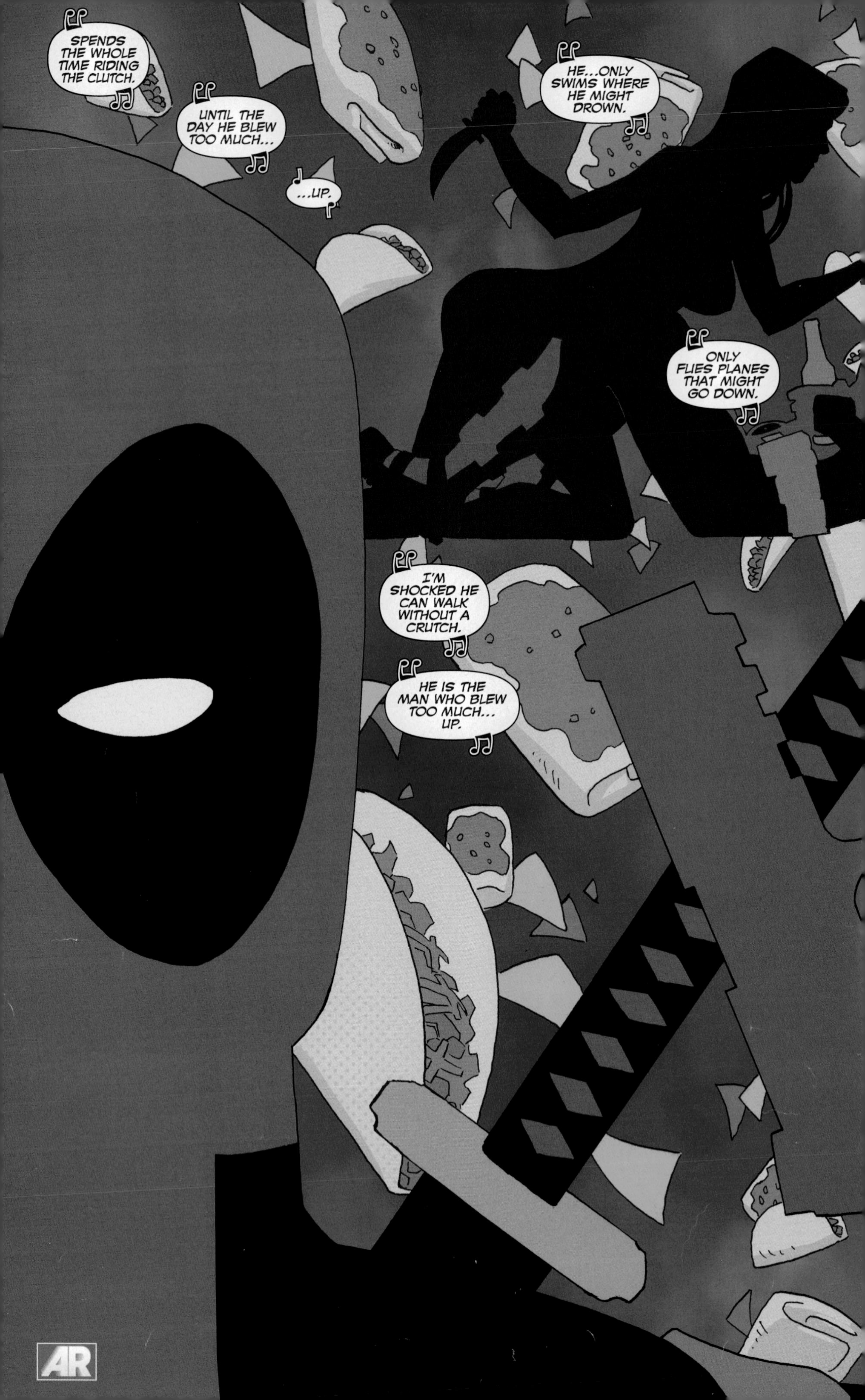
SPENDS THE WHOLE TIME RIDING THE CLUTCH.
UNTIL THE DAY HE BLEW TOO MUCH...
...UP.
HE...ONLY SWIMS WHERE HE MIGHT DROWN.
ONLY FLIES PLANES THAT MIGHT GO DOWN.
I'M SHOCKED HE CAN WALK WITHOUT A CRUTCH.
HE IS THE MAN WHO BLEW TOO MUCH... UP.

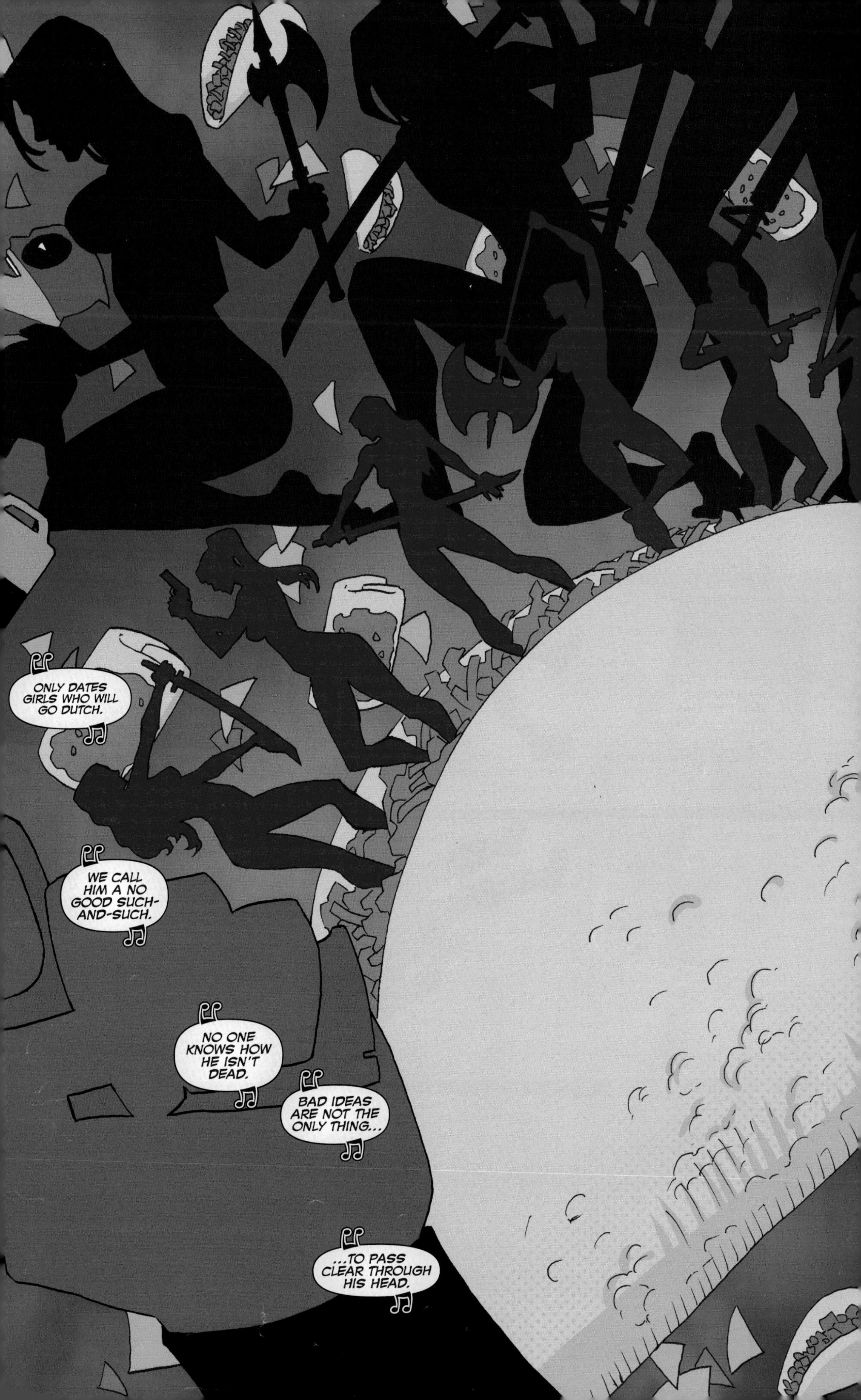
ONLY DATES GIRLS WHO WILL GO DUTCH.
WE CALL HIM A NO GOOD SUCH-AND-SUCH.
NO ONE KNOWS HOW HE ISN'T DEAD.
BAD IDEAS ARE NOT THE ONLY THING...
...TO PASS CLEAR THROUGH HIS HEAD.

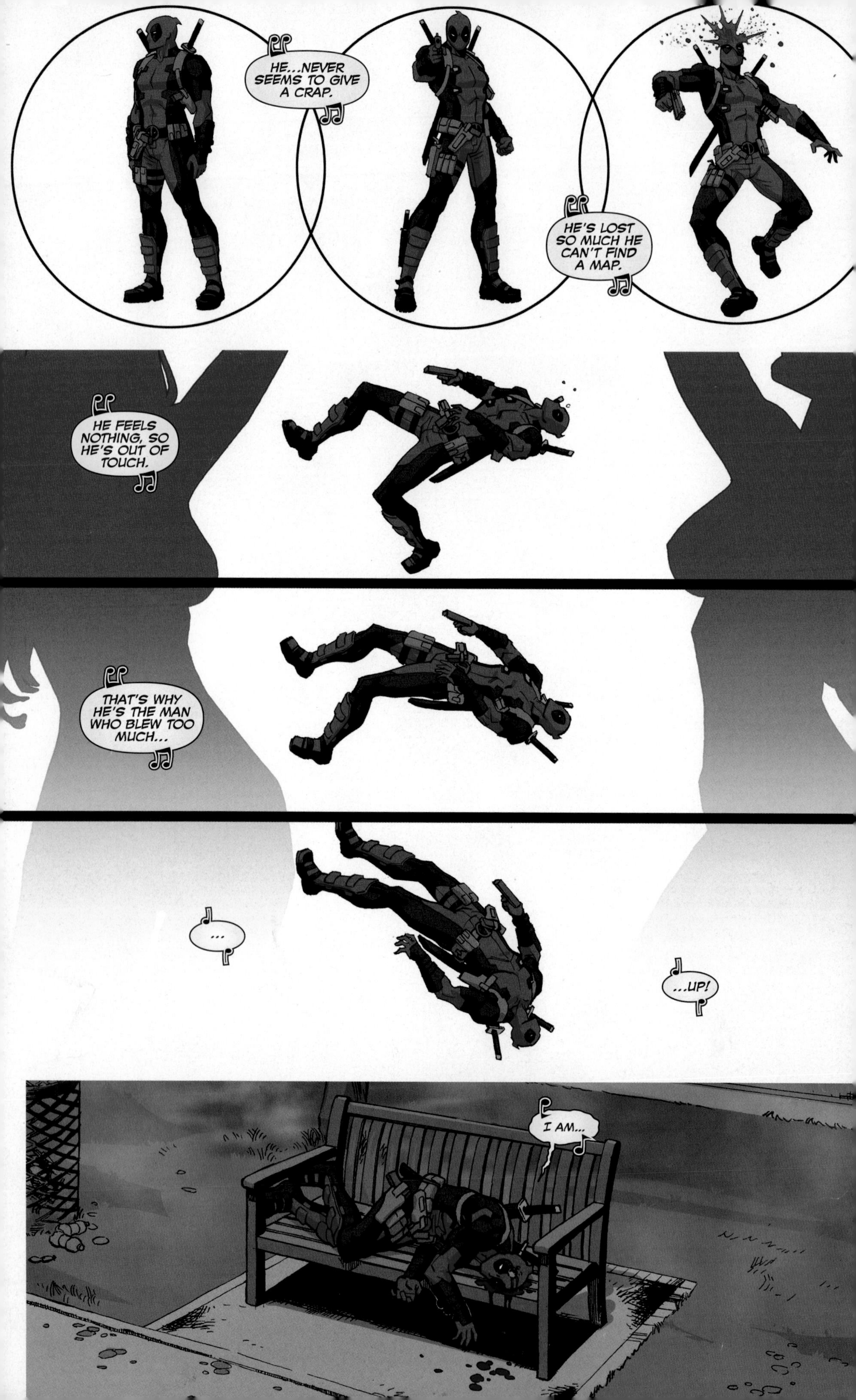
HE...NEVER SEEMS TO GIVE A CRAP.
HE'S LOST SO MUCH HE CAN'T FIND A MAP.
HE FEELS NOTHING, SO HE'S OUT OF TOUCH.
THAT'S WHY HE'S THE MAN WHO BLEW TOO MUCH...
...
...UP!
I AM...

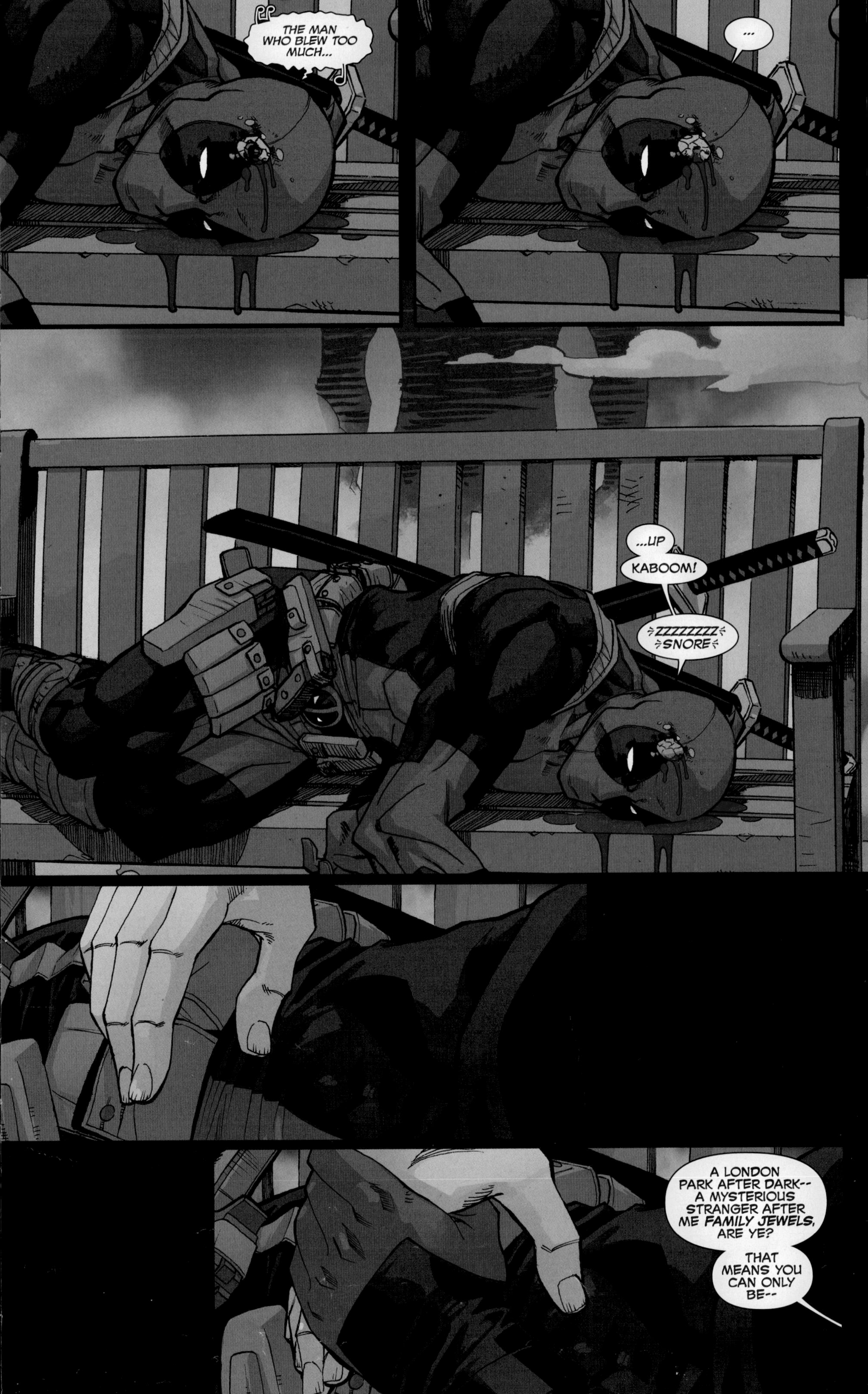
THE MAN WHO BLEW TOO MUCH...
...
...UP
KABOOM!
ZZZZZZZZZ SNORE
A LONDON PARK AFTER DARK-- A MYSTERIOUS STRANGER AFTER ME *FAMILY JEWELS,* ARE YE?
THAT MEANS YOU CAN ONLY BE--

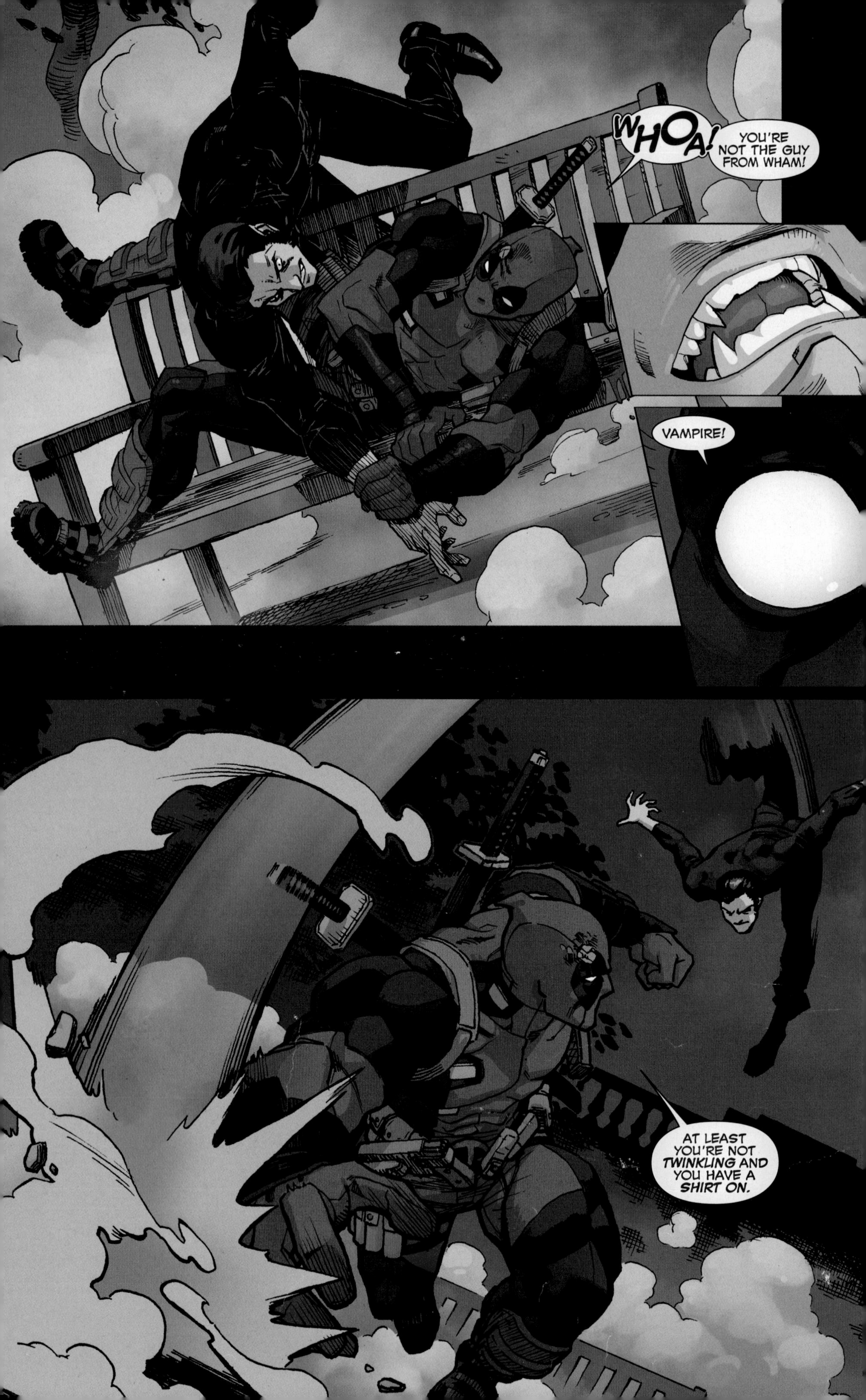
WHOA!
YOU'RE NOT THE GUY FROM WHAM!
VAMPIRE!
AT LEAST YOU'RE NOT TWINKLING AND YOU HAVE A SHIRT ON.

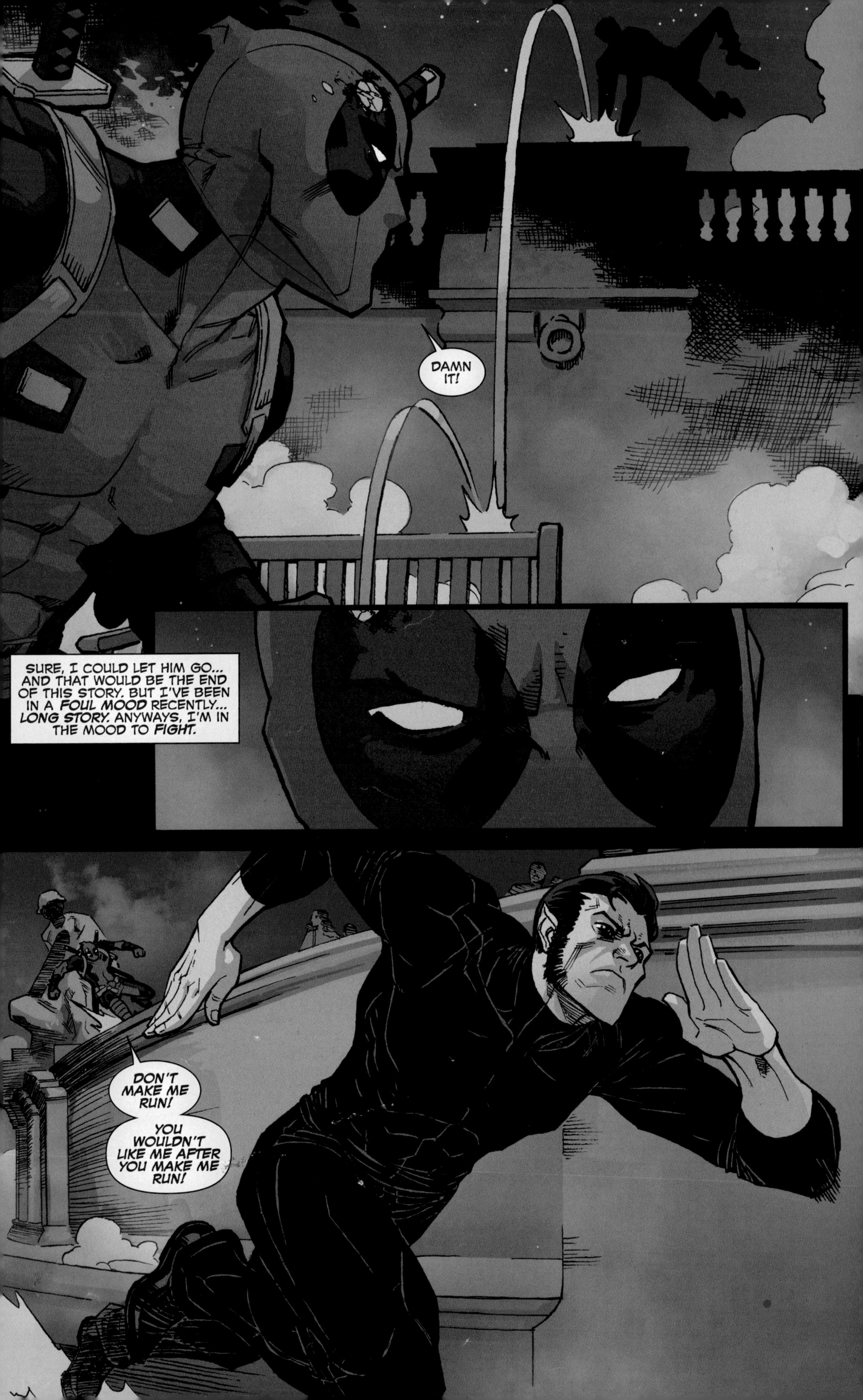
DAMN IT!
SURE, I COULD LET HIM GO... AND THAT WOULD BE THE END OF THIS STORY. BUT I'VE BEEN IN A FOUL MOOD RECENTLY... LONG STORY. ANYWAYS, I'M IN THE MOOD TO FIGHT.
DON'T MAKE ME RUN!
YOU WOULDN'T LIKE ME AFTER YOU MAKE ME RUN!

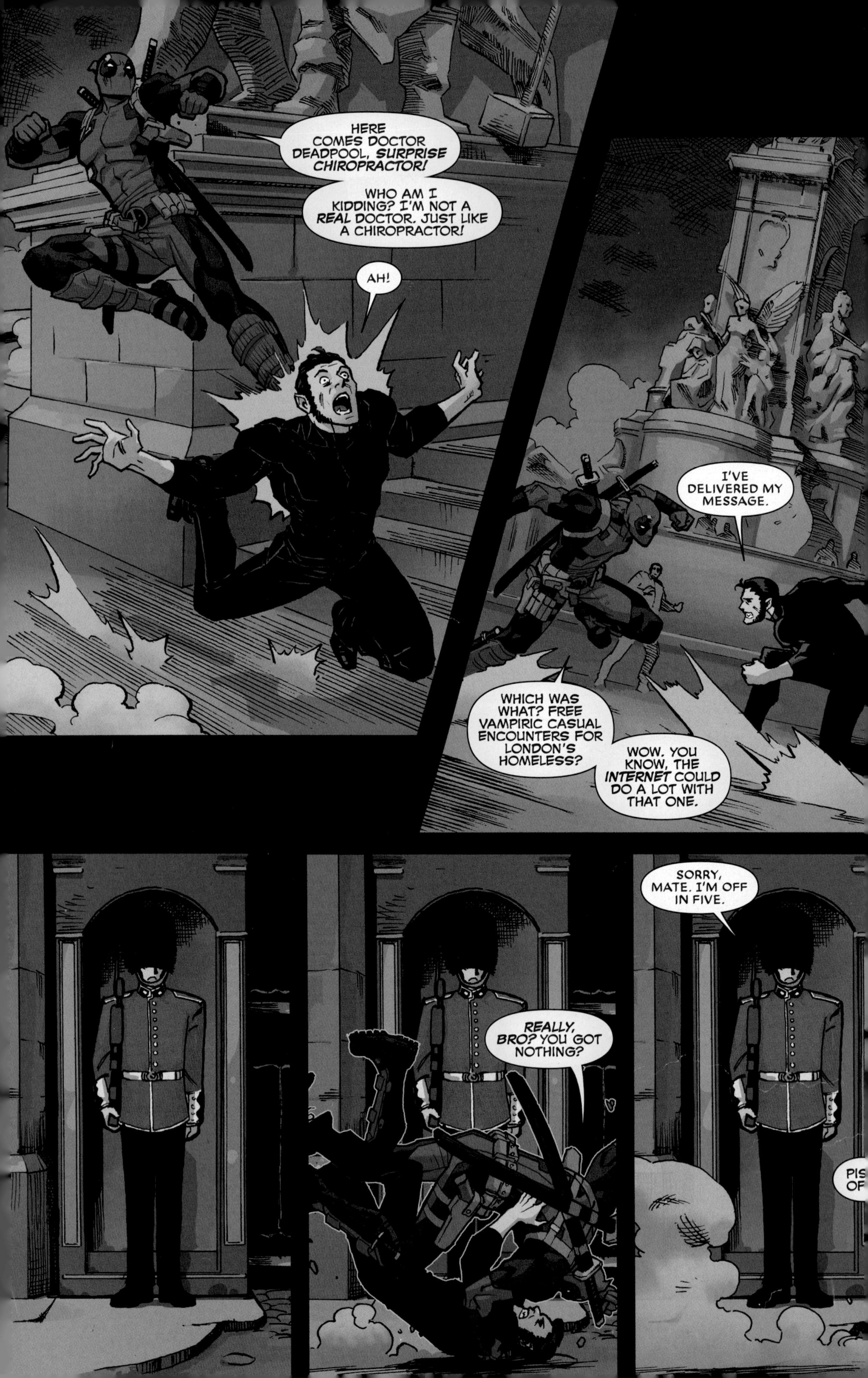
HERE COMES DOCTOR DEADPOOL, SURPRISE CHIROPRACTOR!
WHO AM I KIDDING? I'M NOT A REAL DOCTOR. JUST LIKE A CHIROPRACTOR!
AH!
I'VE DELIVERED MY MESSAGE.
WHICH WAS WHAT? FREE VAMPIRIC CASUAL ENCOUNTERS FOR LONDON'S HOMELESS?
WOW. YOU KNOW, THE INTERNET COULD DO A LOT WITH THAT ONE.
REALLY, BRO? YOU GOT NOTHING?
SORRY, MATE. I'M OFF IN FIVE.

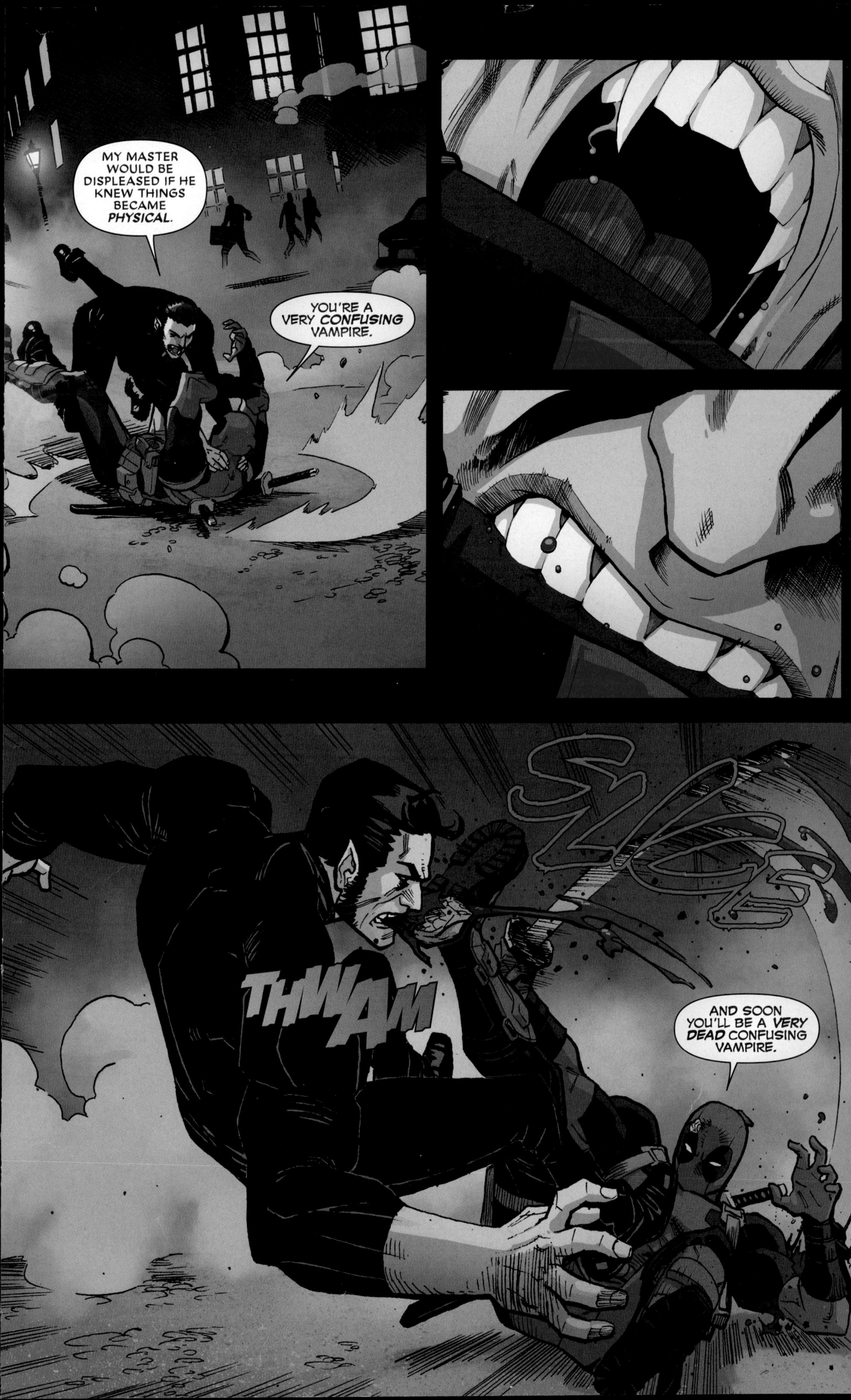
MY MASTER WOULD BE DISPLEASED IF HE KNEW THINGS BECAME PHYSICAL.
YOU'RE A VERY CONFUSING VAMPIRE.
THWAM
AND SOON YOU'LL BE A VERY DEAD CONFUSING VAMPIRE.

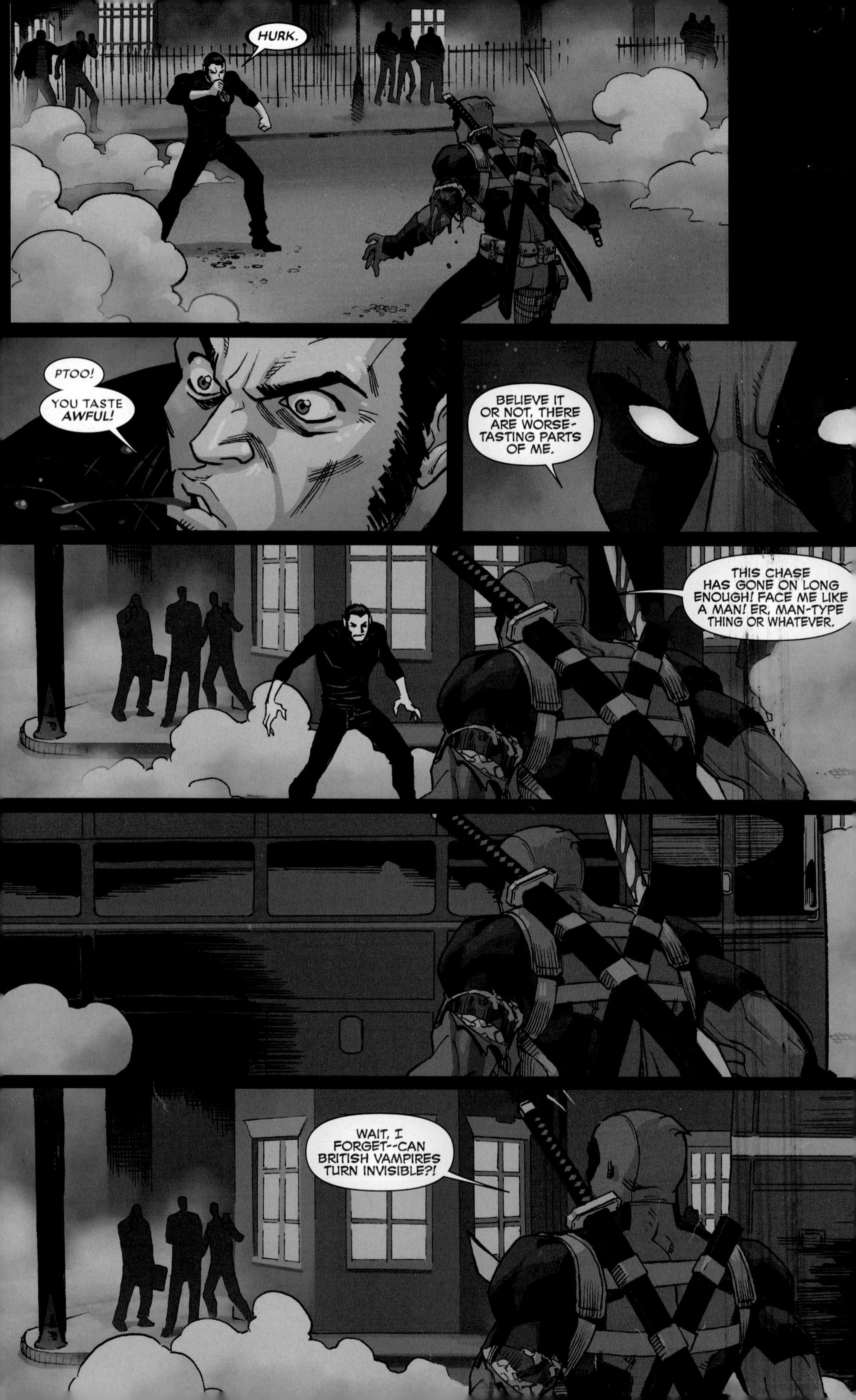
HURK.
PTOO!
YOU TASTE AWFUL!
BELIEVE IT OR NOT, THERE ARE WORSE-TASTING PARTS OF ME.
THIS CHASE HAS GONE ON LONG ENOUGH! FACE ME LIKE A MAN! ER, MAN-TYPE THING OR WHATEVER.
WAIT, I FORGET--CAN BRITISH VAMPIRES TURN INVISIBLE?!

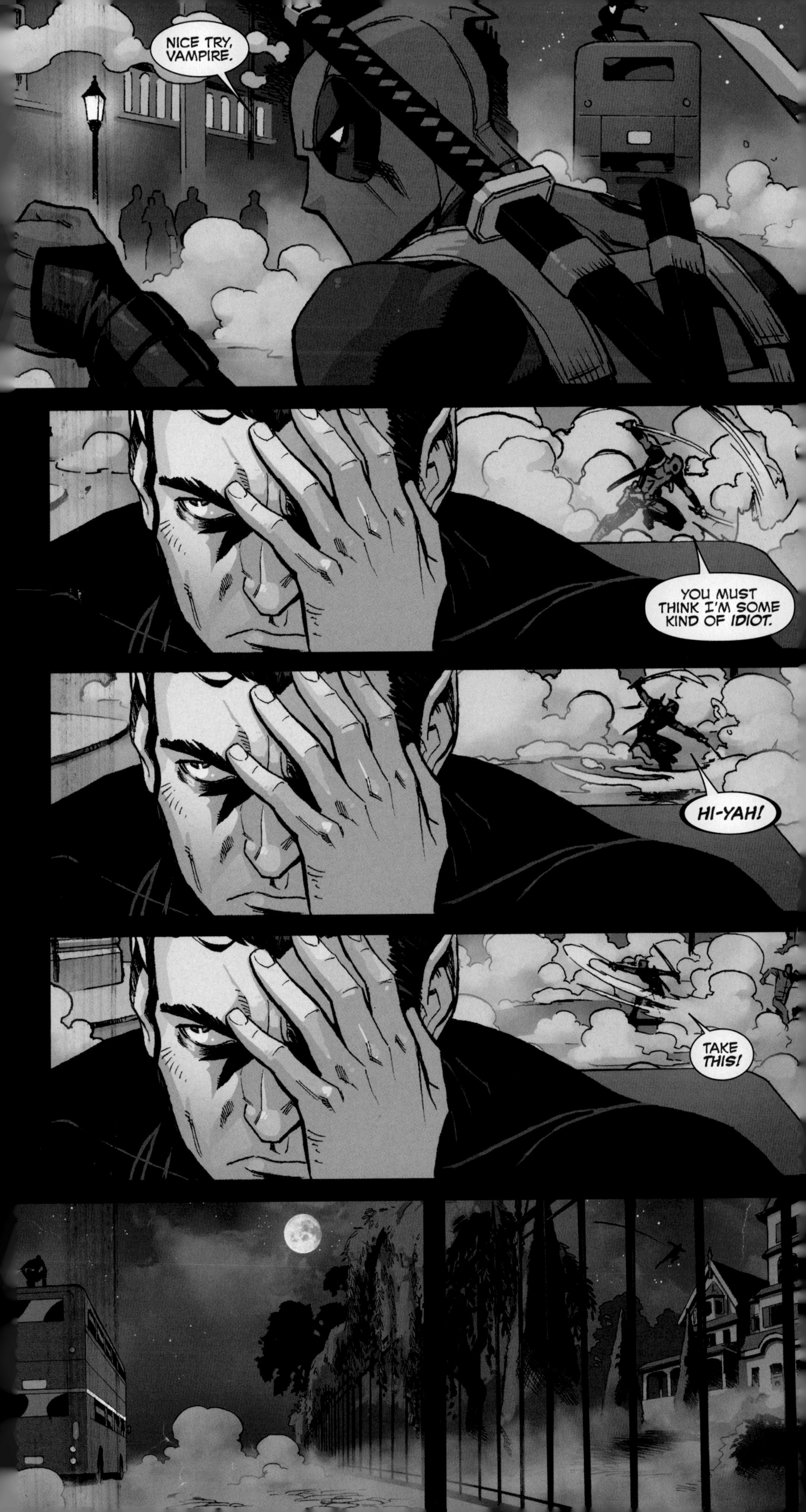
NICE TRY, VAMPIRE.
YOU MUST THINK I'M SOME KIND OF IDIOT.
HI-YAH!
TAKE THIS!

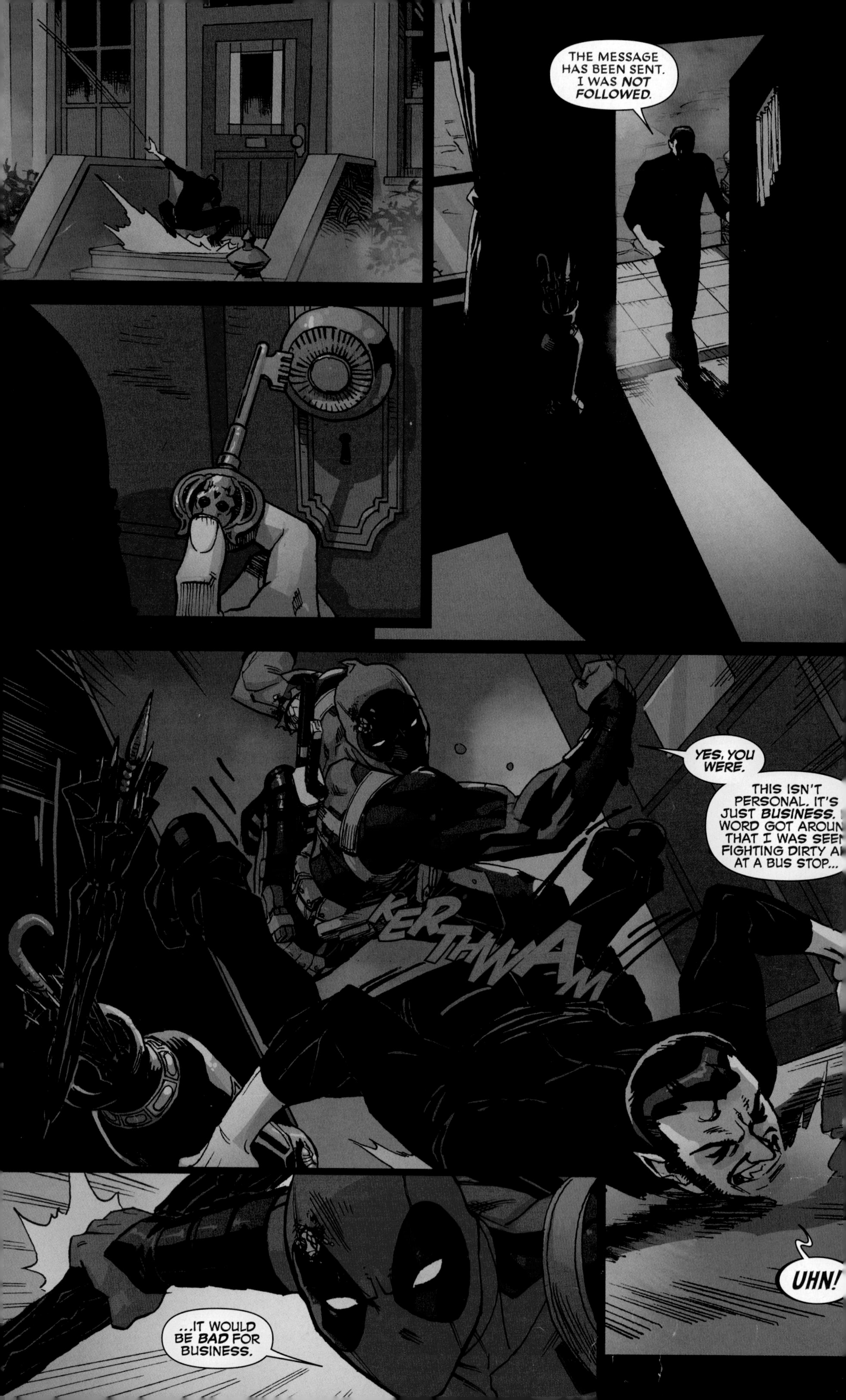
THE MESSAGE HAS BEEN SENT. I WAS NOT FOLLOWED.
YES, YOU WERE.
THIS ISN'T PERSONAL. IT'S JUST BUSINESS. WORD GOT AROUN THAT I WAS SEEN FIGHTING DIRTY A AT A BUS STOP...
KER-THWAM
UHN!
...IT WOULD BE BAD FOR BUSINESS.

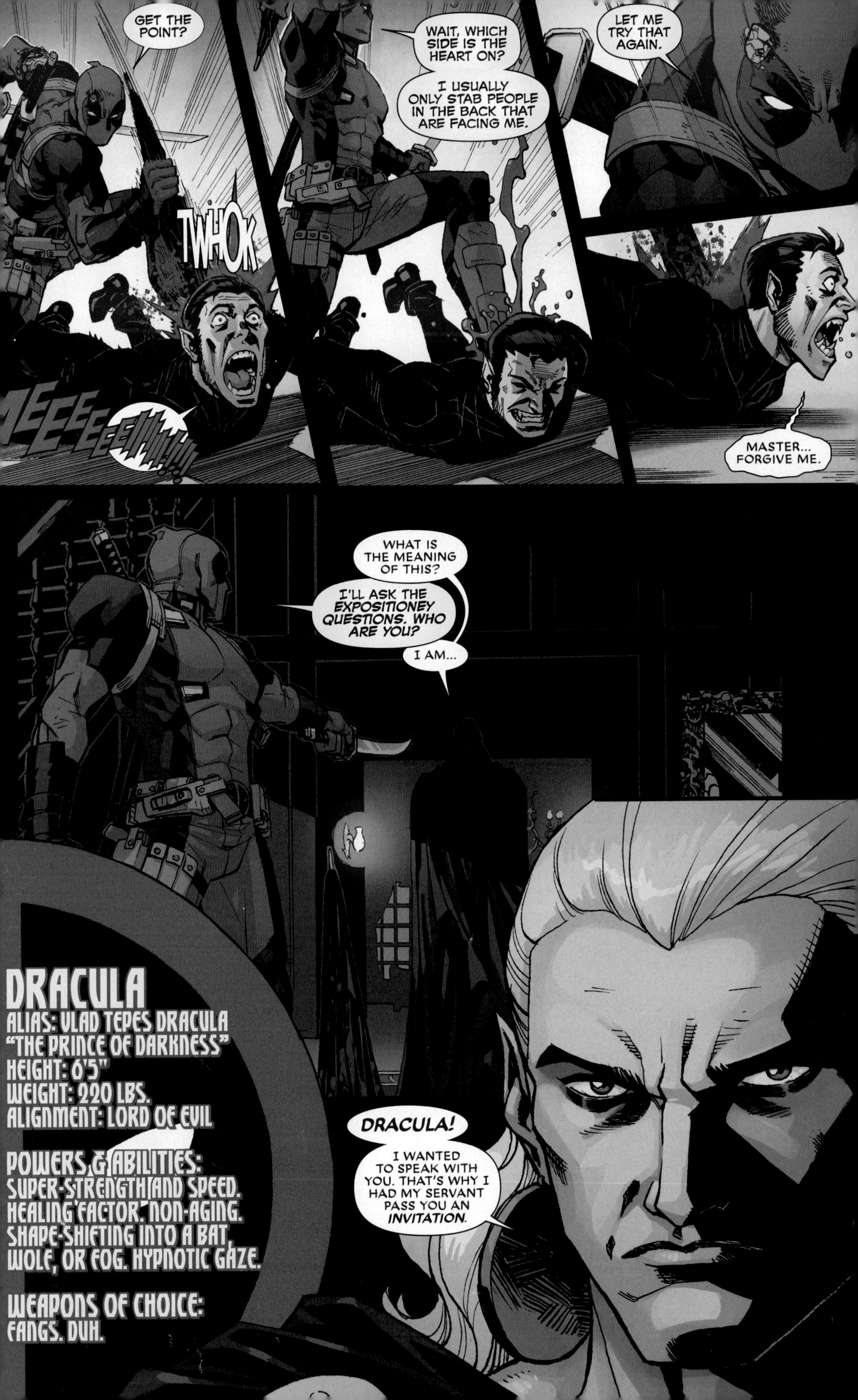
GET THE POINT?
TWHOK
AEEEEEEEIIIIII!!!
WAIT, WHICH SIDE IS THE HEART ON?
I USUALLY ONLY STAB PEOPLE IN THE BACK THAT ARE FACING ME.
LET ME TRY THAT AGAIN.
MASTER... FORGIVE ME.
WHAT IS THE MEANING OF THIS?
I'LL ASK THE EXPOSITIONEY QUESTIONS. WHO ARE YOU?
I AM...
DRACULA
ALIAS: VLAD TEPES DRACULA
"THE PRINCE OF DARKNESS"
HEIGHT: 6'5"
WEIGHT: 220 LBS.
ALIGNMENT: LORD OF EVIL
POWERS & ABILITIES:
SUPER-STRENGTH AND SPEED. HEALING FACTOR. NON-AGING. SHAPE-SHIFTING INTO A BAT, WOLF, OR FOG. HYPNOTIC GAZE.
WEAPONS OF CHOICE:
FANGS. DUH.
DRACULA!
I WANTED TO SPEAK WITH YOU. THAT'S WHY I HAD MY SERVANT PASS YOU AN INVITATION.

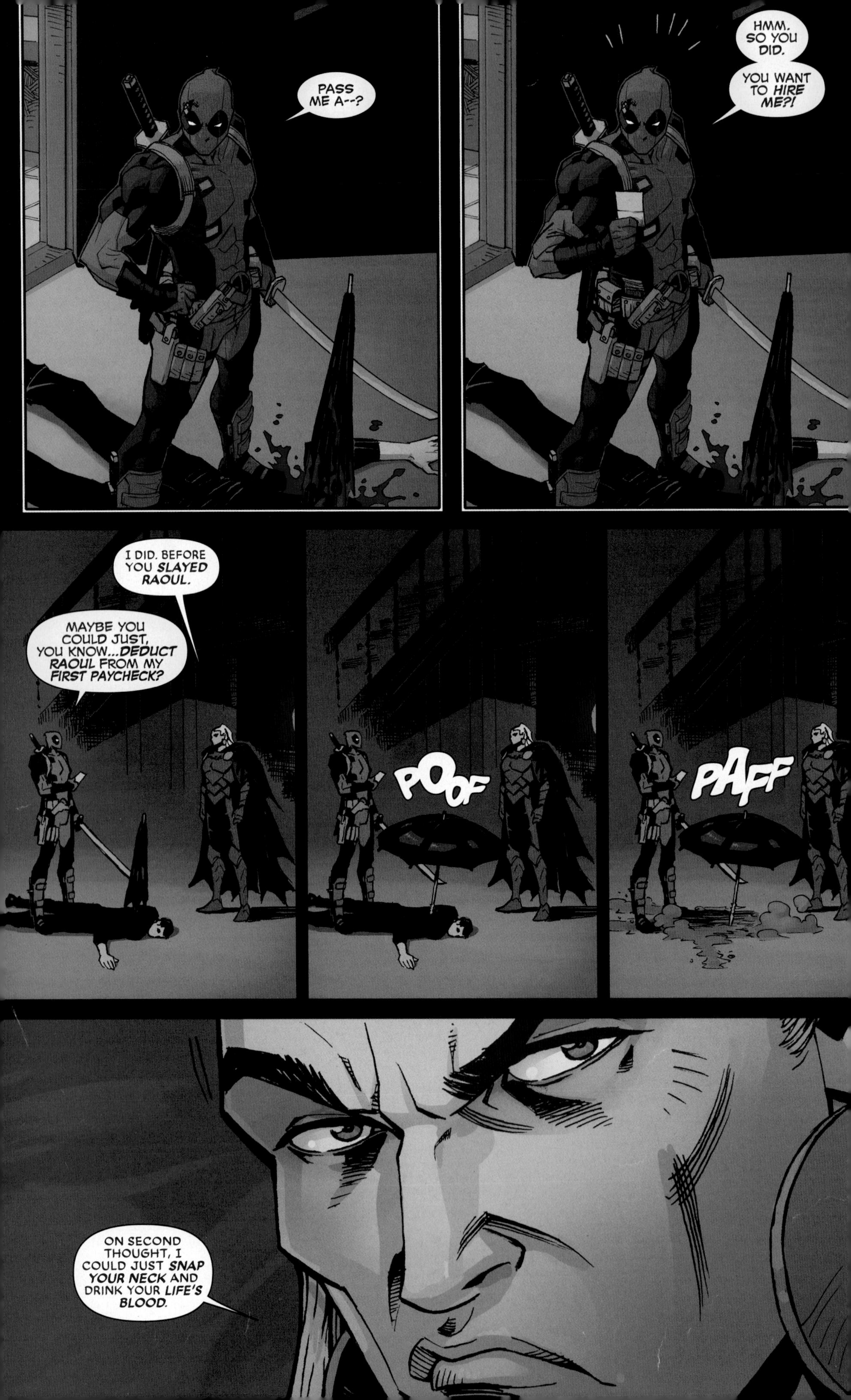
PASS ME A--?
HMM. SO YOU DID.
YOU WANT TO HIRE ME?!
I DID. BEFORE YOU SLAYED RAOUL.
MAYBE YOU COULD JUST, YOU KNOW...DEDUCT RAOUL FROM MY FIRST PAYCHECK?
POOF
PAFF
ON SECOND THOUGHT, I COULD JUST SNAP YOUR NECK AND DRINK YOUR LIFE'S BLOOD.

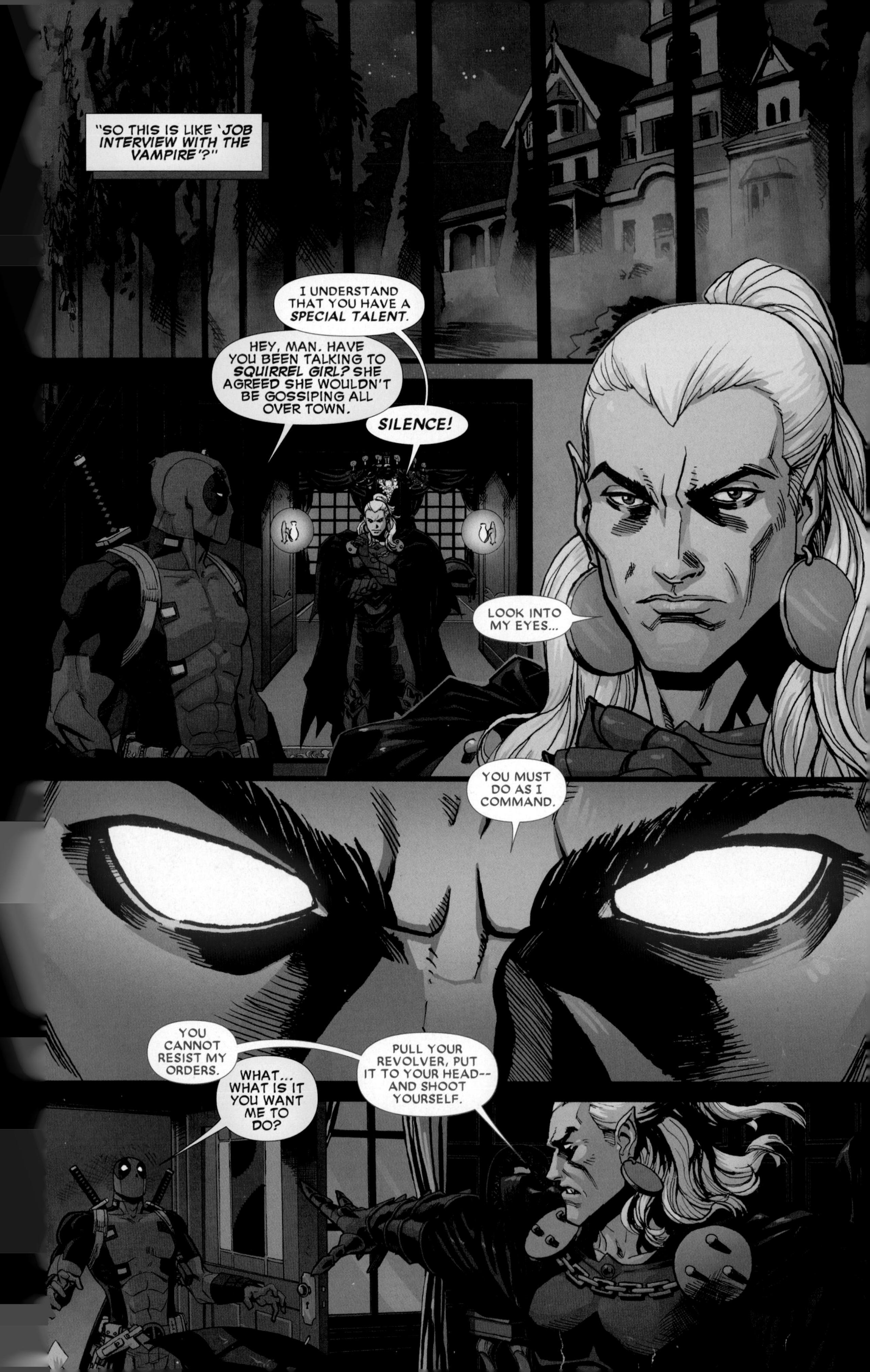
"SO THIS IS LIKE 'JOB INTERVIEW WITH THE VAMPIRE'?"
I UNDERSTAND THAT YOU HAVE A SPECIAL TALENT.
HEY, MAN. HAVE YOU BEEN TALKING TO SQUIRREL GIRL? SHE AGREED SHE WOULDN'T BE GOSSIPING ALL OVER TOWN.
SILENCE!
LOOK INTO MY EYES...
YOU MUST DO AS I COMMAND.
YOU CANNOT RESIST MY ORDERS.
WHAT... WHAT IS IT YOU WANT ME TO DO?
PULL YOUR REVOLVER, PUT IT TO YOUR HEAD-- AND SHOOT YOURSELF.

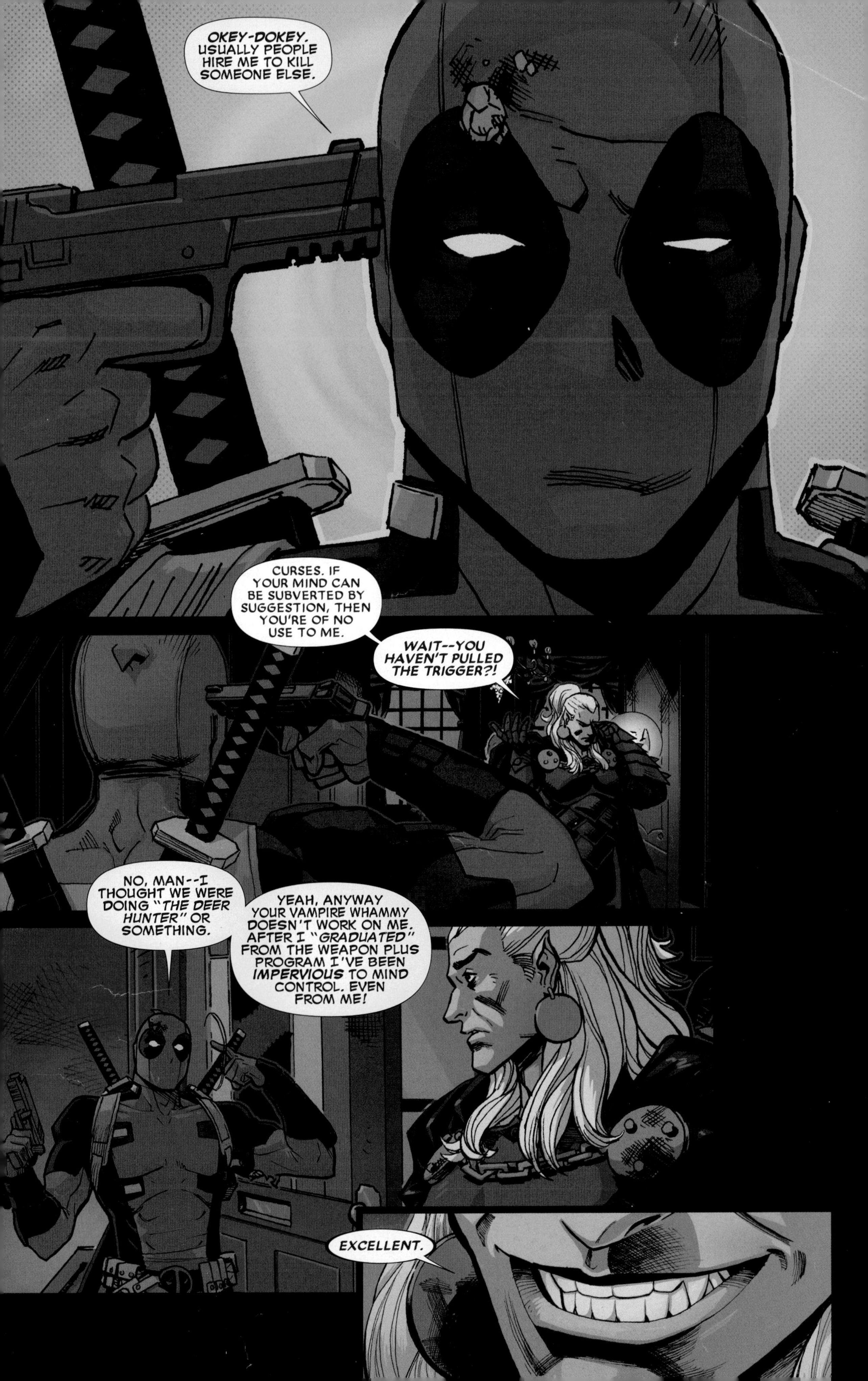
OKEY-DOKEY. USUALLY PEOPLE HIRE ME TO KILL SOMEONE ELSE.
CURSES. IF YOUR MIND CAN BE SUBVERTED BY SUGGESTION, THEN YOU'RE OF NO USE TO ME.
WAIT--YOU HAVEN'T PULLED THE TRIGGER?!
NO, MAN--I THOUGHT WE WERE DOING "THE DEER HUNTER" OR SOMETHING.
YEAH, ANYWAY YOUR VAMPIRE WHAMMY DOESN'T WORK ON ME. AFTER I "GRADUATED" FROM THE WEAPON PLUS PROGRAM I'VE BEEN IMPERVIOUS TO MIND CONTROL. EVEN FROM ME!
EXCELLENT.

DEADPOOL
The Gauntlet

CHAPTER 2:
DEADPOOL & THE TEMPLE OF BOOM!

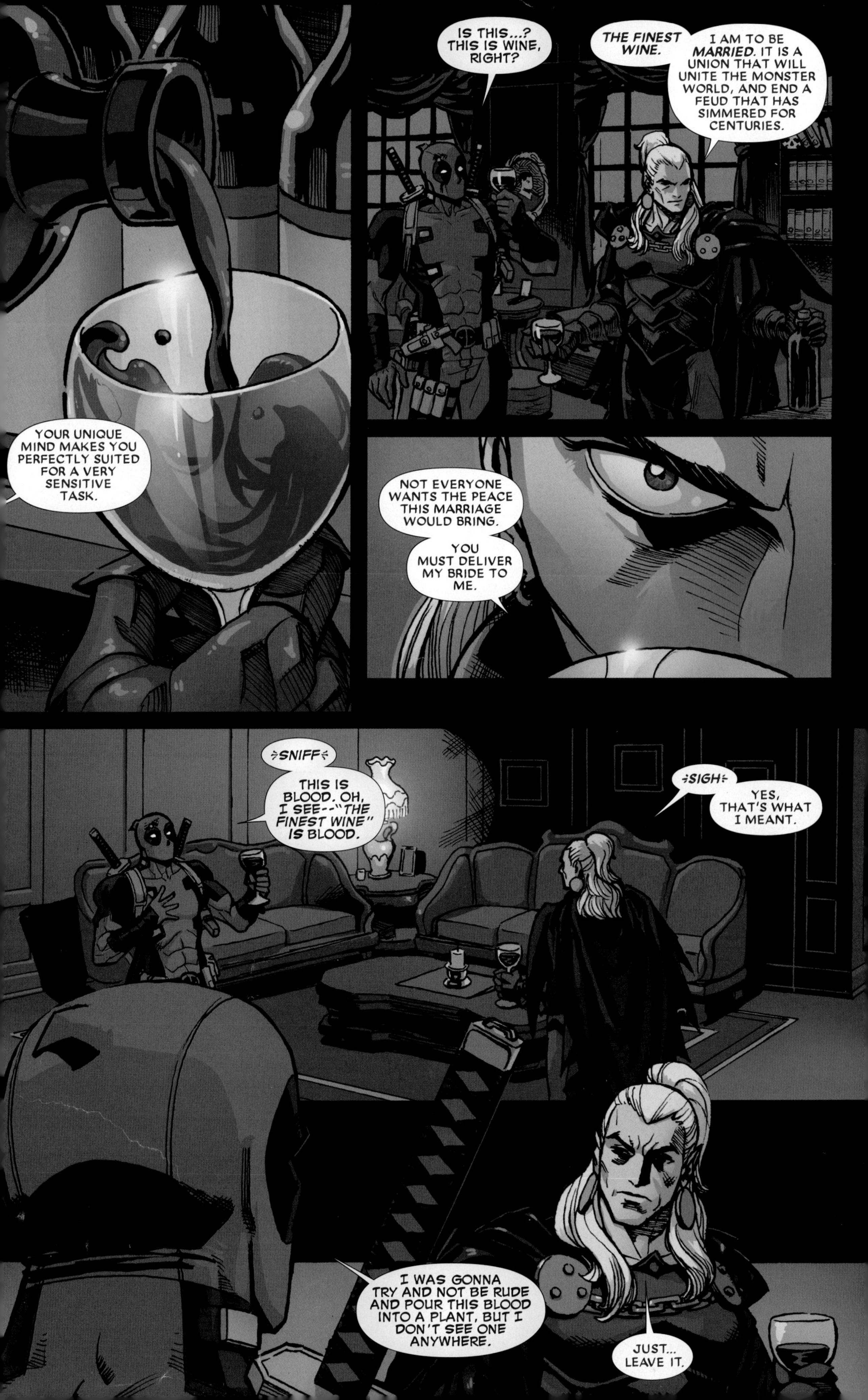
IS THIS...? THIS IS WINE, RIGHT?
THE FINEST WINE.
I AM TO BE MARRIED. IT IS A UNION THAT WILL UNITE THE MONSTER WORLD, AND END A FEUD THAT HAS SIMMERED FOR CENTURIES.
YOUR UNIQUE MIND MAKES YOU PERFECTLY SUITED FOR A VERY SENSITIVE TASK.
NOT EVERYONE WANTS THE PEACE THIS MARRIAGE WOULD BRING.
YOU MUST DELIVER MY BRIDE TO ME.
SNIFF
THIS IS BLOOD. OH, I SEE--"THE FINEST WINE" IS BLOOD.
SIGH
YES, THAT'S WHAT I MEANT.
I WAS GONNA TRY AND NOT BE RUDE AND POUR THIS BLOOD INTO A PLANT, BUT I DON'T SEE ONE ANYWHERE.
JUST... LEAVE IT.

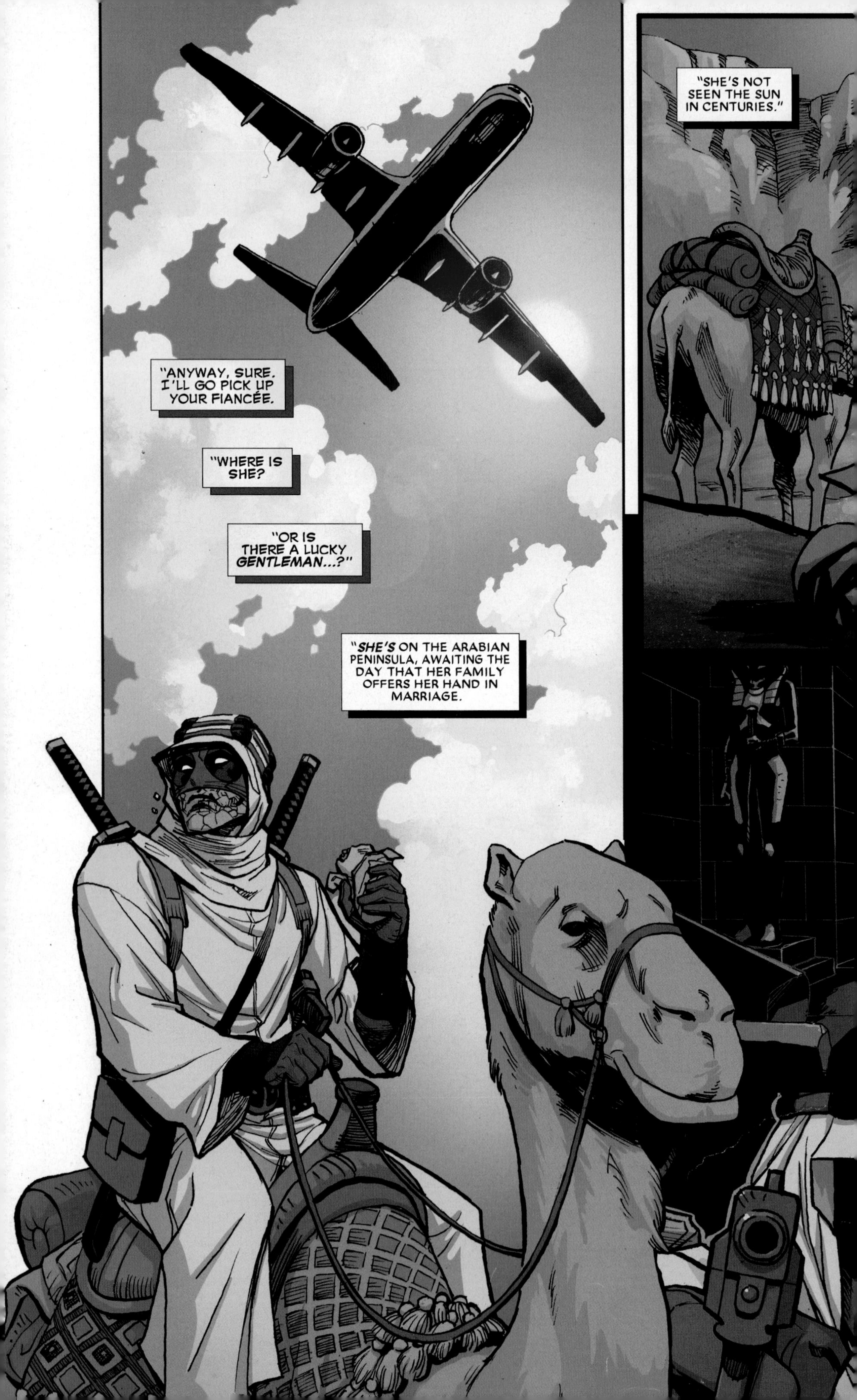
"ANYWAY, SURE. I'LL GO PICK UP YOUR FIANCÉE.
"WHERE IS SHE?
"OR IS THERE A LUCKY GENTLEMAN...?"
"SHE'S ON THE ARABIAN PENINSULA, AWAITING THE DAY THAT HER FAMILY OFFERS HER HAND IN MARRIAGE.
"SHE'S NOT SEEN THE SUN IN CENTURIES."

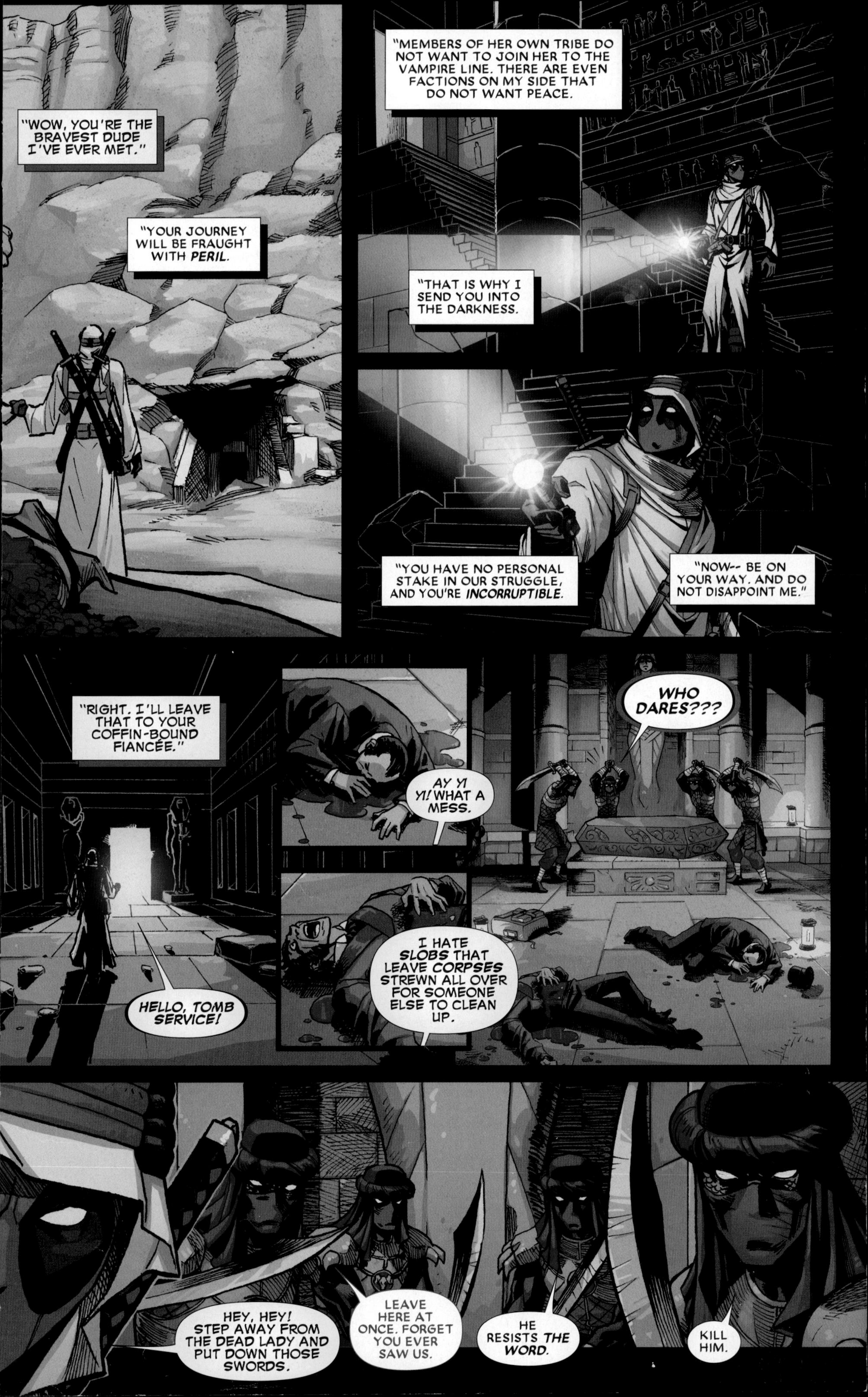
"WOW, YOU'RE THE BRAVEST DUDE I'VE EVER MET."
"YOUR JOURNEY WILL BE FRAUGHT WITH PERIL.
"MEMBERS OF HER OWN TRIBE DO NOT WANT TO JOIN HER TO THE VAMPIRE LINE. THERE ARE EVEN FACTIONS ON MY SIDE THAT DO NOT WANT PEACE.
"THAT IS WHY I SEND YOU INTO THE DARKNESS.
"YOU HAVE NO PERSONAL STAKE IN OUR STRUGGLE, AND YOU'RE INCORRUPTIBLE.
"NOW-- BE ON YOUR WAY. AND DO NOT DISAPPOINT ME."
"RIGHT. I'LL LEAVE THAT TO YOUR COFFIN-BOUND FIANCÉE."
HELLO, TOMB SERVICE!
AY YI YI! WHAT A MESS.
I HATE SLOBS THAT LEAVE CORPSES STREWN ALL OVER FOR SOMEONE ELSE TO CLEAN UP.
WHO DARES???
HEY, HEY! STEP AWAY FROM THE DEAD LADY AND PUT DOWN THOSE SWORDS.
LEAVE HERE AT ONCE. FORGET YOU EVER SAW US.
HE RESISTS THE WORD.
KILL HIM.

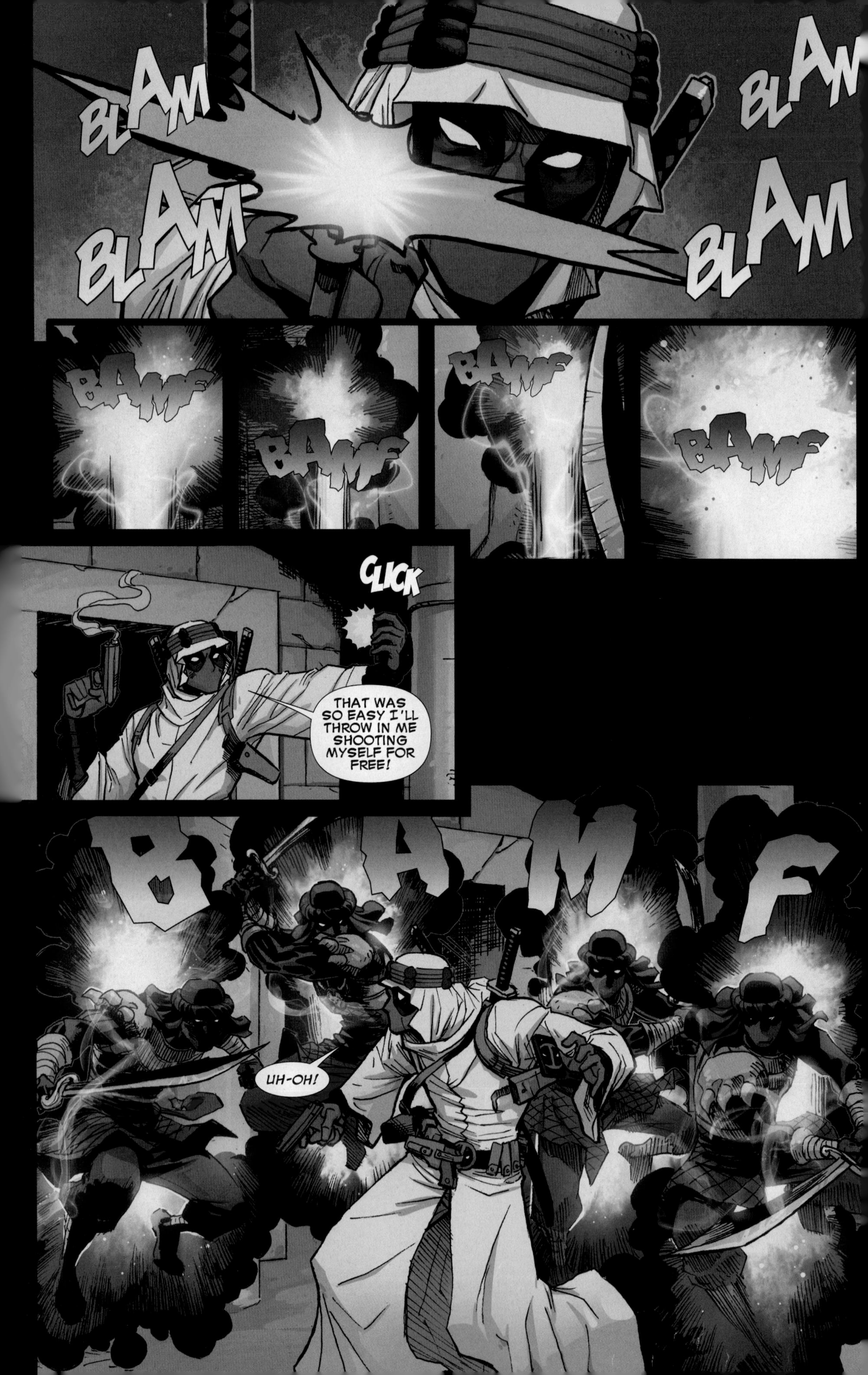
BLAM
BLAM
BLAM
BLAM
BAMF
BAMF
BAMF
BAMF
CLICK
THAT WAS SO EASY I'LL THROW IN ME SHOOTING MYSELF FOR FREE!
BAMF
UH-OH!

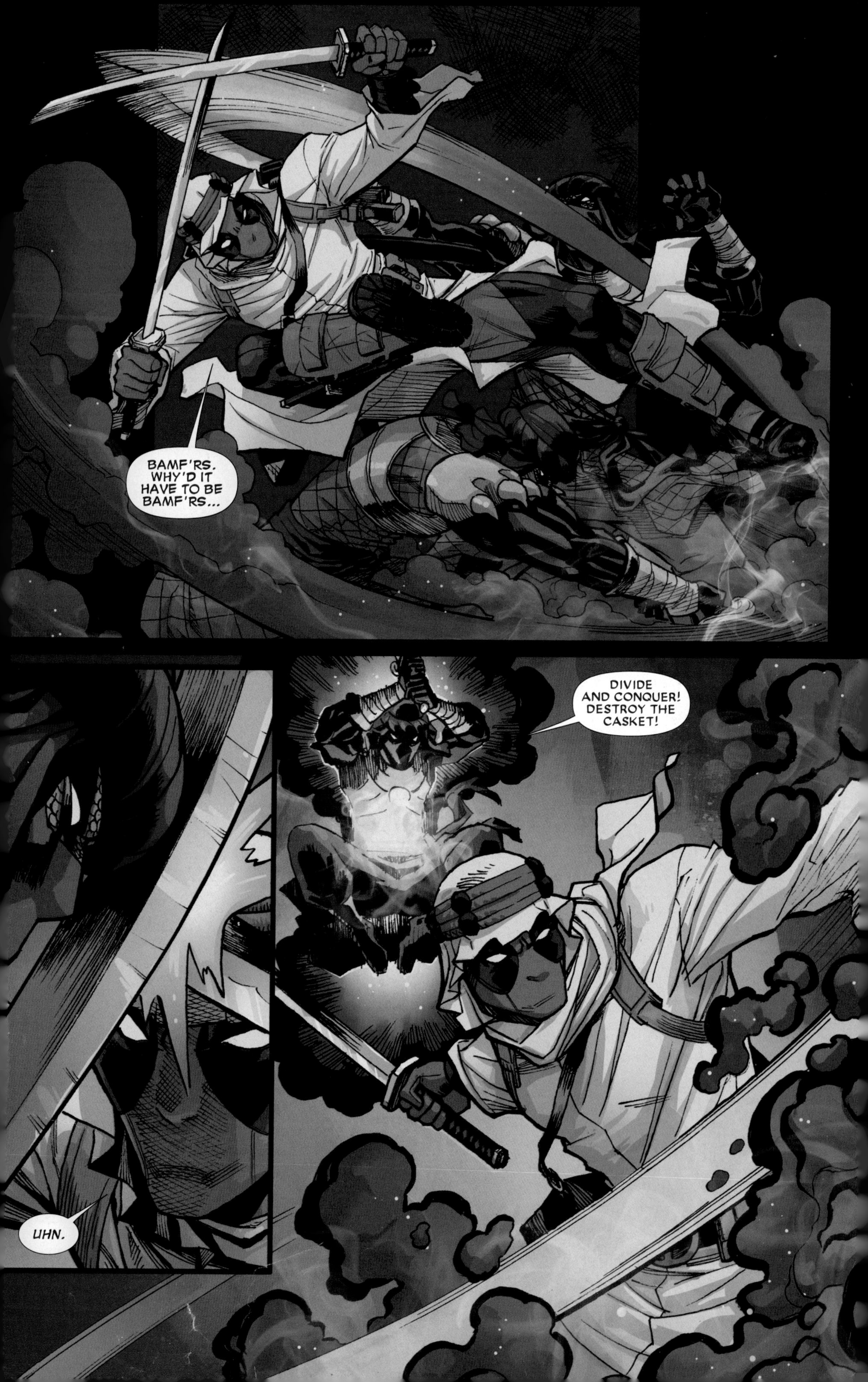
BAMF'RS. WHY'D IT HAVE TO BE BAMF'RS...
UHN.
DIVIDE AND CONQUER! DESTROY THE CASKET!

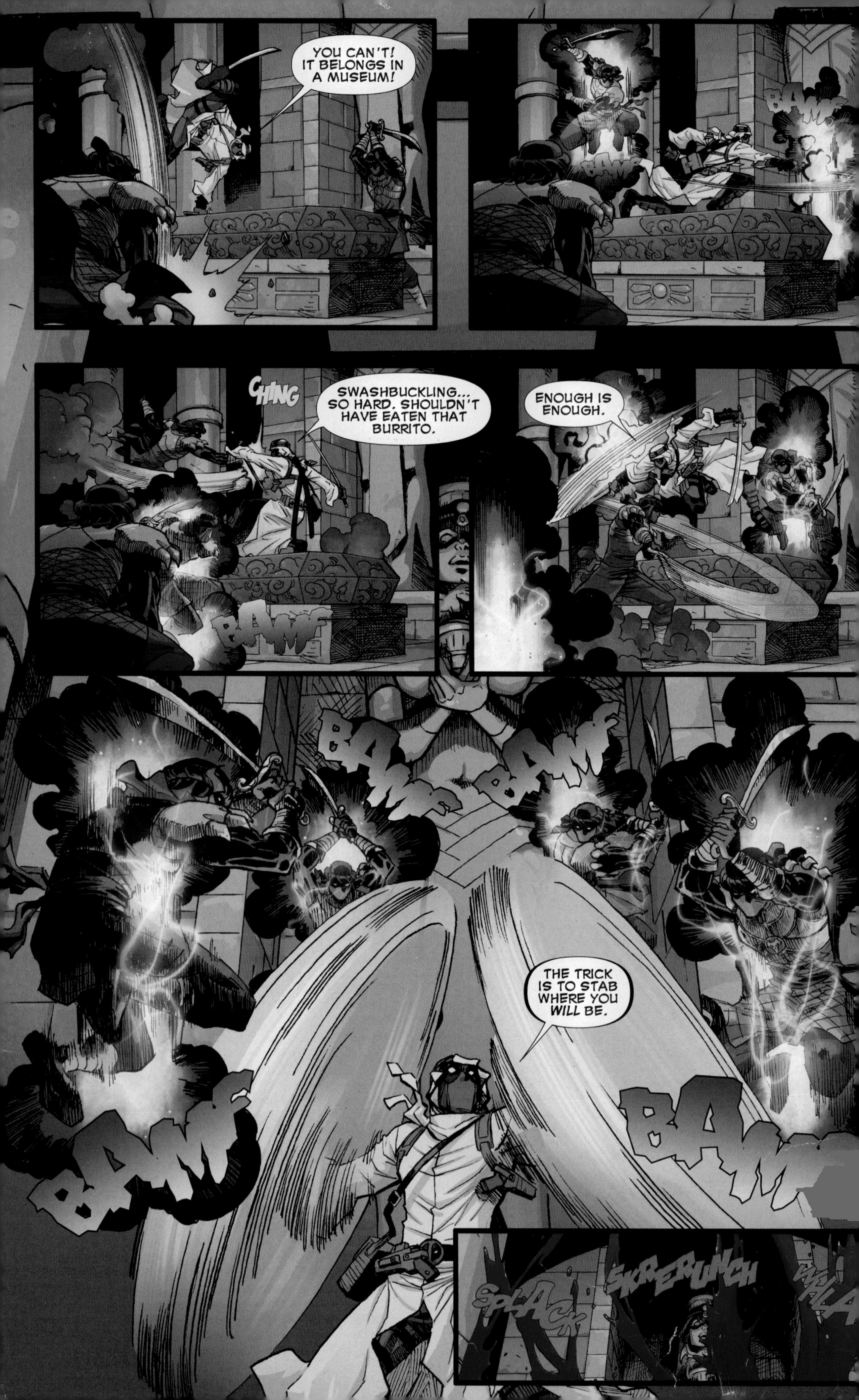

YOU CAN'T! IT BELONGS IN A MUSEUM!
BAMF
BAMF
CHING
SWASHBUCKLING... SO HARD. SHOULDN'T HAVE EATEN THAT BURRITO.
BAMF
ENOUGH IS ENOUGH.
BAMF
BAMF
THE TRICK IS TO STAB WHERE YOU *WILL* BE.
BAMF
SPLACK
SKRERUNCH

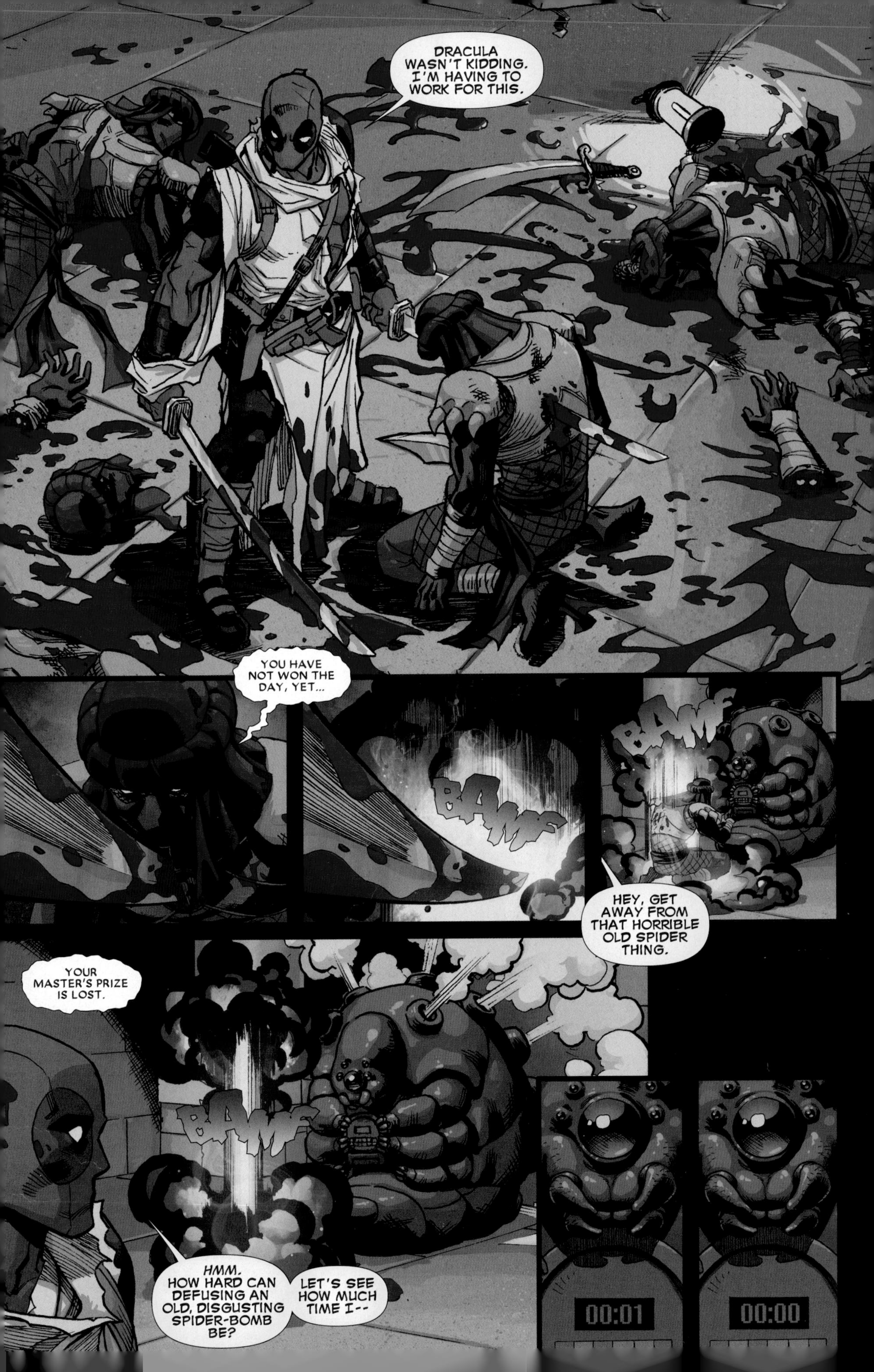
DRACULA WASN'T KIDDING. I'M HAVING TO WORK FOR THIS.
YOU HAVE NOT WON THE DAY, YET...
BAMF
BAMF
HEY, GET AWAY FROM THAT HORRIBLE OLD SPIDER THING.
YOUR MASTER'S PRIZE IS LOST.
BAMF
HMM. HOW HARD CAN DEFUSING AN OLD, DISGUSTING SPIDER-BOMB BE?
LET'S SEE HOW MUCH TIME I--
00:01
00:00

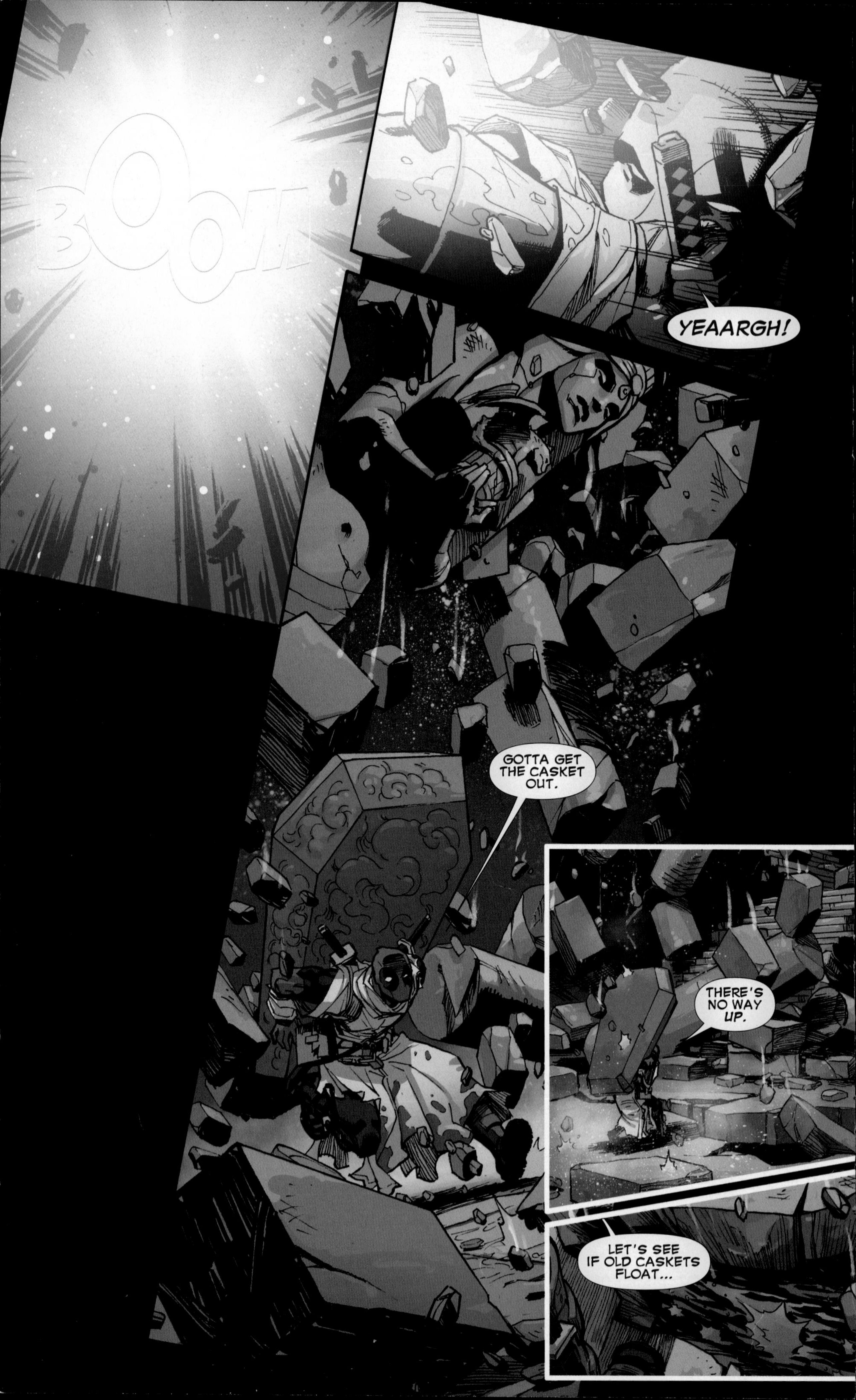
BOOM
YEAARGH!
GOTTA GET THE CASKET OUT.
THERE'S NO WAY UP.
LET'S SEE IF OLD CASKETS FLOAT...

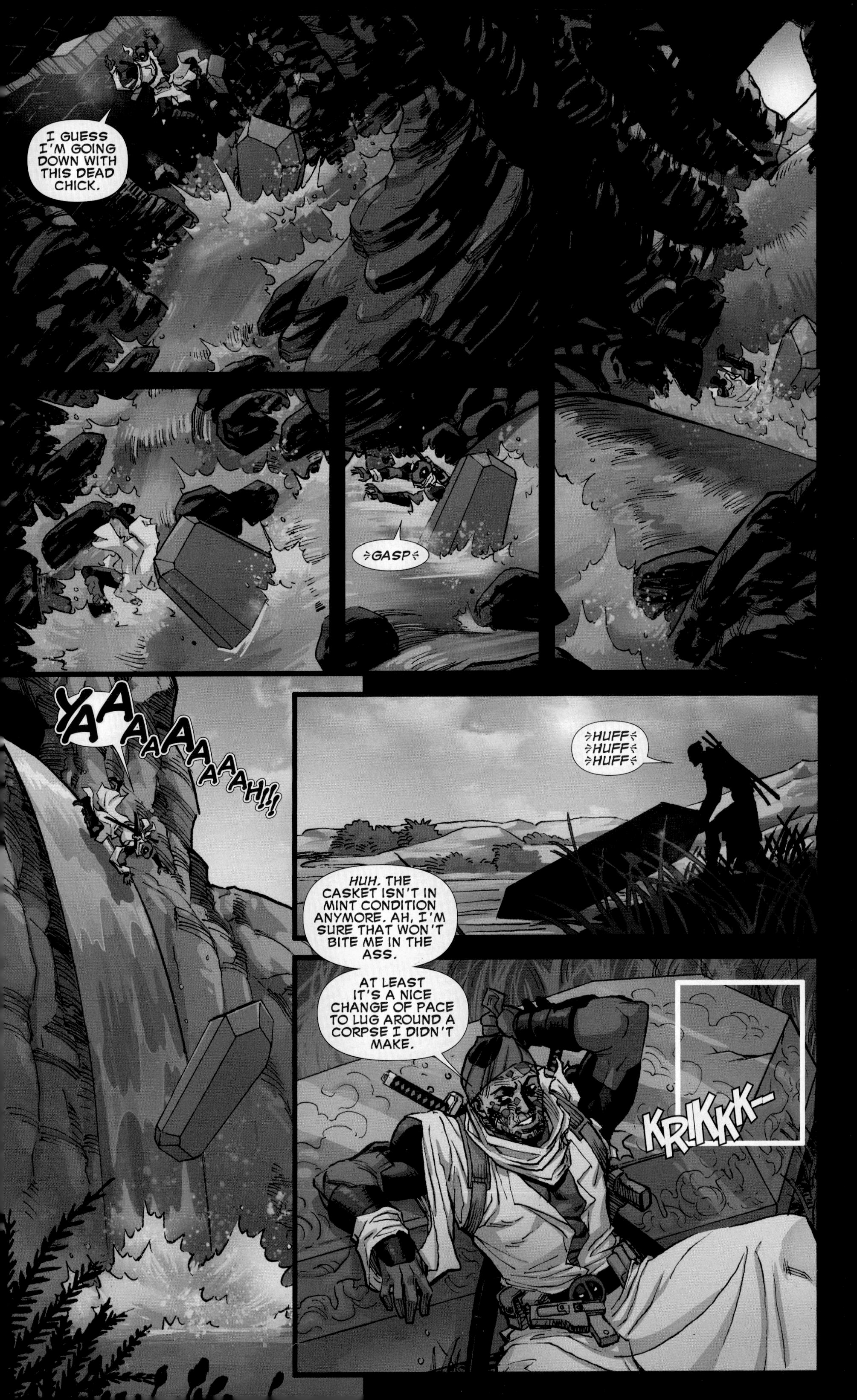

I GUESS I'M GOING DOWN WITH THIS DEAD CHICK.
GASP
YAAAAAAAAAAAH!!!
HUFF HUFF HUFF
HUH. THE CASKET ISN'T IN MINT CONDITION ANYMORE. AH, I'M SURE THAT WON'T BITE ME IN THE ASS.
AT LEAST IT'S A NICE CHANGE OF PACE TO LUG AROUND A CORPSE I DIDN'T MAKE.
KRIKKK-

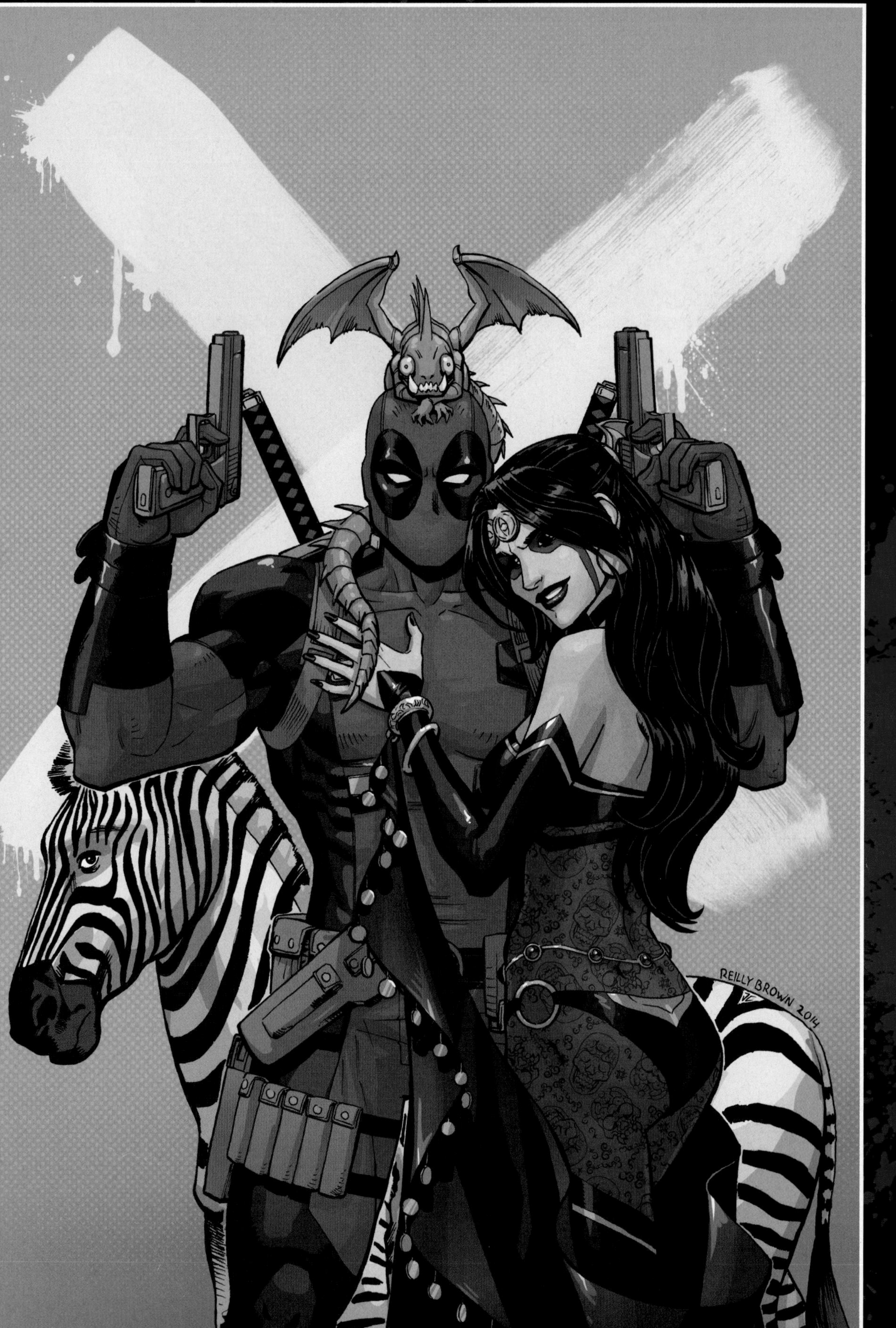
REILLY BROWN 2014

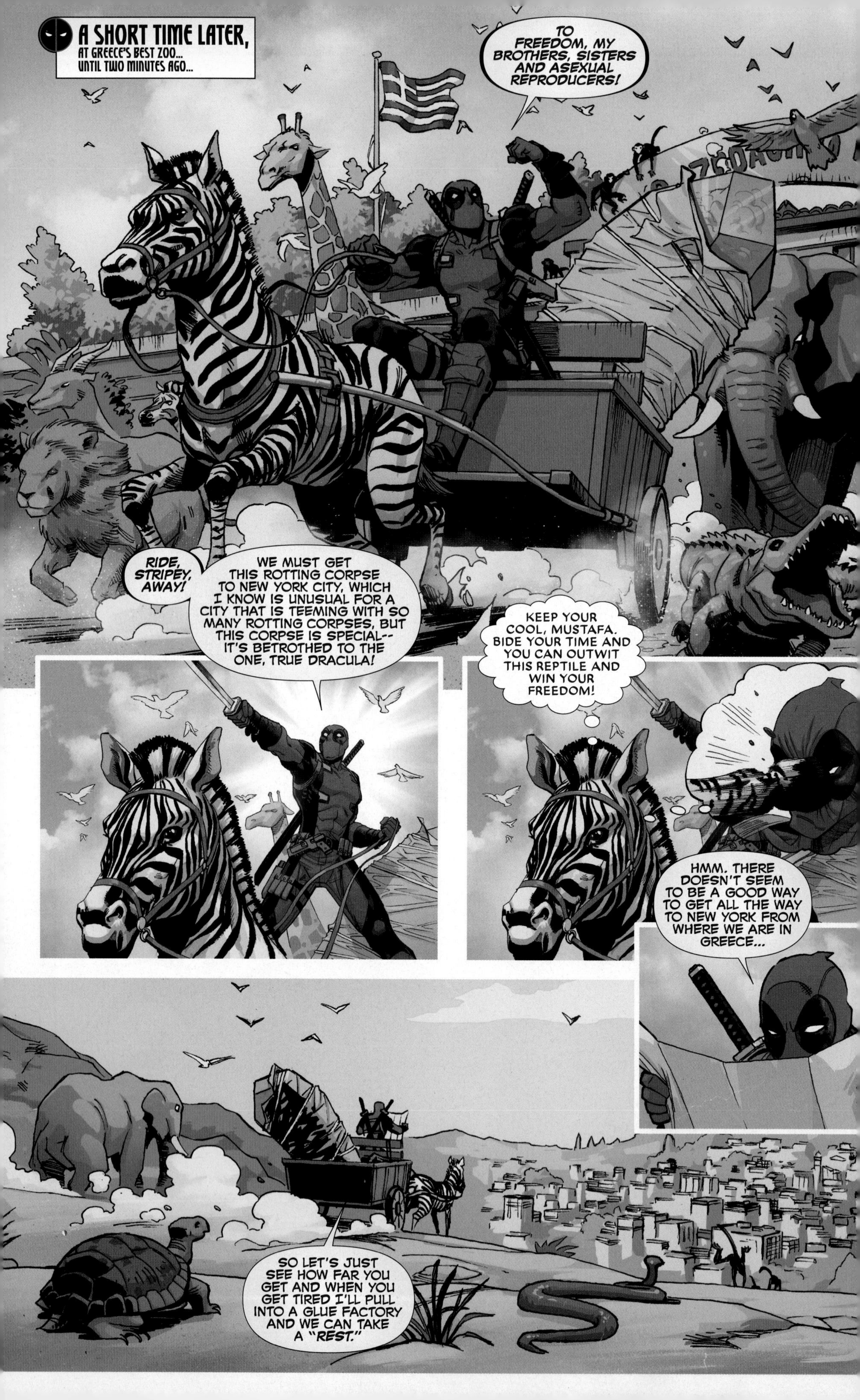
A SHORT TIME LATER,
AT GREECE'S BEST ZOO... UNTIL TWO MINUTES AGO...
TO FREEDOM, MY BROTHERS, SISTERS AND ASEXUAL REPRODUCERS!
RIDE, STRIPEY, AWAY!
WE MUST GET THIS ROTTING CORPSE TO NEW YORK CITY, WHICH I KNOW IS UNUSUAL FOR A CITY THAT IS TEEMING WITH SO MANY ROTTING CORPSES, BUT THIS CORPSE IS SPECIAL-- IT'S BETROTHED TO THE ONE, TRUE DRACULA!
KEEP YOUR COOL, MUSTAFA. BIDE YOUR TIME AND YOU CAN OUTWIT THIS REPTILE AND WIN YOUR FREEDOM!
HMM. THERE DOESN'T SEEM TO BE A GOOD WAY TO GET ALL THE WAY TO NEW YORK FROM WHERE WE ARE IN GREECE...
SO LET'S JUST SEE HOW FAR YOU GET AND WHEN YOU GET TIRED I'LL PULL INTO A GLUE FACTORY AND WE CAN TAKE A "REST."

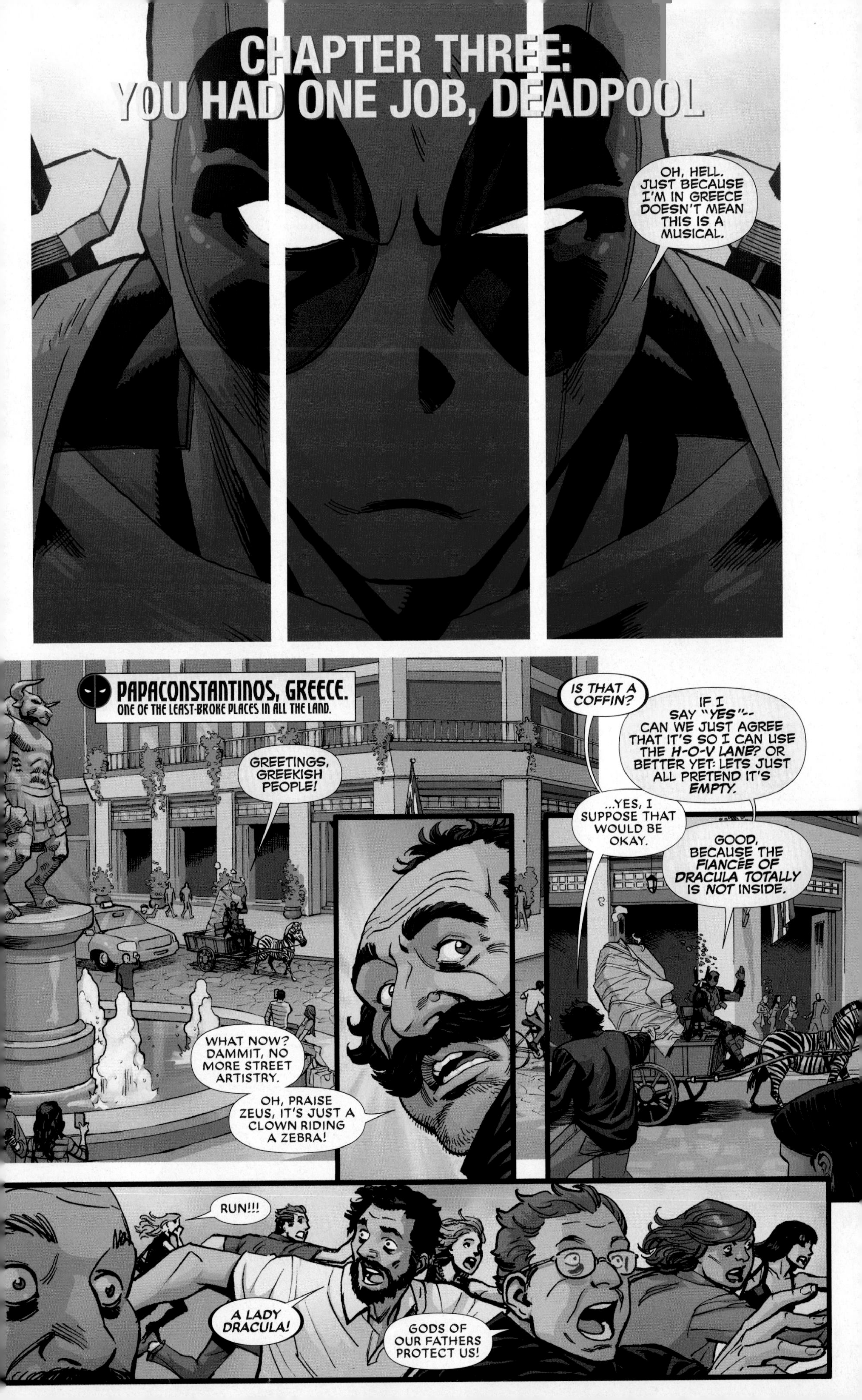
CHAPTER THREE:
YOU HAD ONE JOB, DEADPOOL
OH, HELL. JUST BECAUSE I'M IN GREECE DOESN'T MEAN THIS IS A MUSICAL.
PAPACONSTANTINOS, GREECE.
ONE OF THE LEAST-BROKE PLACES IN ALL THE LAND.
GREETINGS, GREEKISH PEOPLE!
WHAT NOW? DAMMIT, NO MORE STREET ARTISTRY.
OH, PRAISE ZEUS, IT'S JUST A CLOWN RIDING A ZEBRA!
IS THAT A COFFIN?
IF I SAY "YES"-- CAN WE JUST AGREE THAT IT'S SO I CAN USE THE H-O-V LANE? OR BETTER YET: LETS JUST ALL PRETEND IT'S EMPTY.
...YES, I SUPPOSE THAT WOULD BE OKAY.
GOOD, BECAUSE THE FIANCÉE OF DRACULA TOTALLY IS NOT INSIDE.
RUN!!!
A LADY DRACULA!
GODS OF OUR FATHERS PROTECT US!

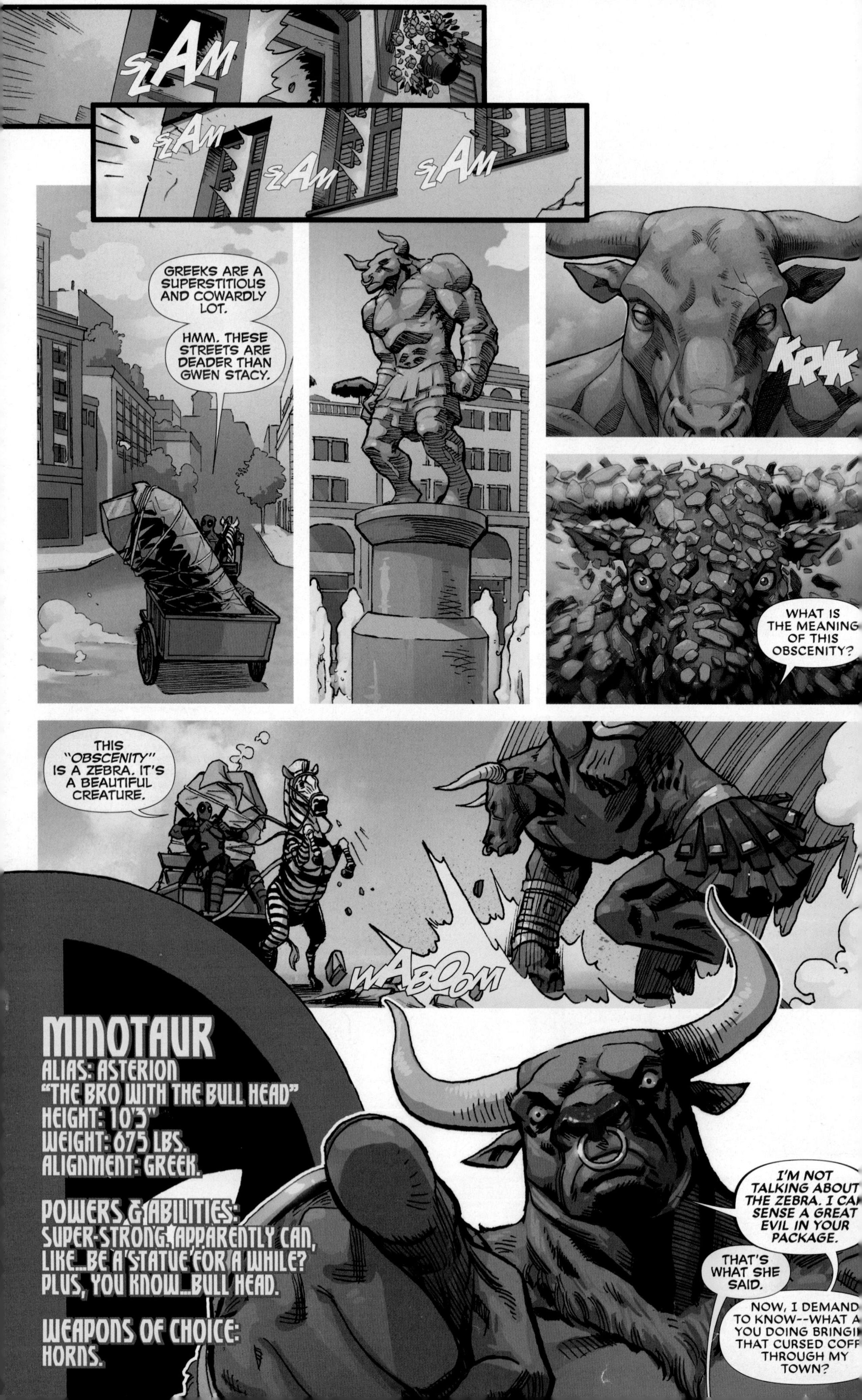
SLAM
SLAM
SLAM
SLAM
GREEKS ARE A SUPERSTITIOUS AND COWARDLY LOT.
HMM. THESE STREETS ARE DEADER THAN GWEN STACY.
KRAK
WHAT IS THE MEANING OF THIS OBSCENITY?
THIS "OBSCENITY" IS A ZEBRA. IT'S A BEAUTIFUL CREATURE.
WABOOM
MINOTAUR
ALIAS: ASTERION
"THE BRO WITH THE BULL HEAD"
HEIGHT: 10'3"
WEIGHT: 675 LBS.
ALIGNMENT: GREEK.
POWERS & ABILITIES:
SUPER-STRONG, APPARENTLY CAN, LIKE...BE A STATUE FOR A WHILE? PLUS, YOU KNOW...BULL HEAD.
WEAPONS OF CHOICE:
HORNS.
I'M NOT TALKING ABOUT THE ZEBRA. I CAN SENSE A GREAT EVIL IN YOUR PACKAGE.
THAT'S WHAT SHE SAID.
NOW, I DEMAND TO KNOW--WHAT ARE YOU DOING BRINGING THAT CURSED COFFIN THROUGH MY TOWN?

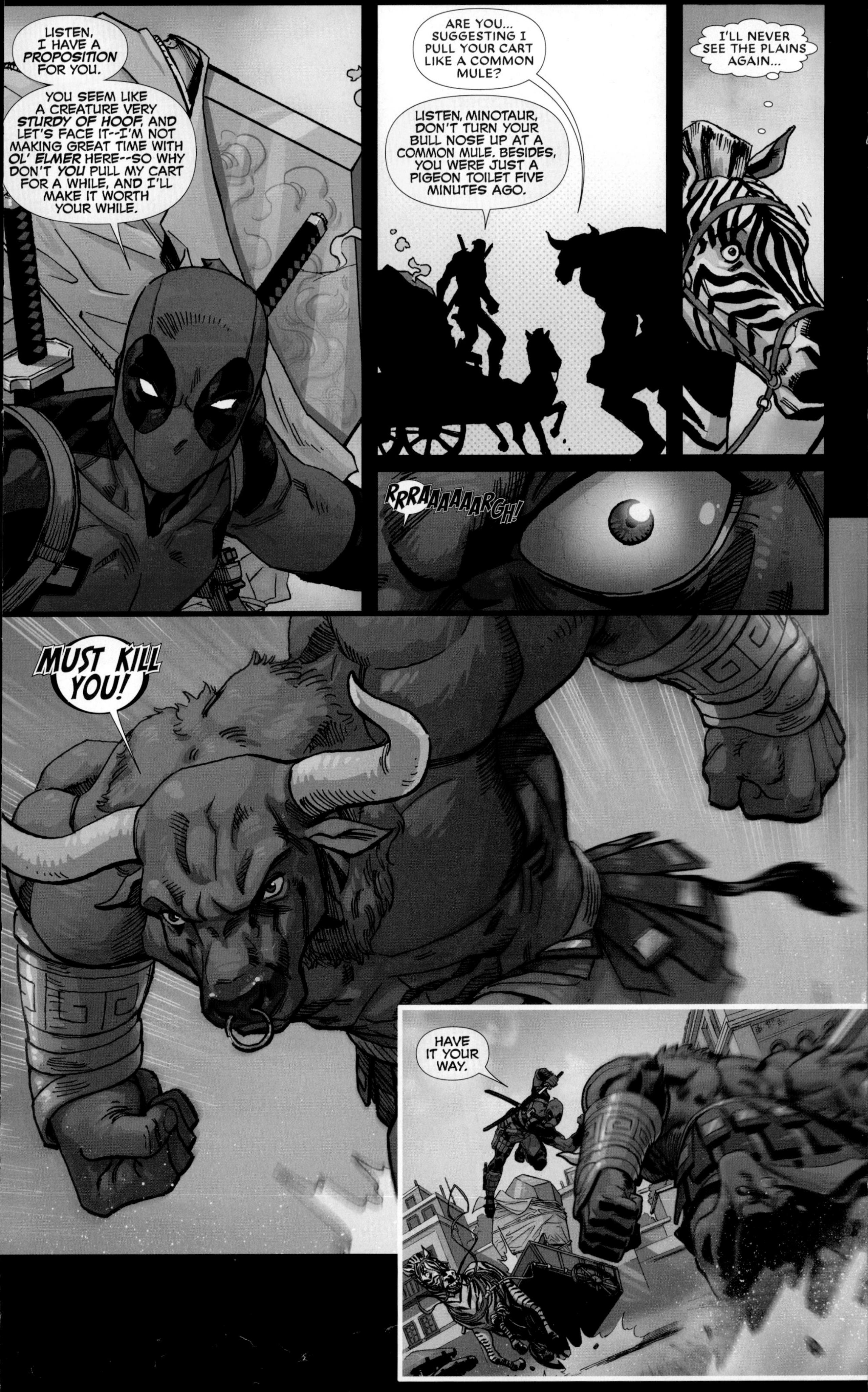
LISTEN, I HAVE A PROPOSITION FOR YOU.
YOU SEEM LIKE A CREATURE VERY STURDY OF HOOF, AND LET'S FACE IT--I'M NOT MAKING GREAT TIME WITH OL' ELMER HERE--SO WHY DON'T YOU PULL MY CART FOR A WHILE, AND I'LL MAKE IT WORTH YOUR WHILE.
ARE YOU... SUGGESTING I PULL YOUR CART LIKE A COMMON MULE?
LISTEN, MINOTAUR, DON'T TURN YOUR BULL NOSE UP AT A COMMON MULE. BESIDES, YOU WERE JUST A PIGEON TOILET FIVE MINUTES AGO.
I'LL NEVER SEE THE PLAINS AGAIN...
RRRAAAAAARGH!
MUST KILL YOU!
HAVE IT YOUR WAY.

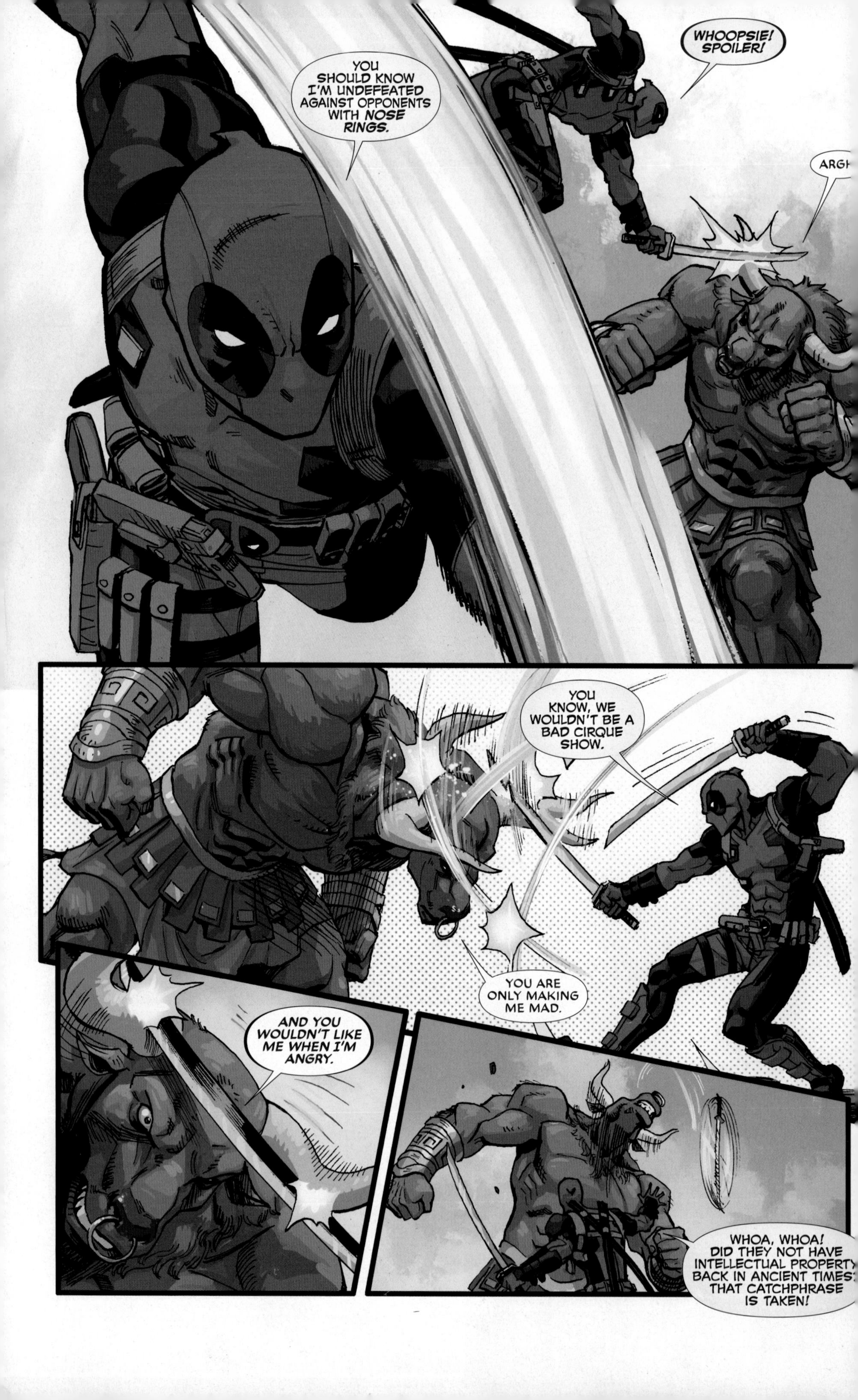
YOU SHOULD KNOW I'M UNDEFEATED AGAINST OPPONENTS WITH NOSE RINGS.
WHOOPSIE! SPOILER!
ARGH
YOU KNOW, WE WOULDN'T BE A BAD CIRQUE SHOW.
YOU ARE ONLY MAKING ME MAD.
AND YOU WOULDN'T LIKE ME WHEN I'M ANGRY.
WHOA, WHOA! DID THEY NOT HAVE INTELLECTUAL PROPERTY BACK IN ANCIENT TIMES? THAT CATCHPHRASE IS TAKEN!

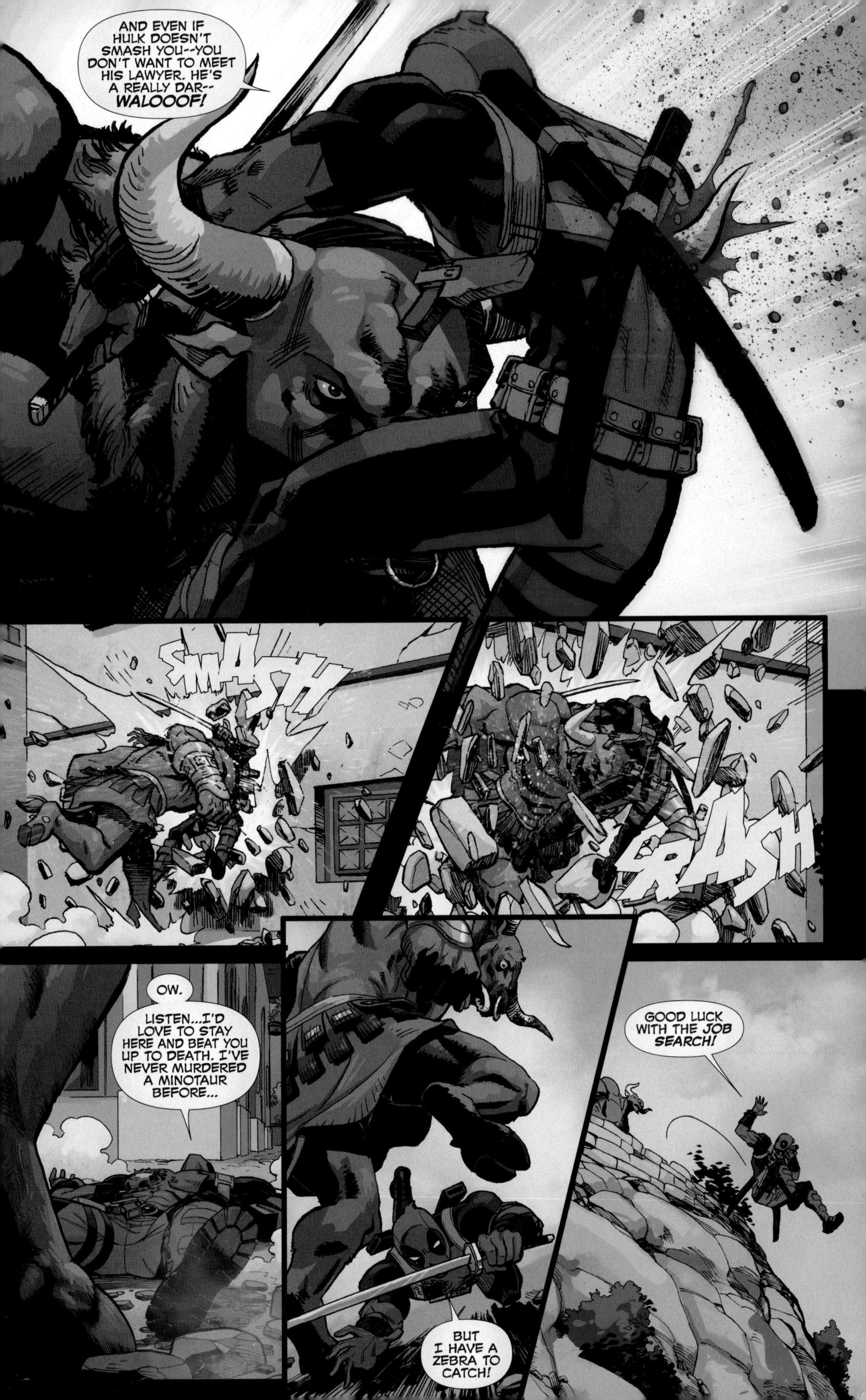
AND EVEN IF HULK DOESN'T SMASH YOU--YOU DON'T WANT TO MEET HIS LAWYER. HE'S A REALLY DAR-- WALOOOF!
SMASH
CRASH
OW.
LISTEN...I'D LOVE TO STAY HERE AND BEAT YOU UP TO DEATH. I'VE NEVER MURDERED A MINOTAUR BEFORE...
BUT I HAVE A ZEBRA TO CATCH!
GOOD LUCK WITH THE JOB SEARCH!

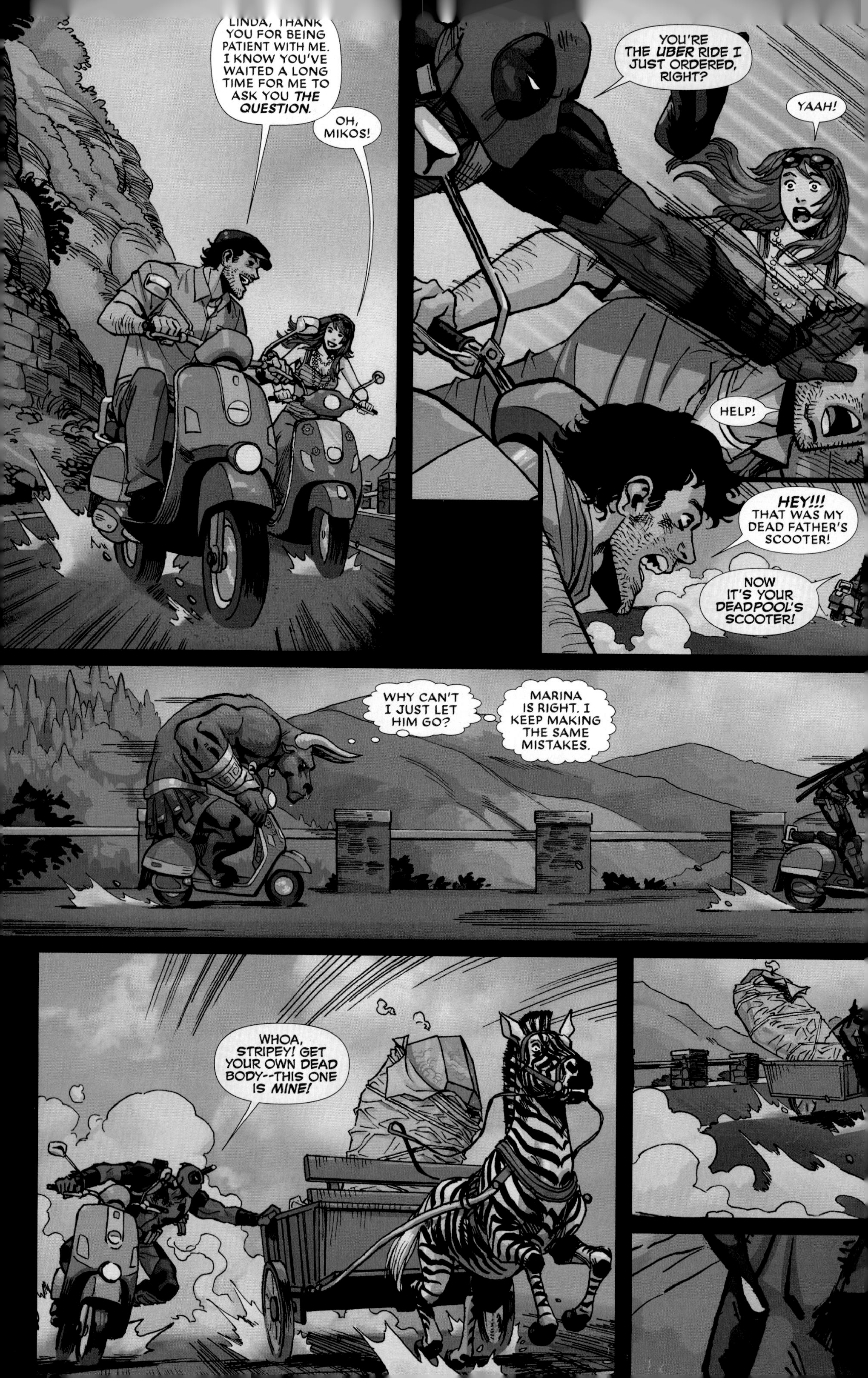
LINDA, THANK YOU FOR BEING PATIENT WITH ME. I KNOW YOU'VE WAITED A LONG TIME FOR ME TO ASK YOU THE QUESTION.
OH, MIKOS!
YOU'RE THE UBER RIDE I JUST ORDERED, RIGHT?
YAAH!
HELP!
HEY!!! THAT WAS MY DEAD FATHER'S SCOOTER!
NOW IT'S YOUR DEADPOOL'S SCOOTER!
WHY CAN'T I JUST LET HIM GO?
MARINA IS RIGHT. I KEEP MAKING THE SAME MISTAKES.
WHOA, STRIPEY! GET YOUR OWN DEAD BODY--THIS ONE IS MINE!

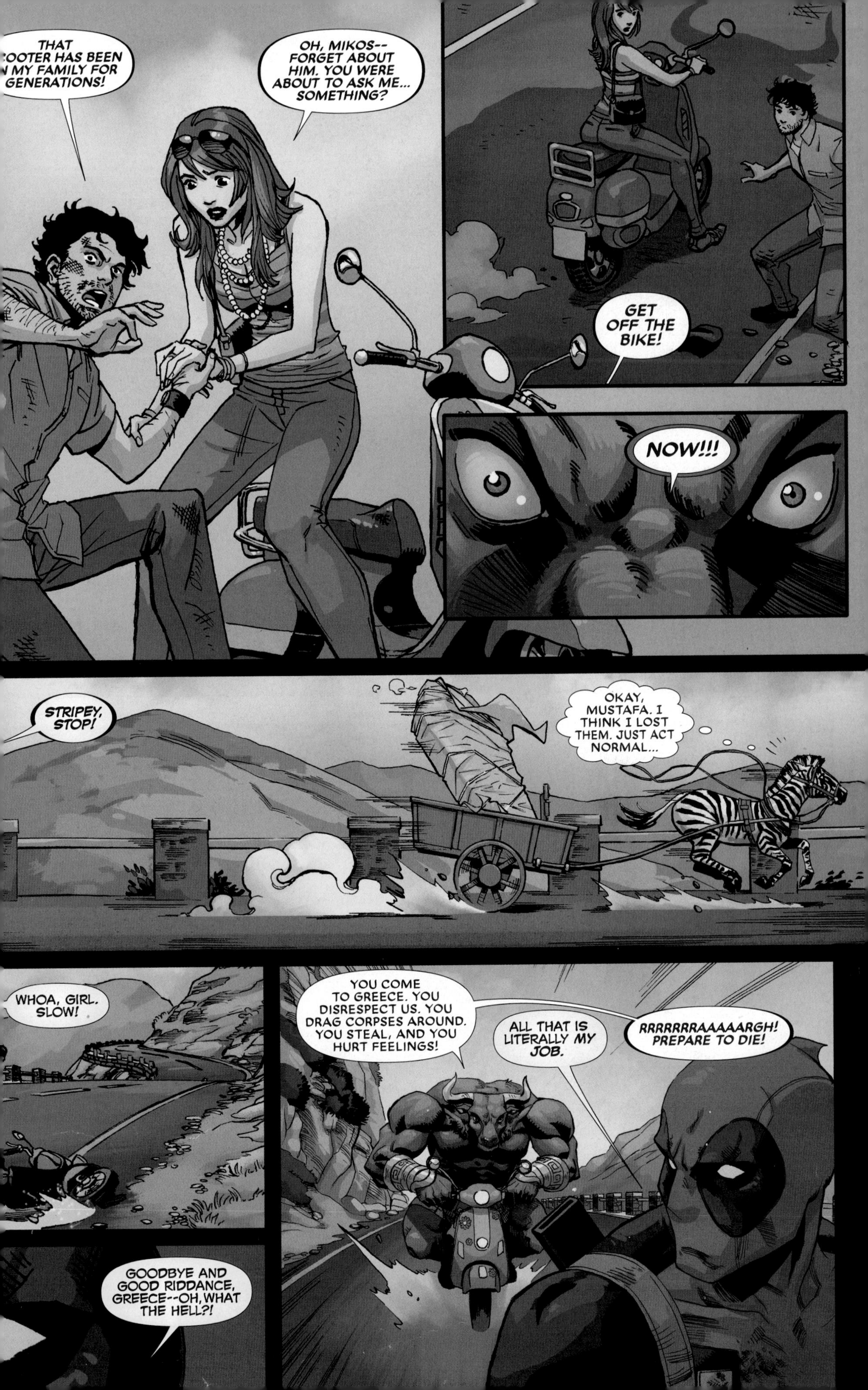
THAT COOTER HAS BEEN N MY FAMILY FOR GENERATIONS!
OH, MIKOS-- FORGET ABOUT HIM. YOU WERE ABOUT TO ASK ME... SOMETHING?
GET OFF THE BIKE!
NOW!!!
STRIPEY, STOP!
OKAY, MUSTAFA. I THINK I LOST THEM. JUST ACT NORMAL...
WHOA, GIRL. SLOW!
GOODBYE AND GOOD RIDDANCE, GREECE--OH, WHAT THE HELL?!
YOU COME TO GREECE. YOU DISRESPECT US. YOU DRAG CORPSES AROUND. YOU STEAL, AND YOU HURT FEELINGS!
ALL THAT IS LITERALLY MY JOB.
RRRRRRRAAAAARGH! PREPARE TO DIE!

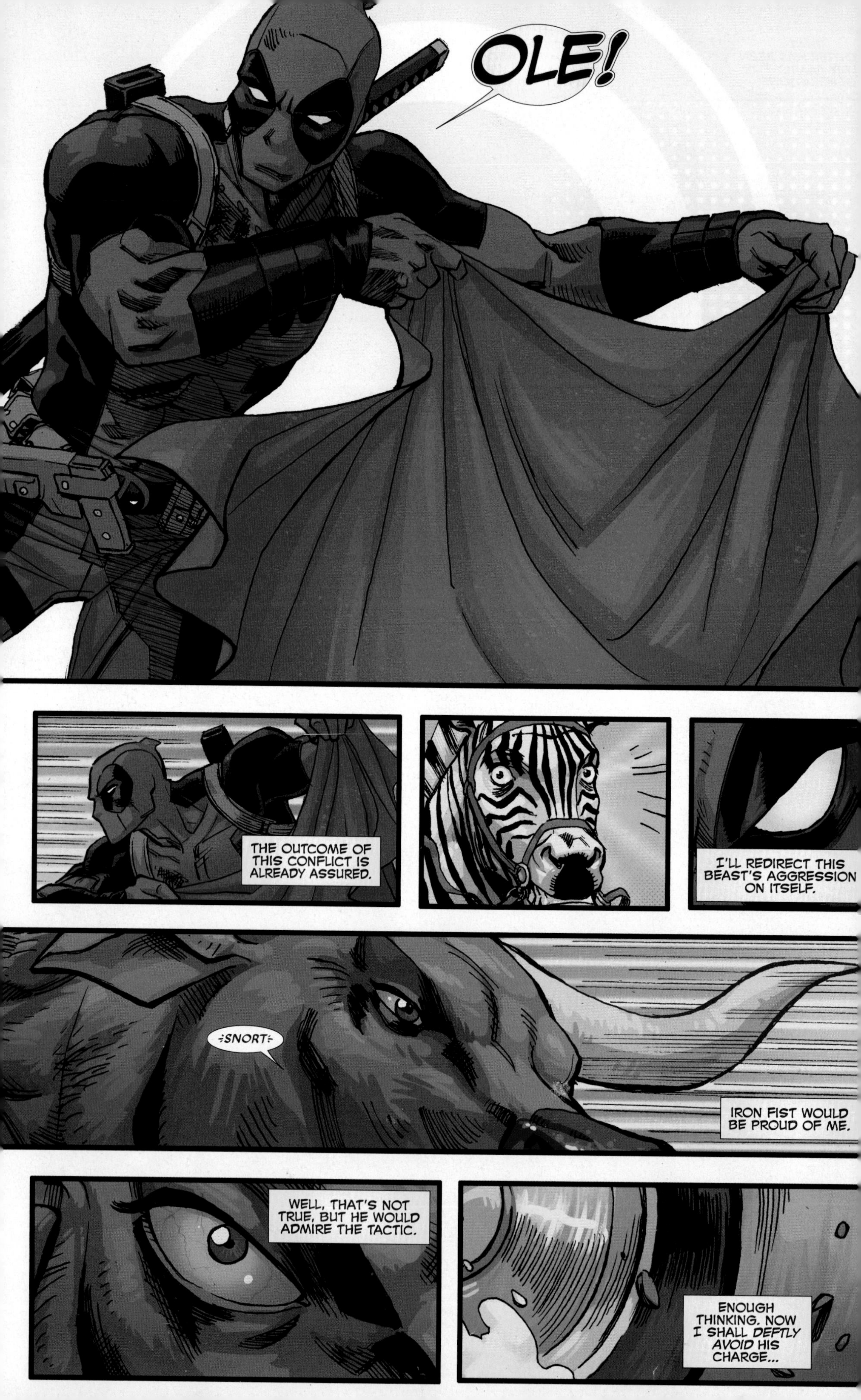
OLE!
THE OUTCOME OF THIS CONFLICT IS ALREADY ASSURED.
I'LL REDIRECT THIS BEAST'S AGGRESSION ON ITSELF.
SNORT
IRON FIST WOULD BE PROUD OF ME.
WELL, THAT'S NOT TRUE, BUT HE WOULD ADMIRE THE TACTIC.
ENOUGH THINKING. NOW I SHALL DEFTLY AVOID HIS CHARGE...

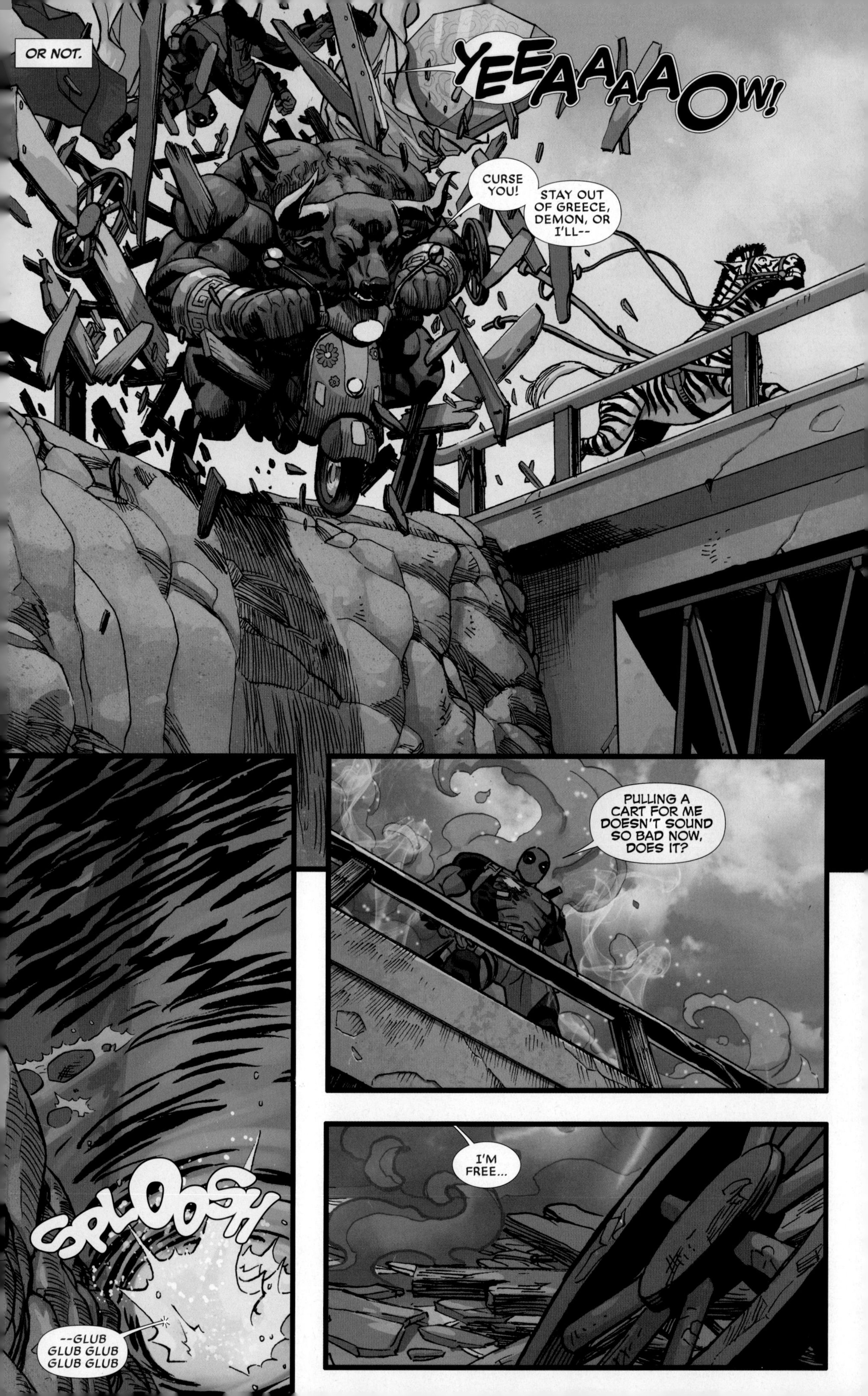
OR NOT.
YEEAAAAAOW!
CURSE YOU!
STAY OUT OF GREECE, DEMON, OR I'LL--
SPLOOSH
--GLUB GLUB GLUB GLUB GLUB
PULLING A CART FOR ME DOESN'T SOUND SO BAD NOW, DOES IT?
I'M FREE...

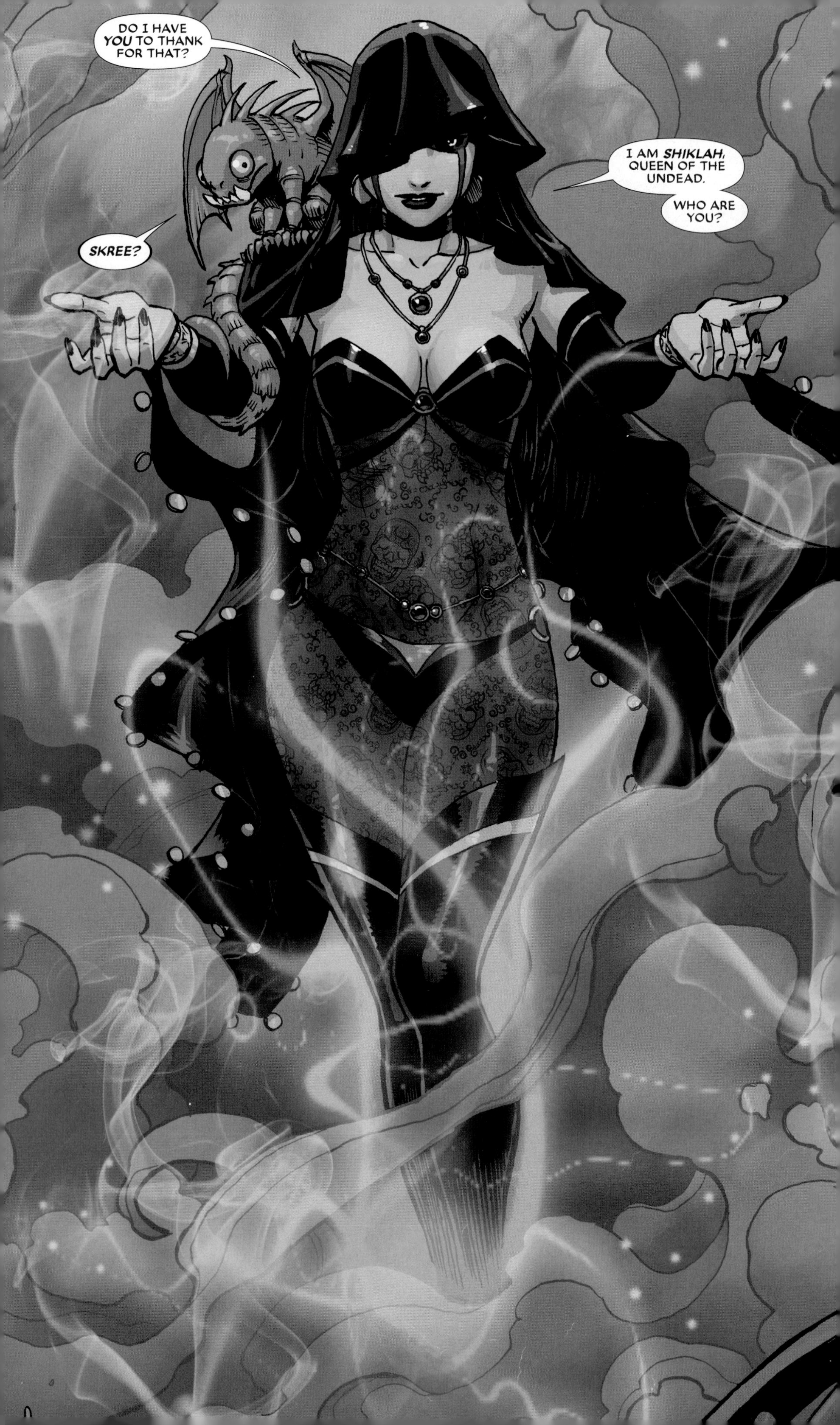
DO I HAVE YOU TO THANK FOR THAT?
SKREE?
I AM SHIKLAH, QUEEN OF THE UNDEAD.
WHO ARE YOU?

MEANWHILE, BACK IN THE DESERT...

A BURRITO.

THERE'S ONLY ONE THING THAT COULD MEAN.

BLADE
ALIAS: ERIC BROOKS "THE DAYWALKER"
HEIGHT: 6'2"
WEIGHT: 215 LBS.
ALIGNMENT: GOOD, IF YOU'RE NOT A VAMPIRE. USUALLY.

POWERS & ABILITIES:
ALL THE POWERS
(AND BEVERAGE PREFERENCES)
OF YOUR AVERAGE VAMPIRE...
PLUS, HE CAN GO OUT IN THE SUN.

WEAPONS OF CHOICE:
WORDS & STAKES.

DEADPOOL. IF YOU'RE HELPING SHIKLAH, THEN BLADE'S COMING FOR YOU.

COUNT ON IT.

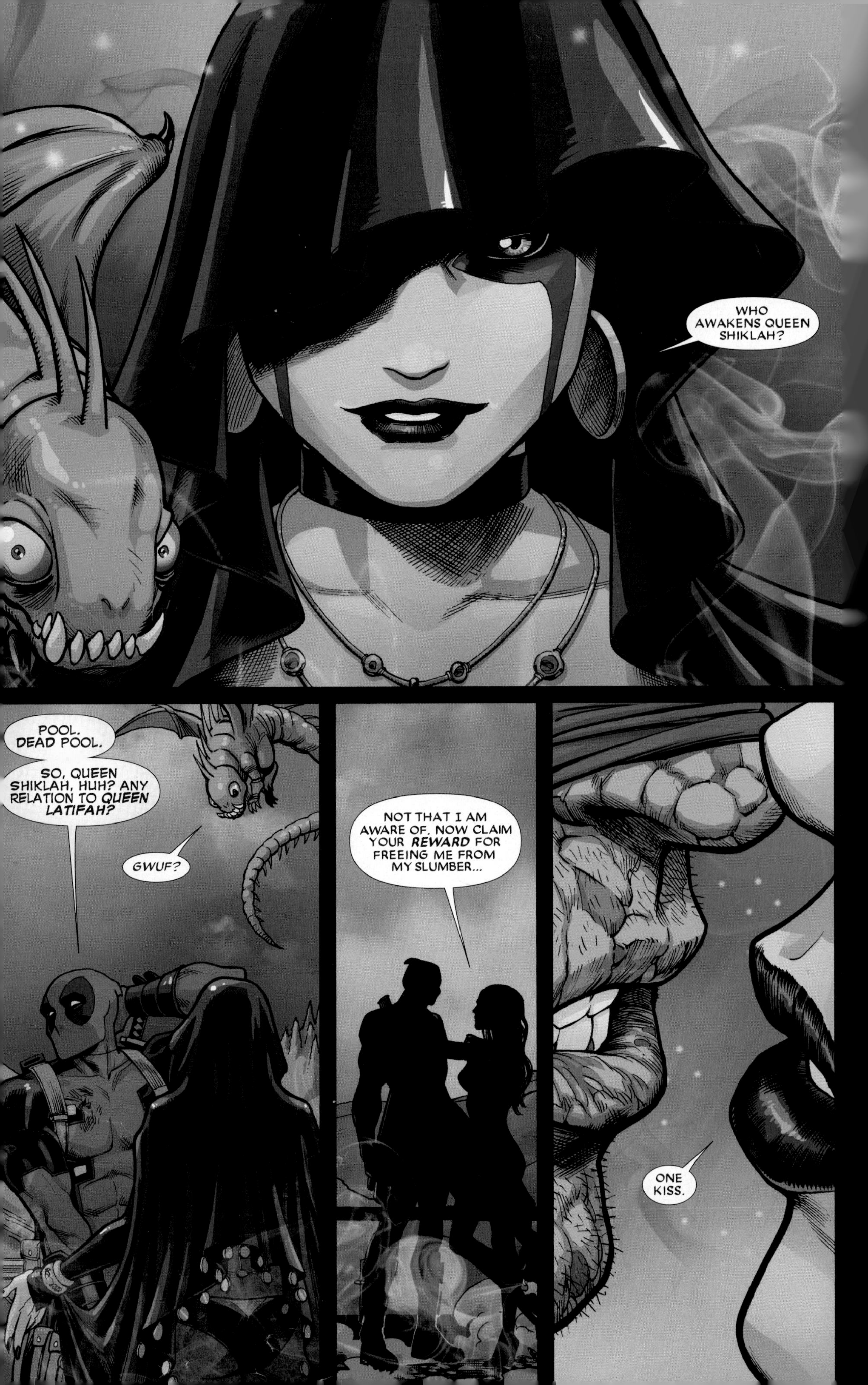

WHO AWAKENS QUEEN SHIKLAH?
POOL. DEAD POOL.
SO, QUEEN SHIKLAH, HUH? ANY RELATION TO *QUEEN LATIFAH?*
GWUF?
NOT THAT I AM AWARE OF. NOW CLAIM YOUR *REWARD* FOR FREEING ME FROM MY SLUMBER...
ONE KISS.

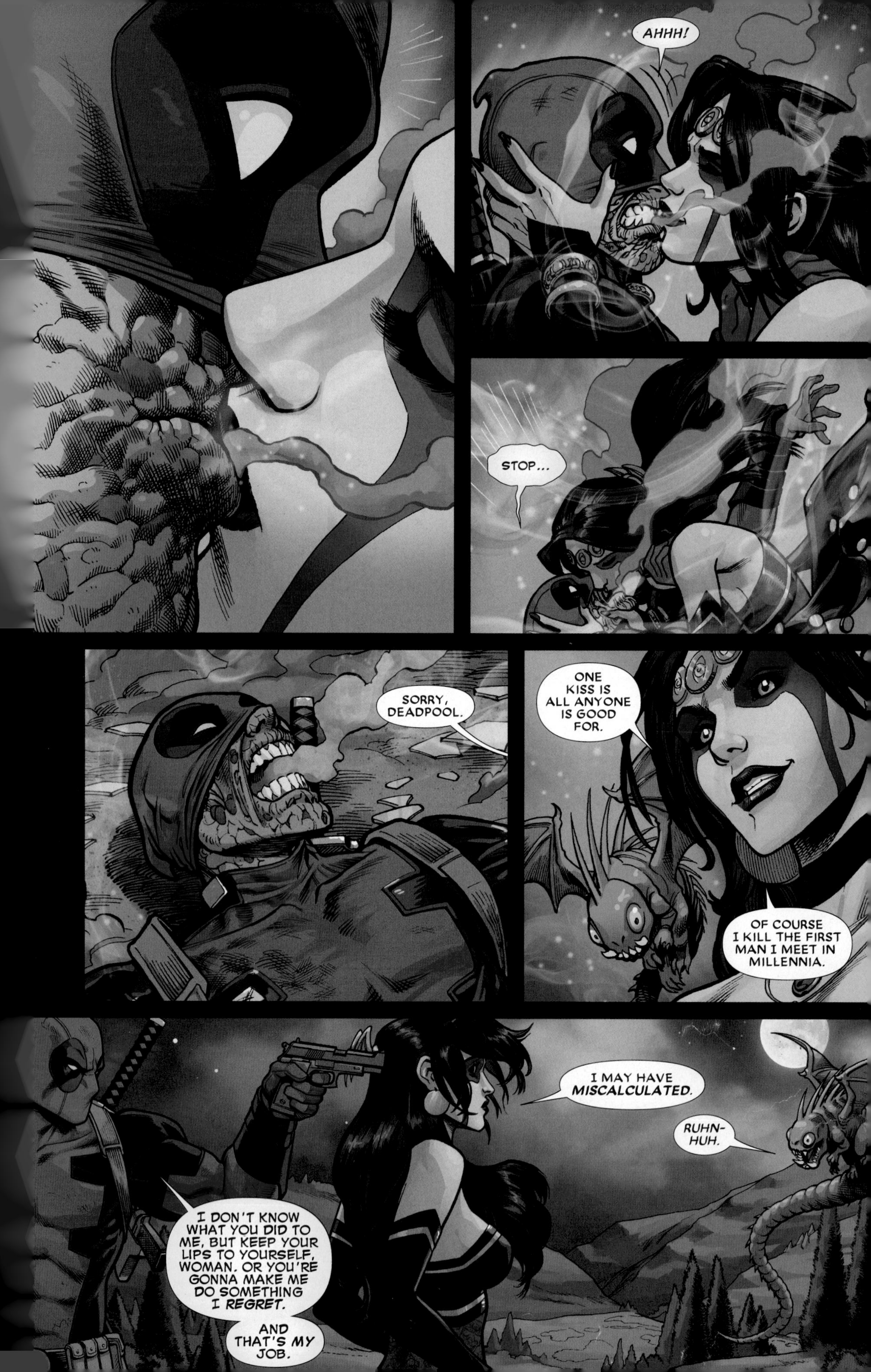
AHHH!
STOP...
SORRY, DEADPOOL.
ONE KISS IS ALL ANYONE IS GOOD FOR.
OF COURSE I KILL THE FIRST MAN I MEET IN MILLENNIA.
I MAY HAVE *MISCALCULATED*.
RUHN-HUH.
I DON'T KNOW WHAT YOU DID TO ME, BUT KEEP YOUR LIPS TO YOURSELF, WOMAN. OR YOU'RE GONNA MAKE ME DO SOMETHING I *REGRET*.
AND THAT'S *MY* JOB.

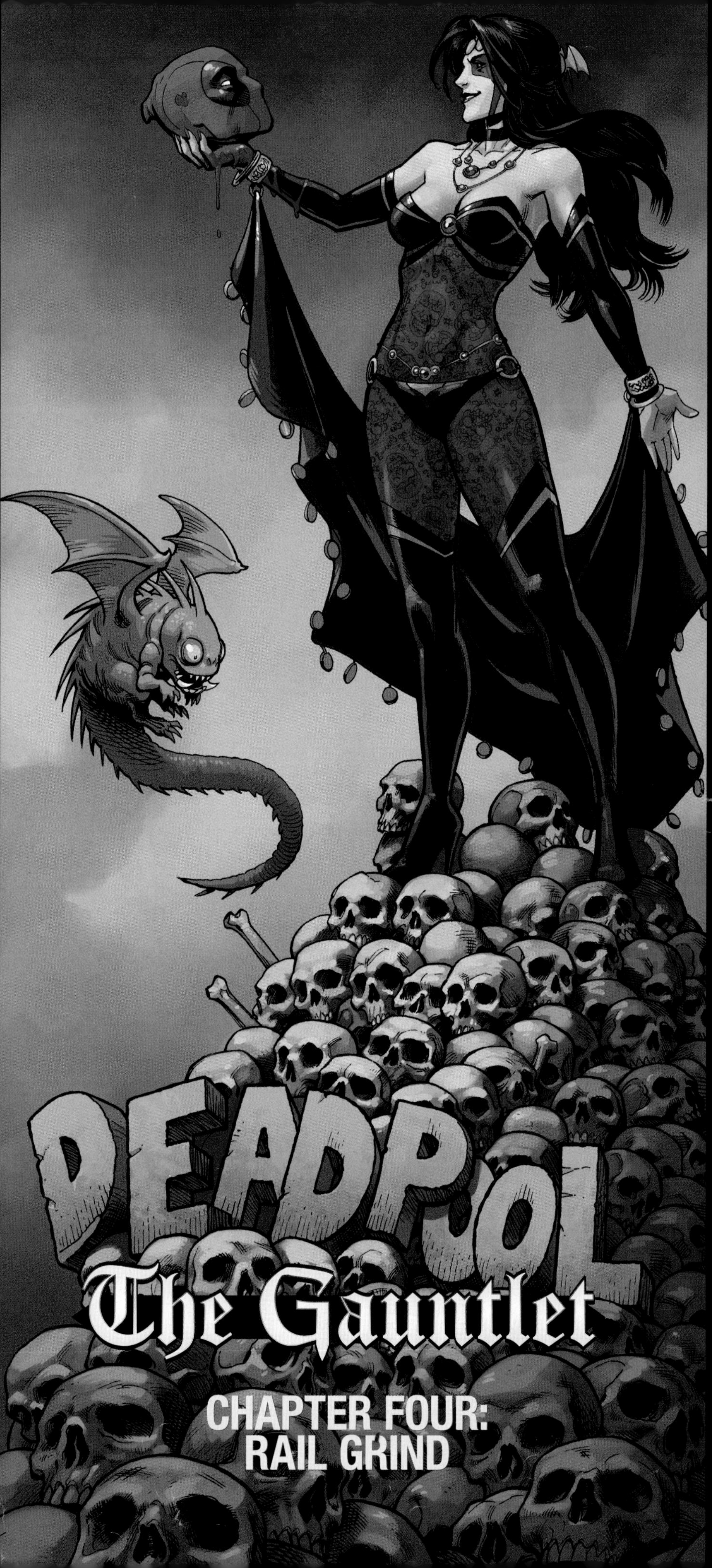
DEADPOOL
The Gauntlet
CHAPTER FOUR:
RAIL GRIND

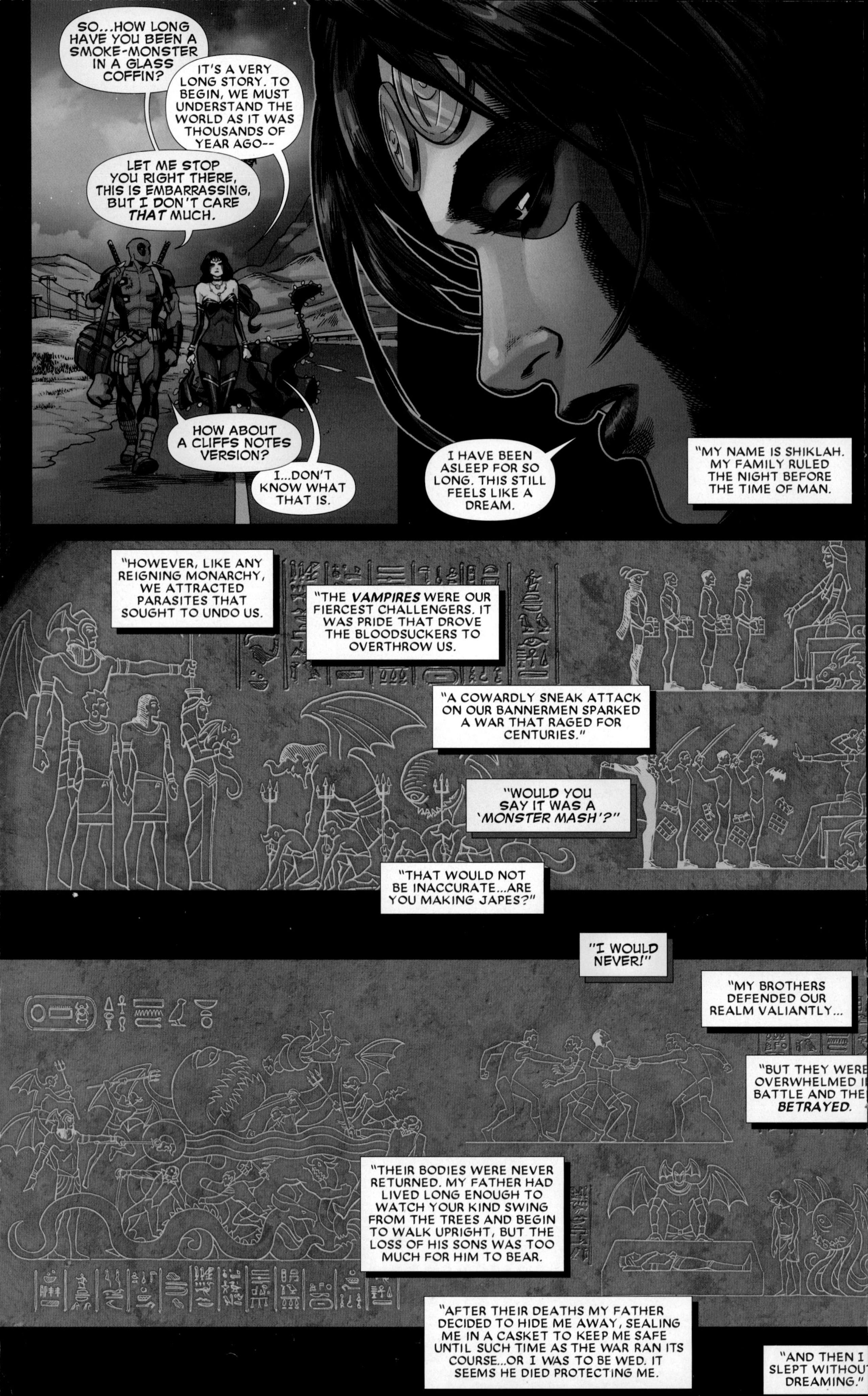
SO...HOW LONG HAVE YOU BEEN A SMOKE-MONSTER IN A GLASS COFFIN?
IT'S A VERY LONG STORY. TO BEGIN, WE MUST UNDERSTAND THE WORLD AS IT WAS THOUSANDS OF YEAR AGO--
LET ME STOP YOU RIGHT THERE, THIS IS EMBARRASSING, BUT I DON'T CARE THAT MUCH.
HOW ABOUT A CLIFFS NOTES VERSION?
I...DON'T KNOW WHAT THAT IS.
I HAVE BEEN ASLEEP FOR SO LONG. THIS STILL FEELS LIKE A DREAM.
"MY NAME IS SHIKLAH. MY FAMILY RULED THE NIGHT BEFORE THE TIME OF MAN.
"HOWEVER, LIKE ANY REIGNING MONARCHY, WE ATTRACTED PARASITES THAT SOUGHT TO UNDO US.
"THE VAMPIRES WERE OUR FIERCEST CHALLENGERS. IT WAS PRIDE THAT DROVE THE BLOODSUCKERS TO OVERTHROW US.
"A COWARDLY SNEAK ATTACK ON OUR BANNERMEN SPARKED A WAR THAT RAGED FOR CENTURIES."
"WOULD YOU SAY IT WAS A 'MONSTER MASH'?"
"THAT WOULD NOT BE INACCURATE...ARE YOU MAKING JAPES?"
"I WOULD NEVER!"
"MY BROTHERS DEFENDED OUR REALM VALIANTLY...
"BUT THEY WERE OVERWHELMED IN BATTLE AND THE BETRAYED.
"THEIR BODIES WERE NEVER RETURNED. MY FATHER HAD LIVED LONG ENOUGH TO WATCH YOUR KIND SWING FROM THE TREES AND BEGIN TO WALK UPRIGHT, BUT THE LOSS OF HIS SONS WAS TOO MUCH FOR HIM TO BEAR.
"AFTER THEIR DEATHS MY FATHER DECIDED TO HIDE ME AWAY, SEALING ME IN A CASKET TO KEEP ME SAFE UNTIL SUCH TIME AS THE WAR RAN ITS COURSE...OR I WAS TO BE WED. IT SEEMS HE DIED PROTECTING ME.
"AND THEN I SLEPT WITHOUT DREAMING."

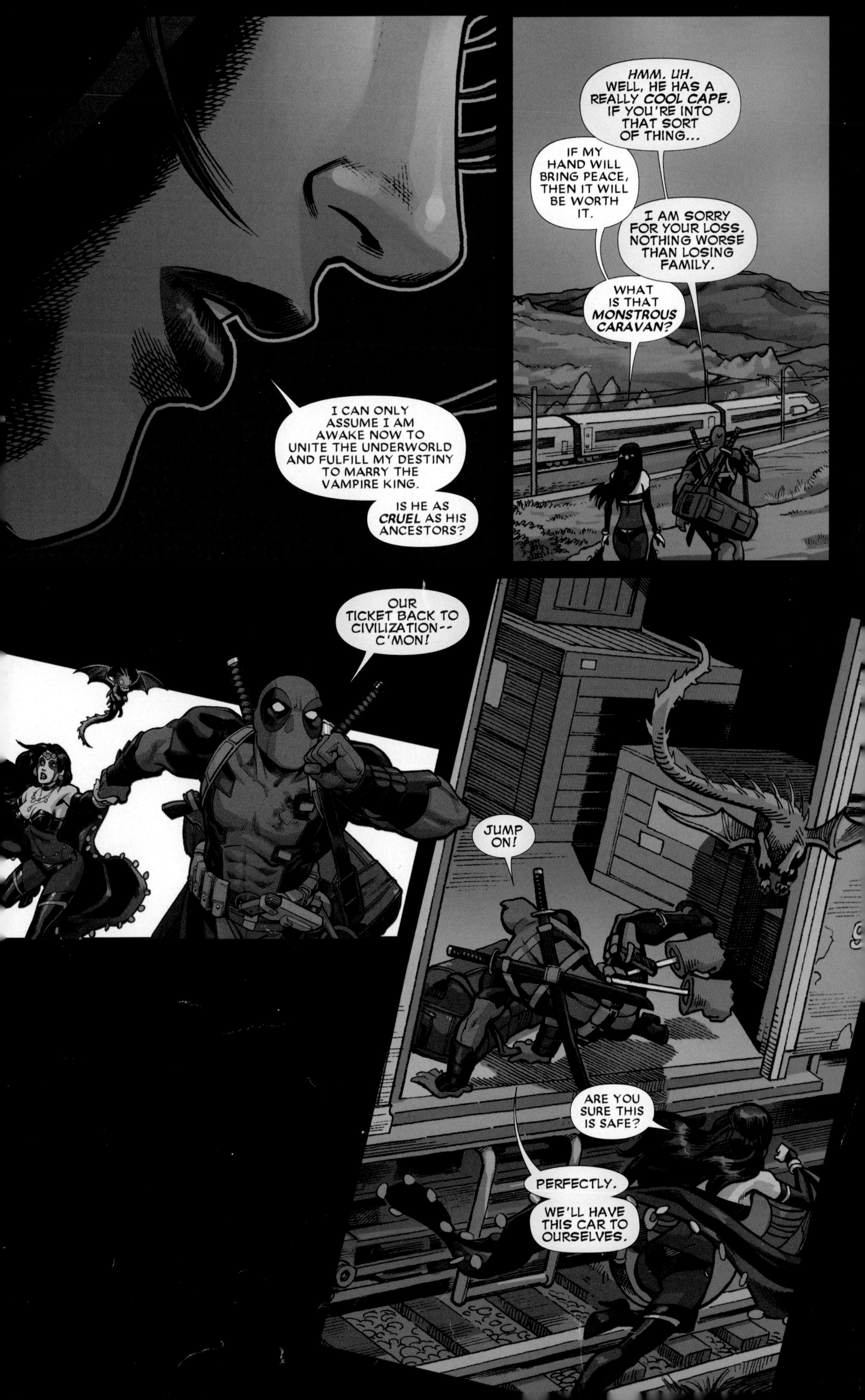
I CAN ONLY ASSUME I AM AWAKE NOW TO UNITE THE UNDERWORLD AND FULFILL MY DESTINY TO MARRY THE VAMPIRE KING.
IS HE AS *CRUEL* AS HIS ANCESTORS?
HMM. UH. WELL, HE HAS A REALLY *COOL CAPE.* IF YOU'RE INTO THAT SORT OF THING...
IF MY HAND WILL BRING PEACE, THEN IT WILL BE WORTH IT.
I AM SORRY FOR YOUR LOSS. NOTHING WORSE THAN LOSING FAMILY.
WHAT IS THAT *MONSTROUS CARAVAN?*
OUR TICKET BACK TO CIVILIZATION-- C'MON!
JUMP ON!
ARE YOU SURE THIS IS SAFE?
PERFECTLY.
WE'LL HAVE THIS CAR TO OURSELVES.

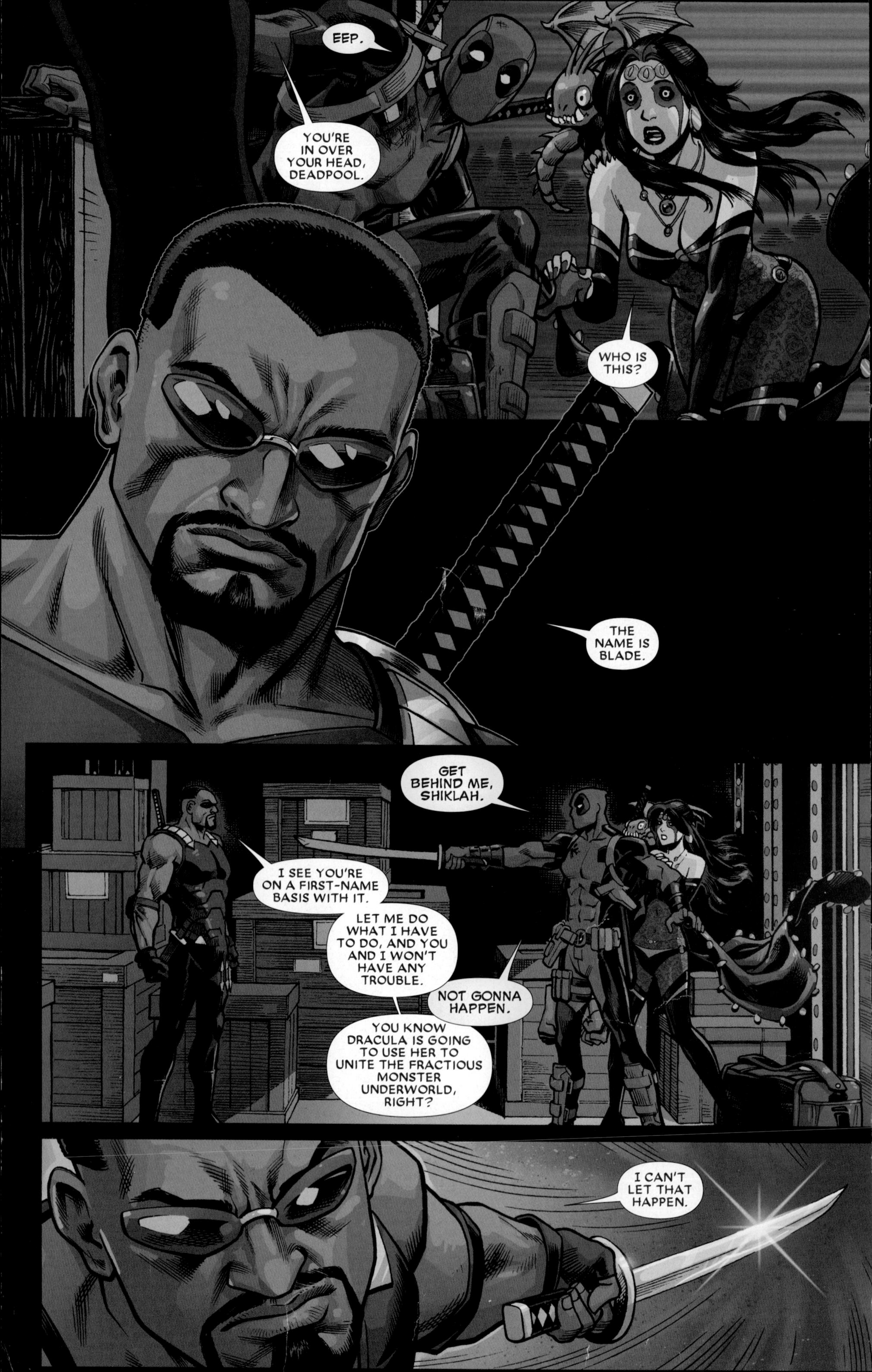
EEP.
YOU'RE IN OVER YOUR HEAD, DEADPOOL.
WHO IS THIS?
THE NAME IS BLADE.
GET BEHIND ME, SHIKLAH.
I SEE YOU'RE ON A FIRST-NAME BASIS WITH IT.
LET ME DO WHAT I HAVE TO DO, AND YOU AND I WON'T HAVE ANY TROUBLE.
NOT GONNA HAPPEN.
YOU KNOW DRACULA IS GOING TO USE HER TO UNITE THE FRACTIOUS MONSTER UNDERWORLD, RIGHT?
I CAN'T LET THAT HAPPEN.

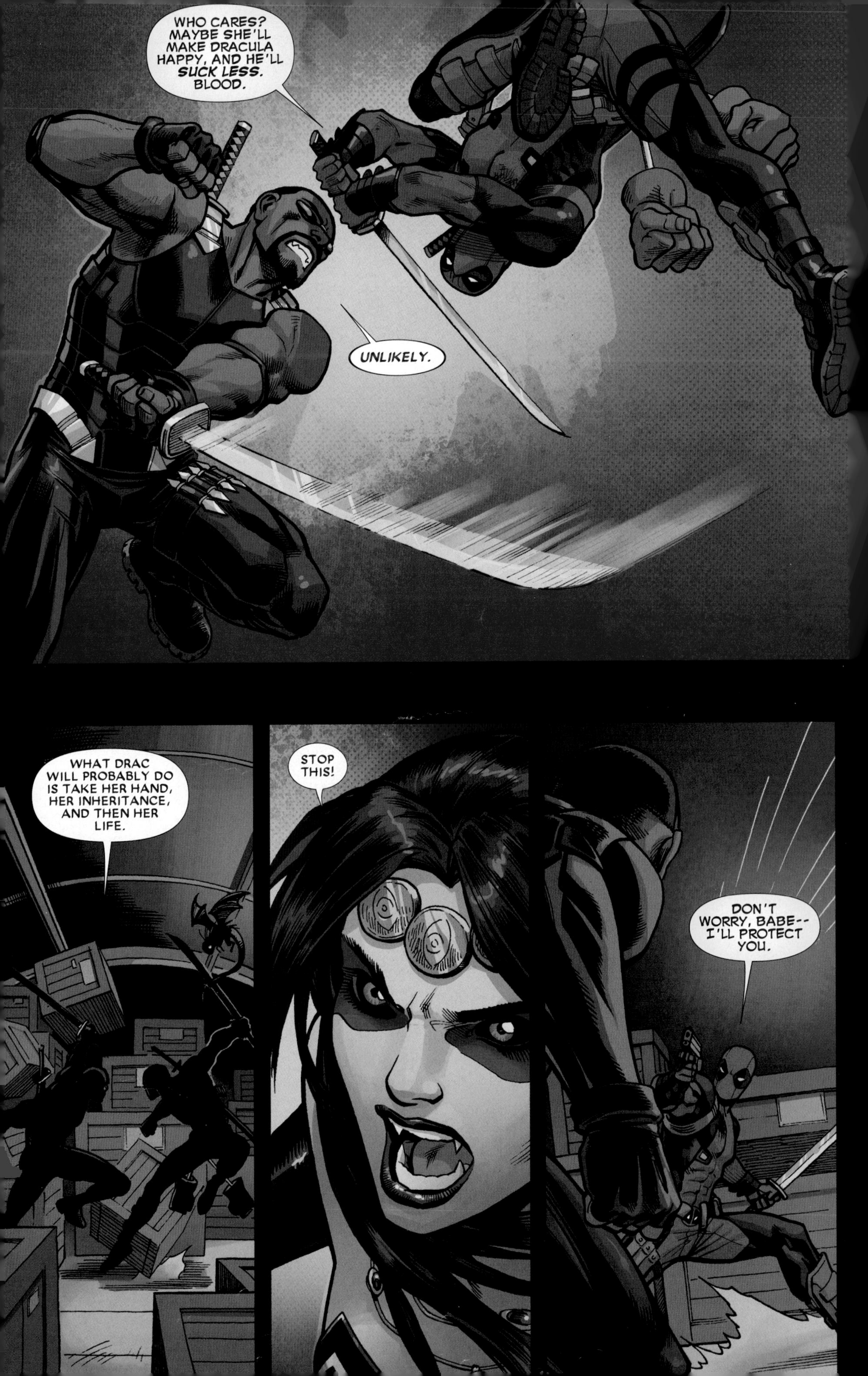
WHO CARES? MAYBE SHE'LL MAKE DRACULA HAPPY, AND HE'LL *SUCK LESS.* BLOOD.
UNLIKELY.
WHAT DRAC WILL PROBABLY DO IS TAKE HER HAND, HER INHERITANCE, AND THEN HER LIFE.
STOP THIS!
DON'T WORRY, BABE-- I'LL PROTECT YOU.

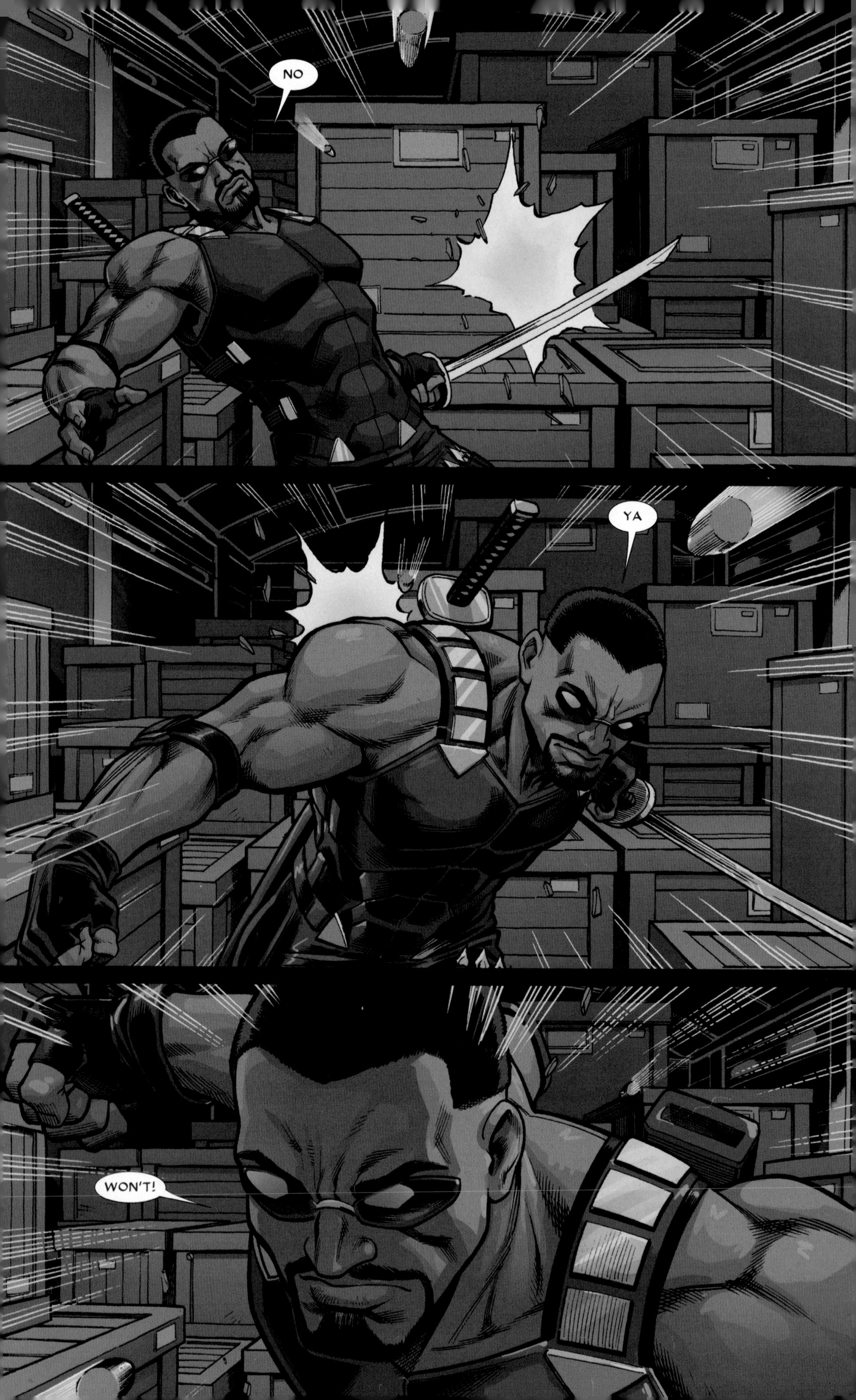
NO
YA
WON'T!

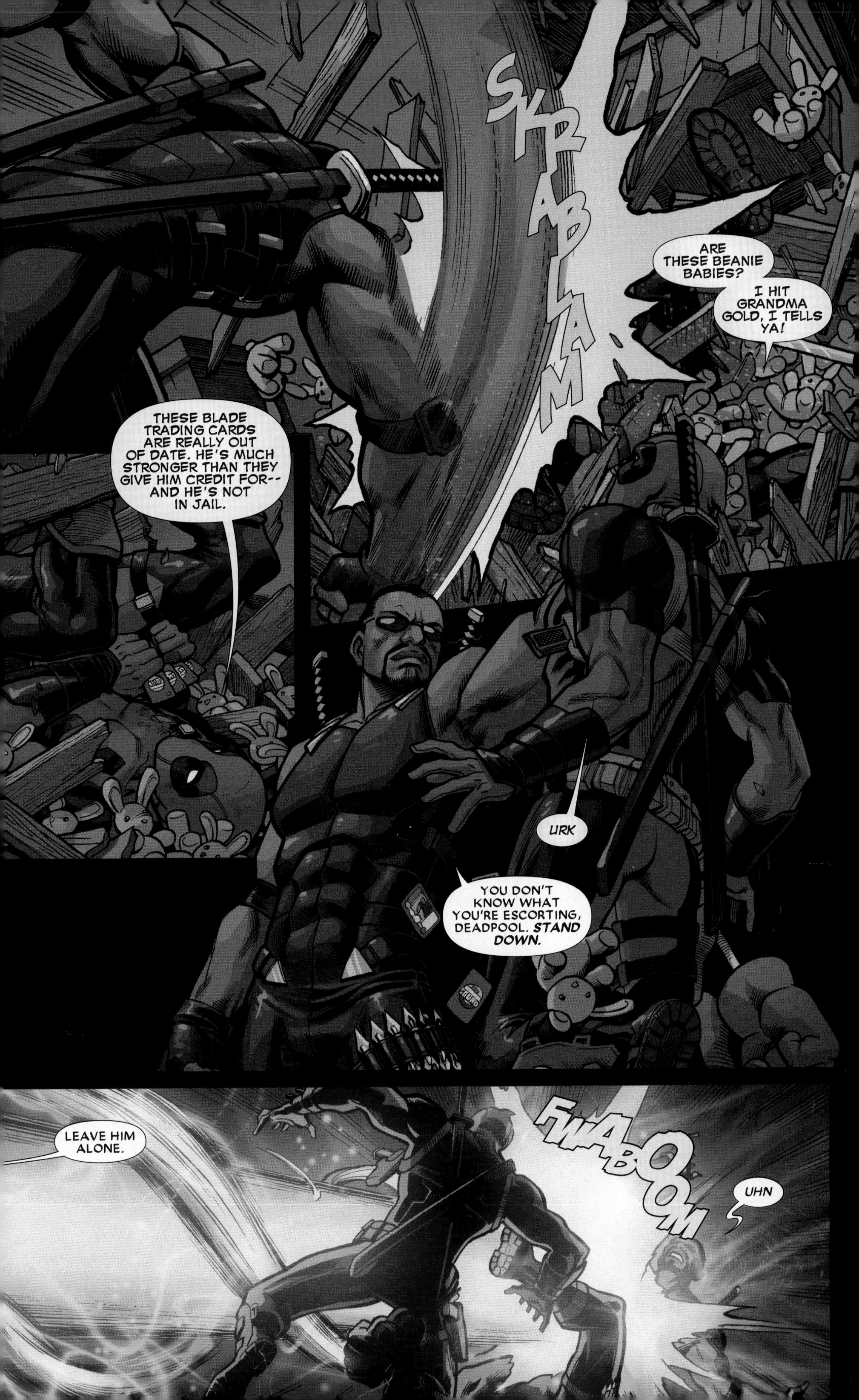
SKRABLAM
ARE THESE BEANIE BABIES?
I HIT GRANDMA GOLD, I TELLS YA!
THESE BLADE TRADING CARDS ARE REALLY OUT OF DATE. HE'S MUCH STRONGER THAN THEY GIVE HIM CREDIT FOR--AND HE'S NOT IN JAIL.
URK
YOU DON'T KNOW WHAT YOU'RE ESCORTING, DEADPOOL. STAND DOWN.
LEAVE HIM ALONE.
FWABOOM
UHN

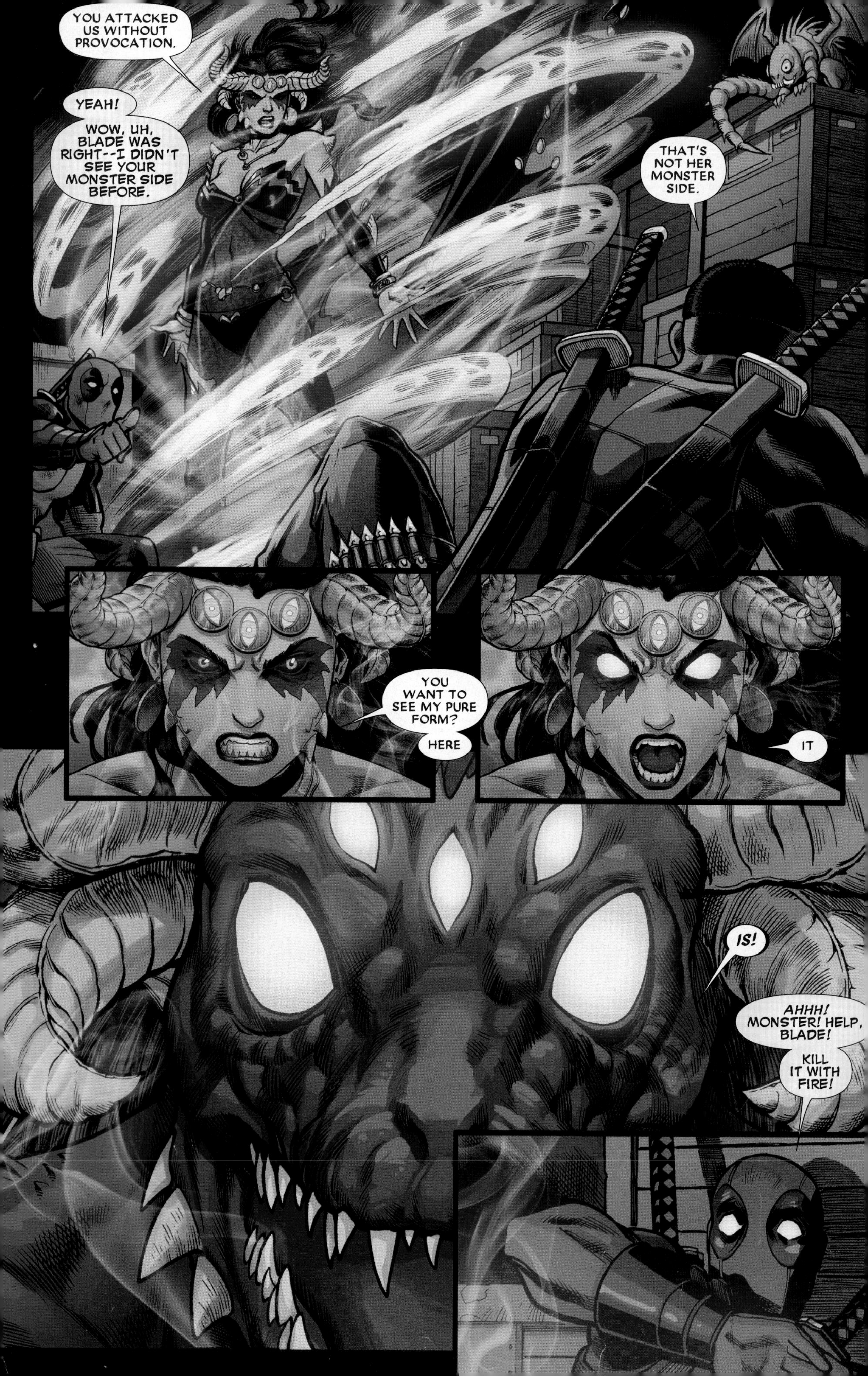
YOU ATTACKED US WITHOUT PROVOCATION.
YEAH!
WOW, UH, BLADE WAS RIGHT--I DIDN'T SEE YOUR MONSTER SIDE BEFORE.
THAT'S NOT HER MONSTER SIDE.
YOU WANT TO SEE MY PURE FORM?
HERE
IT
IS!
AHHH! MONSTER! HELP, BLADE!
KILL IT WITH FIRE!

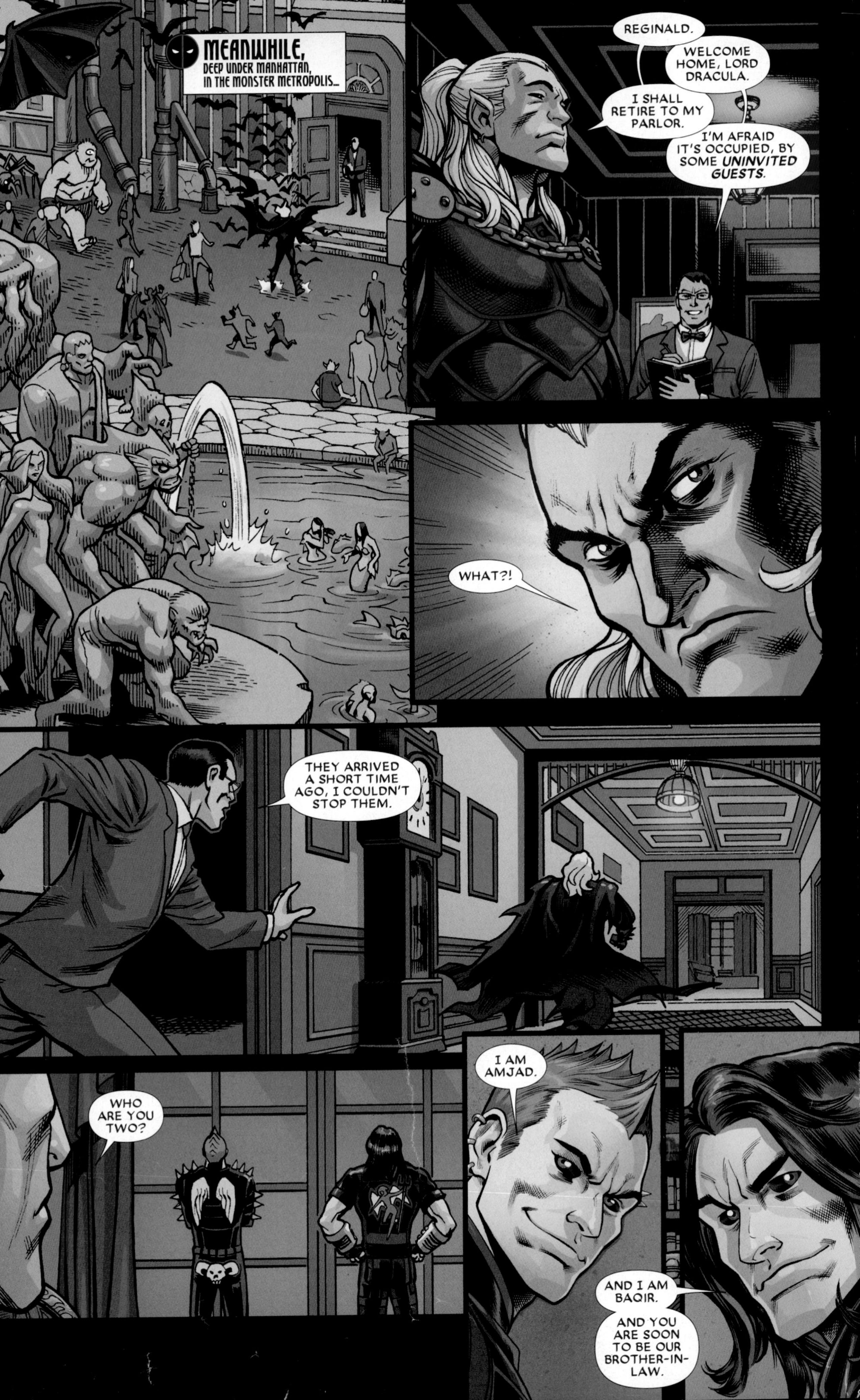
MEANWHILE,
DEEP UNDER MANHATTAN,
IN THE MONSTER METROPOLIS...
REGINALD.
WELCOME HOME, LORD DRACULA.
I SHALL RETIRE TO MY PARLOR.
I'M AFRAID IT'S OCCUPIED, BY SOME UNINVITED GUESTS.
WHAT?!
THEY ARRIVED A SHORT TIME AGO, I COULDN'T STOP THEM.
WHO ARE YOU TWO?
I AM AMJAD.
AND I AM BAQIR.
AND YOU ARE SOON TO BE OUR BROTHER-IN-LAW.

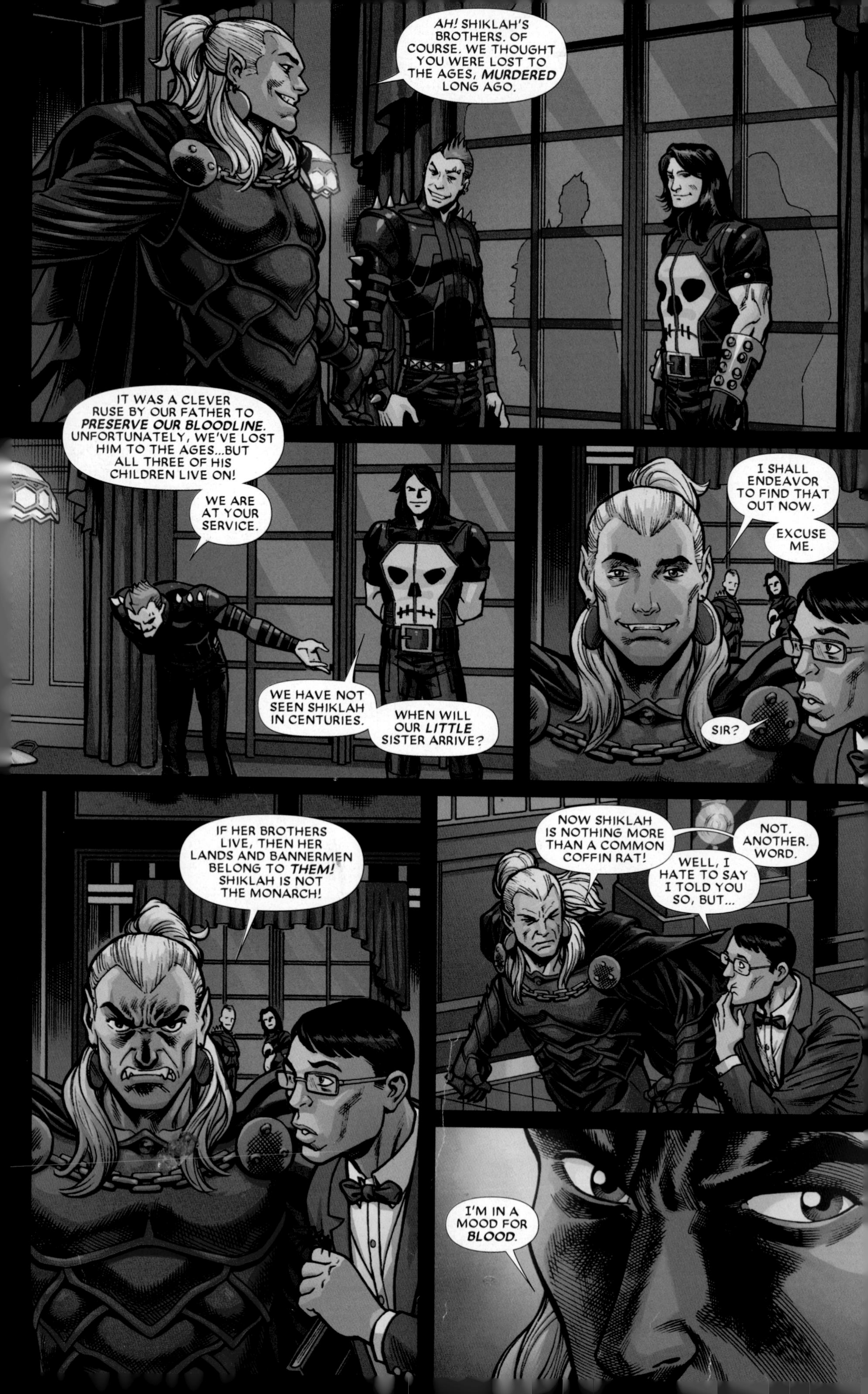
AH! SHIKLAH'S BROTHERS, OF COURSE. WE THOUGHT YOU WERE LOST TO THE AGES, MURDERED LONG AGO.
IT WAS A CLEVER RUSE BY OUR FATHER TO PRESERVE OUR BLOODLINE. UNFORTUNATELY, WE'VE LOST HIM TO THE AGES...BUT ALL THREE OF HIS CHILDREN LIVE ON!
WE ARE AT YOUR SERVICE.
WE HAVE NOT SEEN SHIKLAH IN CENTURIES.
WHEN WILL OUR LITTLE SISTER ARRIVE?
I SHALL ENDEAVOR TO FIND THAT OUT NOW.
EXCUSE ME.
SIR?
IF HER BROTHERS LIVE, THEN HER LANDS AND BANNERMEN BELONG TO THEM! SHIKLAH IS NOT THE MONARCH!
NOW SHIKLAH IS NOTHING MORE THAN A COMMON COFFIN RAT!
WELL, I HATE TO SAY I TOLD YOU SO, BUT...
NOT. ANOTHER. WORD.
I'M IN A MOOD FOR BLOOD.

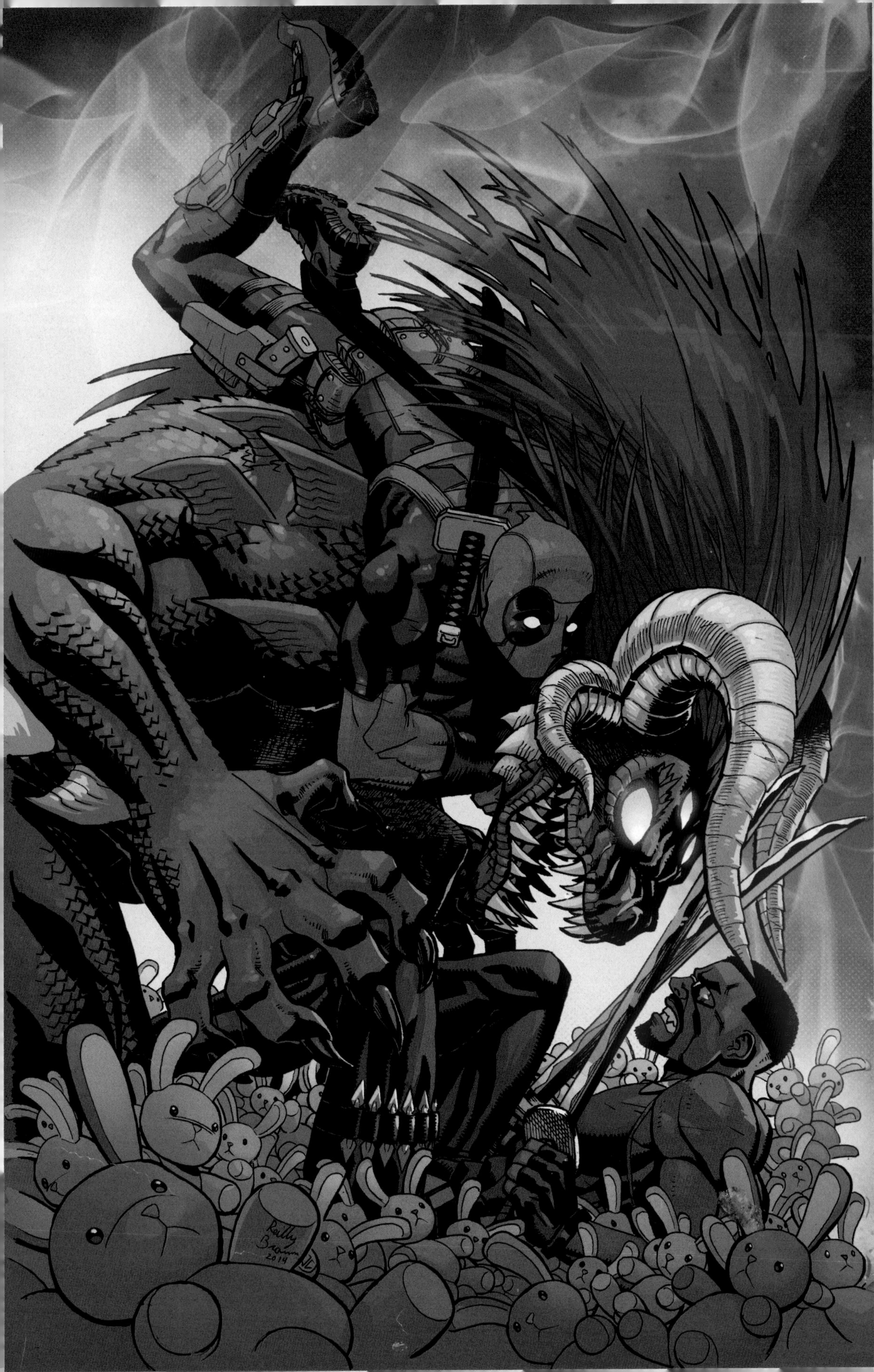
Reilly Brown 2014

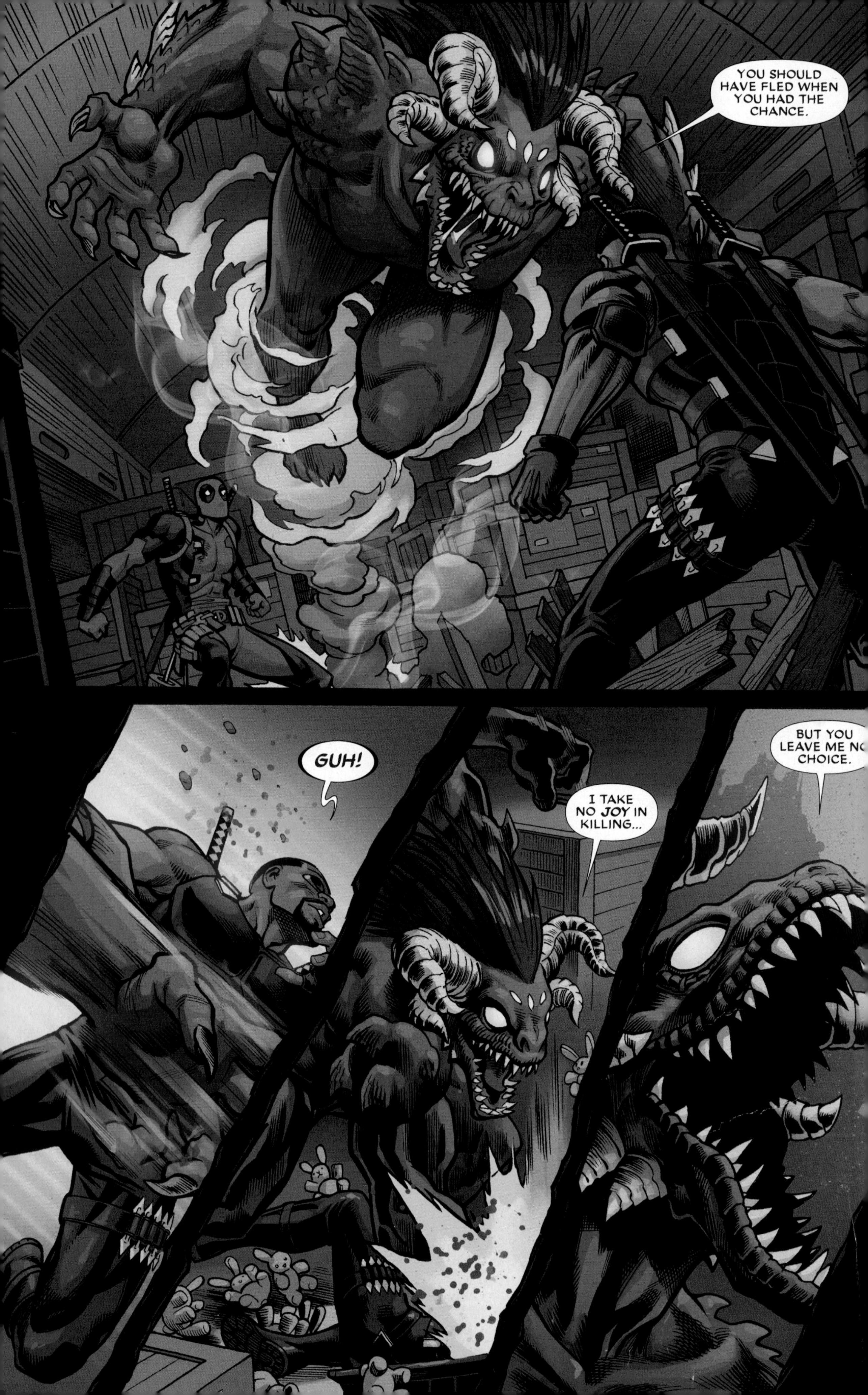
YOU SHOULD HAVE FLED WHEN YOU HAD THE CHANCE.
GUH!
I TAKE NO JOY IN KILLING...
BUT YOU LEAVE ME NO CHOICE.

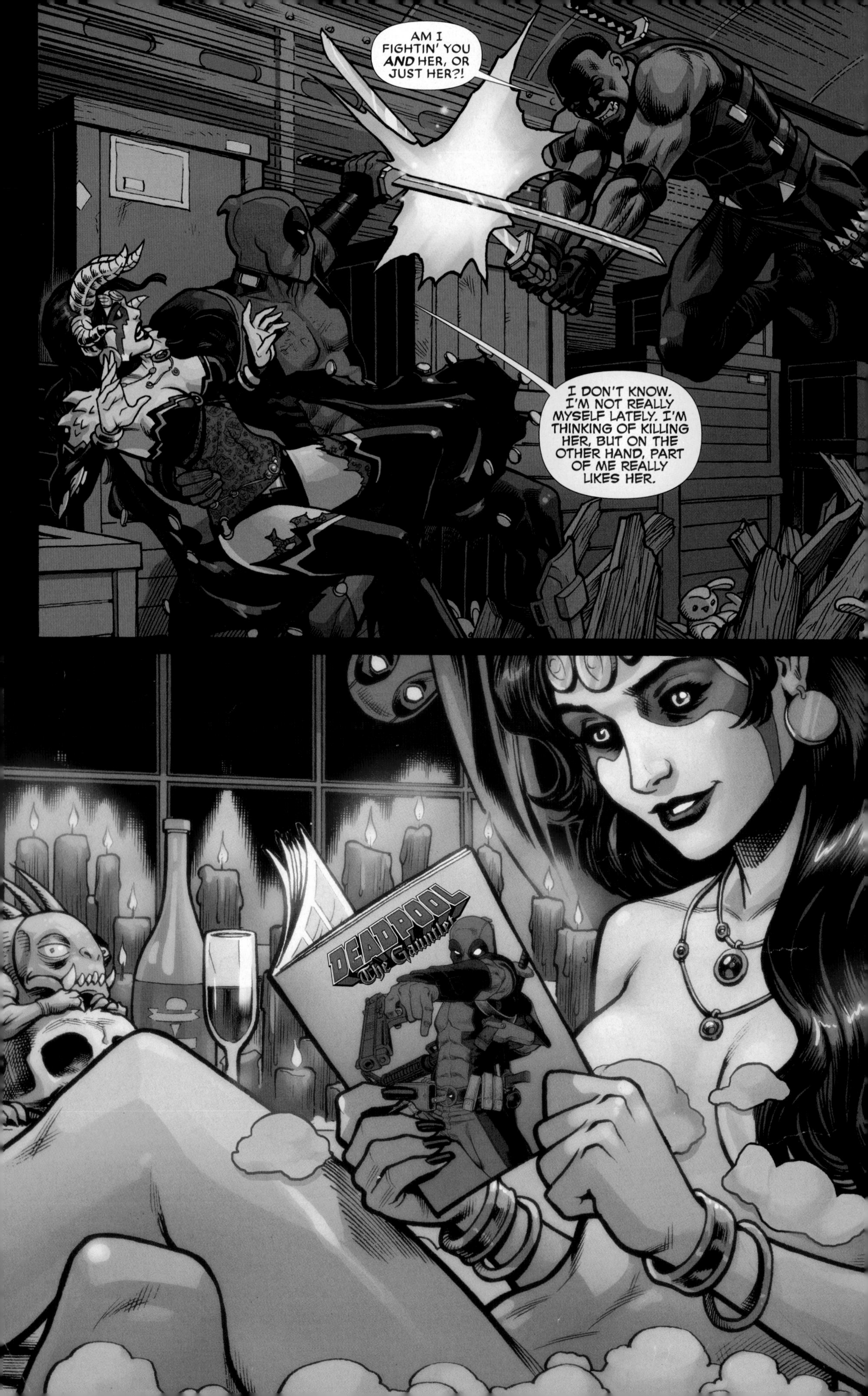
AM I FIGHTIN' YOU AND HER, OR JUST HER?!
I DON'T KNOW. I'M NOT REALLY MYSELF LATELY. I'M THINKING OF KILLING HER, BUT ON THE OTHER HAND, PART OF ME REALLY LIKES HER.
DEADPOOL
The Gauntlet

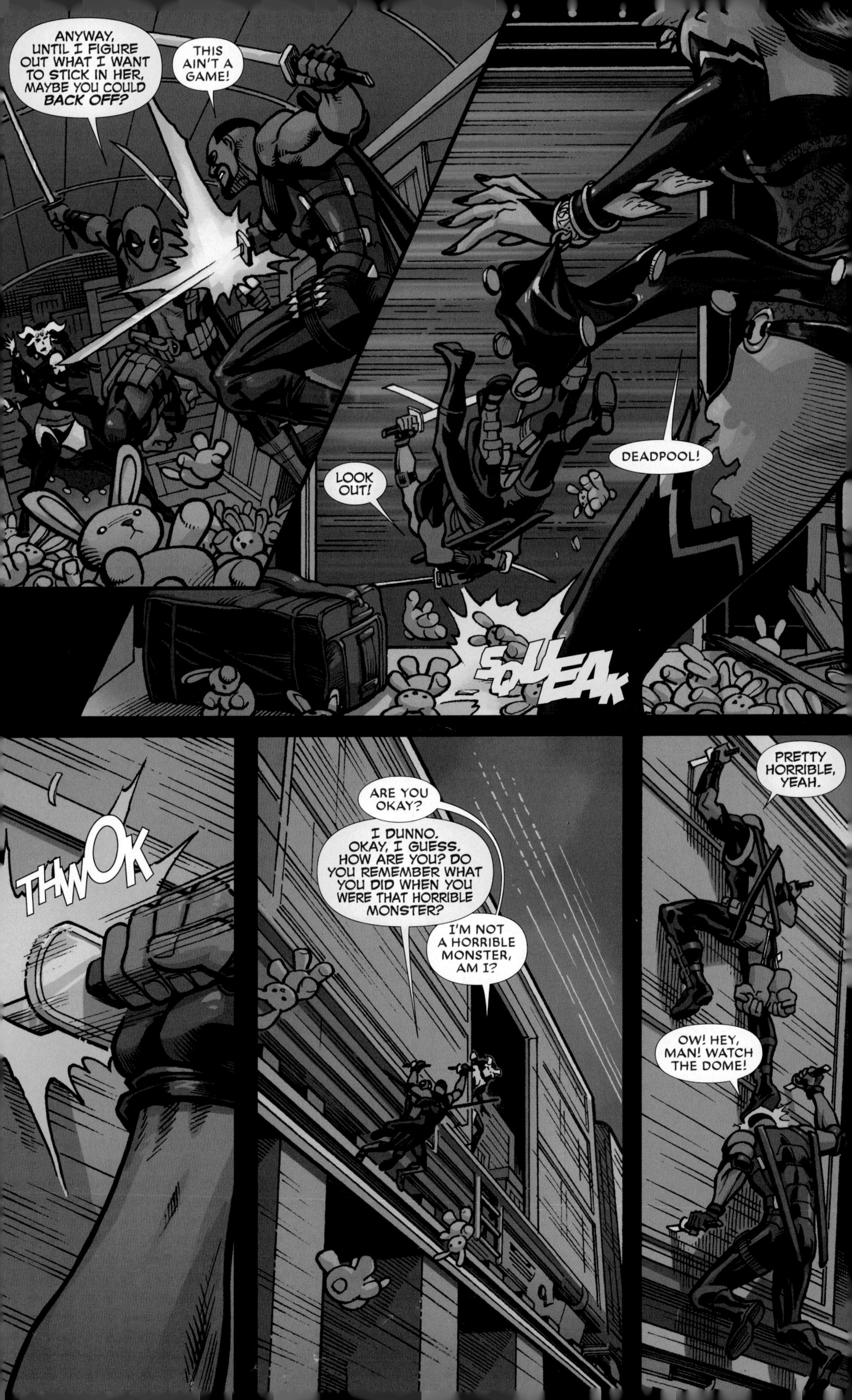
ANYWAY, UNTIL I FIGURE OUT WHAT I WANT TO STICK IN HER, MAYBE YOU COULD BACK OFF?
THIS AIN'T A GAME!
LOOK OUT!
DEADPOOL!
SQUEAK
THWOK
ARE YOU OKAY?
I DUNNO. OKAY, I GUESS. HOW ARE YOU? DO YOU REMEMBER WHAT YOU DID WHEN YOU WERE THAT HORRIBLE MONSTER?
I'M NOT A HORRIBLE MONSTER, AM I?
PRETTY HORRIBLE, YEAH.
OW! HEY, MAN! WATCH THE DOME!

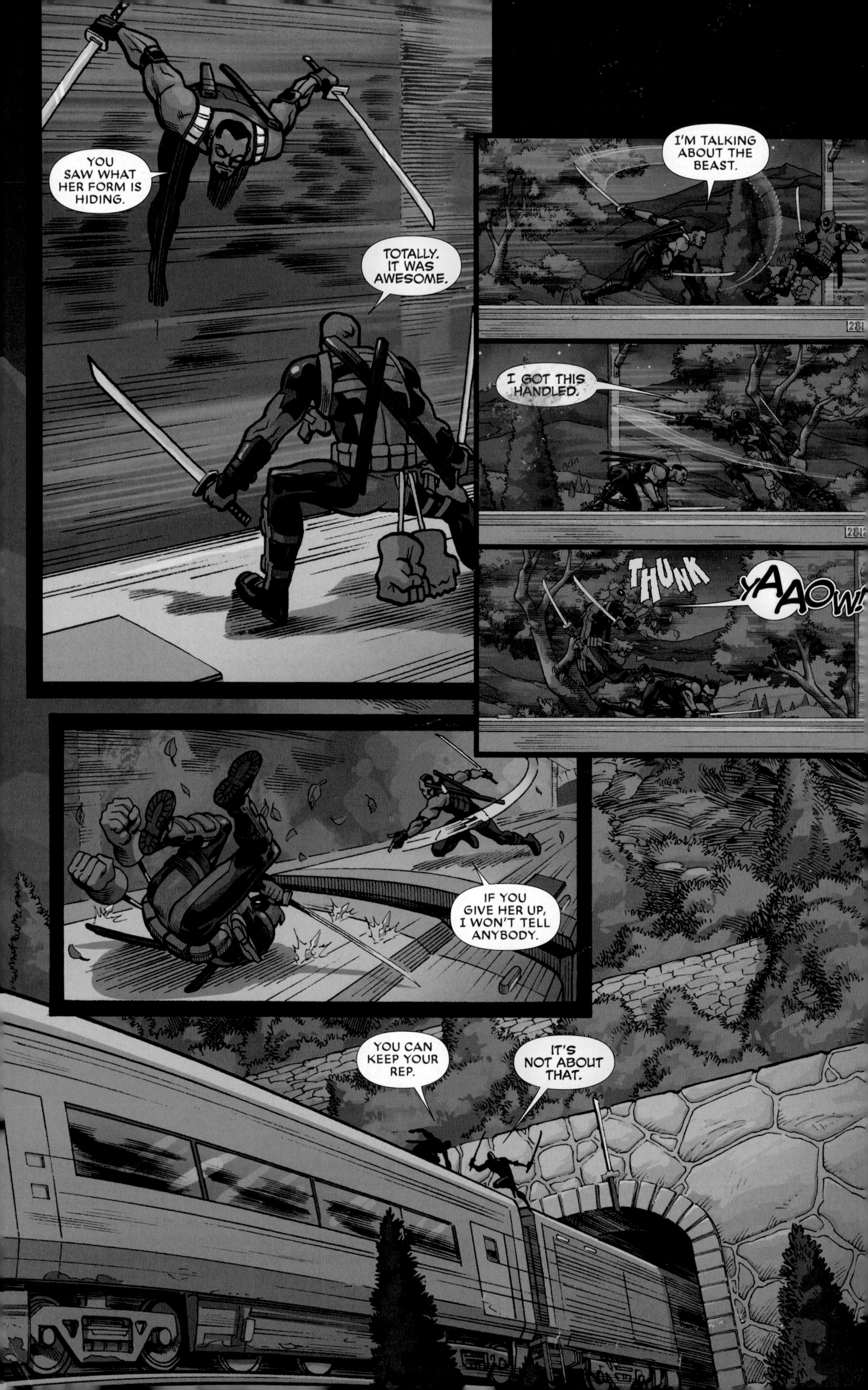
YOU SAW WHAT HER FORM IS HIDING.
TOTALLY. IT WAS AWESOME.
I'M TALKING ABOUT THE BEAST.
I GOT THIS HANDLED.
THUNK
YAAOW!
IF YOU GIVE HER UP, I WON'T TELL ANYBODY.
YOU CAN KEEP YOUR REP.
IT'S NOT ABOUT THAT.

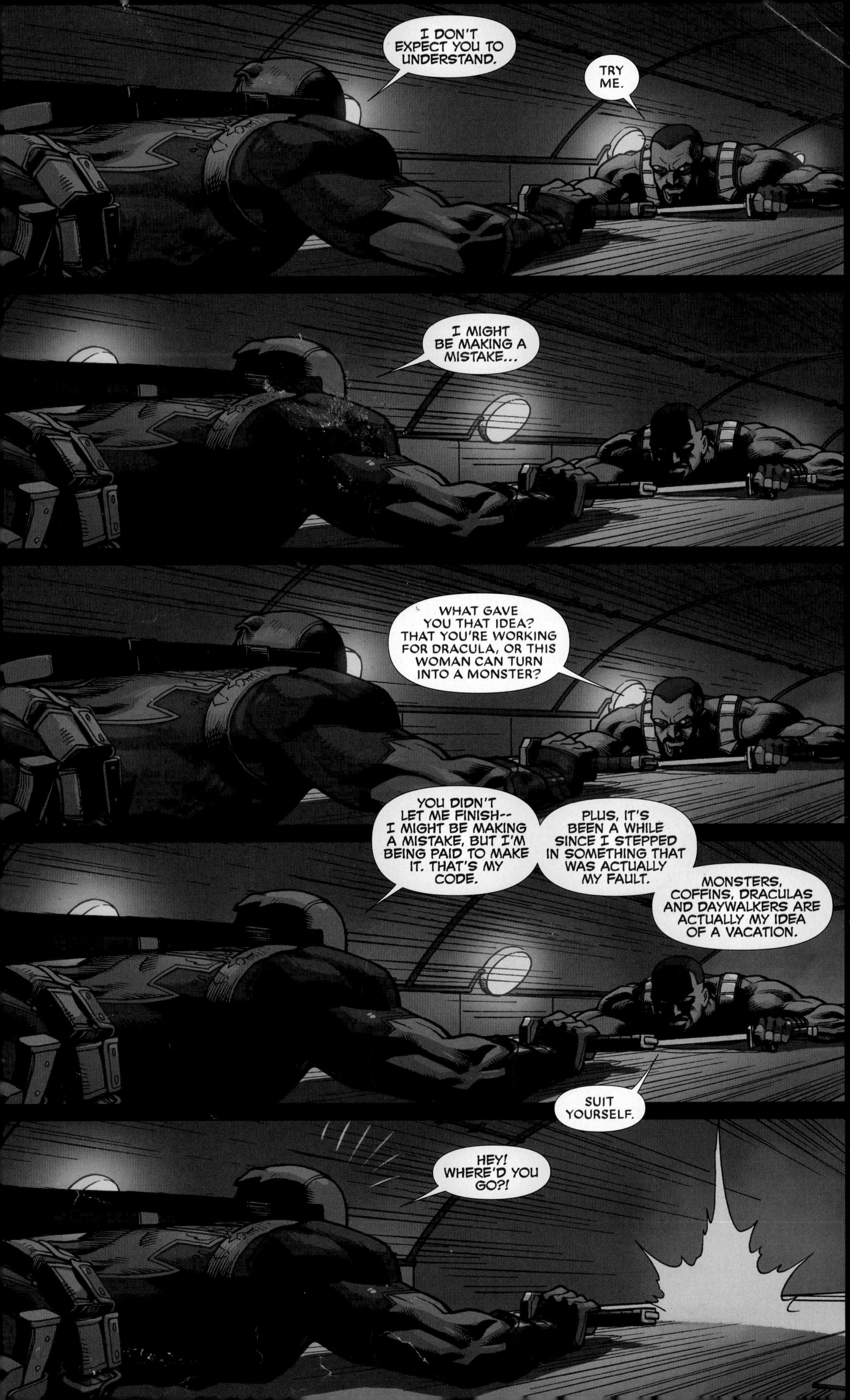
I DON'T EXPECT YOU TO UNDERSTAND.
TRY ME.
I MIGHT BE MAKING A MISTAKE...
WHAT GAVE YOU THAT IDEA? THAT YOU'RE WORKING FOR DRACULA, OR THIS WOMAN CAN TURN INTO A MONSTER?
YOU DIDN'T LET ME FINISH-- I MIGHT BE MAKING A MISTAKE, BUT I'M BEING PAID TO MAKE IT. THAT'S MY CODE.
PLUS, IT'S BEEN A WHILE SINCE I STEPPED IN SOMETHING THAT WAS ACTUALLY MY FAULT.
MONSTERS, COFFINS, DRACULAS AND DAYWALKERS ARE ACTUALLY MY IDEA OF A VACATION.
SUIT YOURSELF.
HEY! WHERE'D YOU GO?!

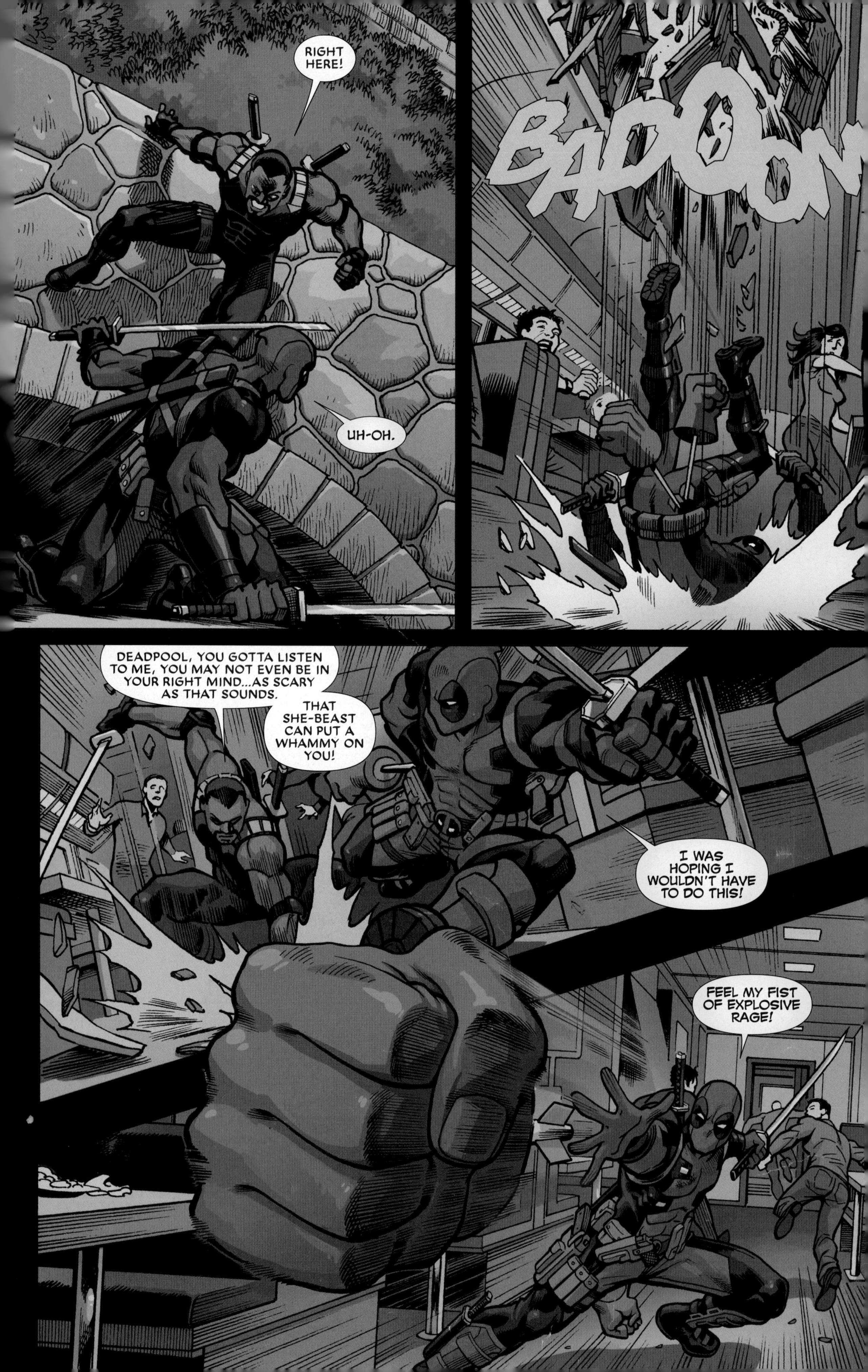
RIGHT HERE!
UH-OH.
BADOOM
DEADPOOL, YOU GOTTA LISTEN TO ME, YOU MAY NOT EVEN BE IN YOUR RIGHT MIND...AS SCARY AS THAT SOUNDS.
THAT SHE-BEAST CAN PUT A WHAMMY ON YOU!
I WAS HOPING I WOULDN'T HAVE TO DO THIS!
FEEL MY FIST OF EXPLOSIVE RAGE!

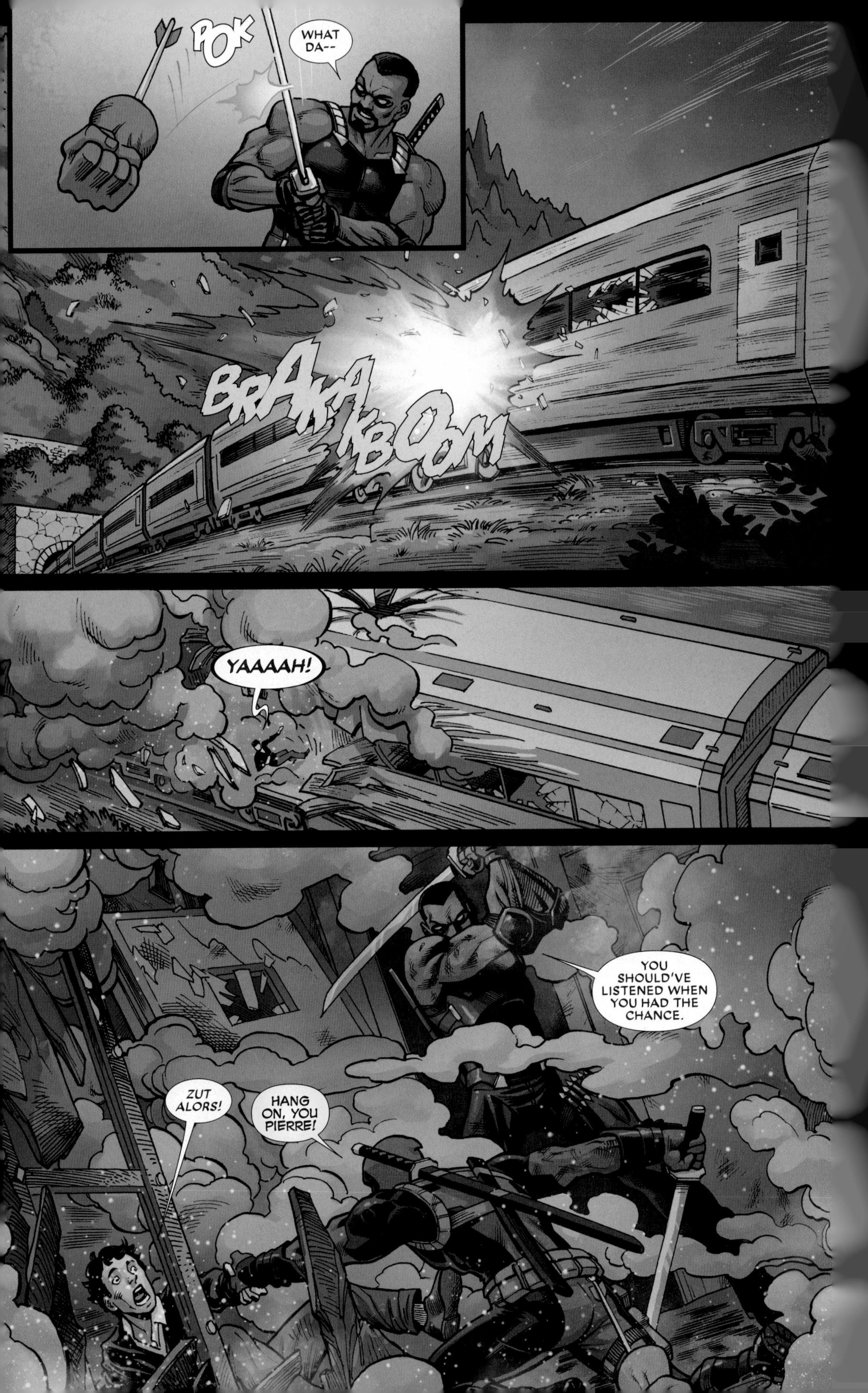
POK
WHAT DA--
BRAKA KBOOM
YAAAAH!
YOU SHOULD'VE LISTENED WHEN YOU HAD THE CHANCE.
ZUT ALORS!
HANG ON, YOU PIERRE!

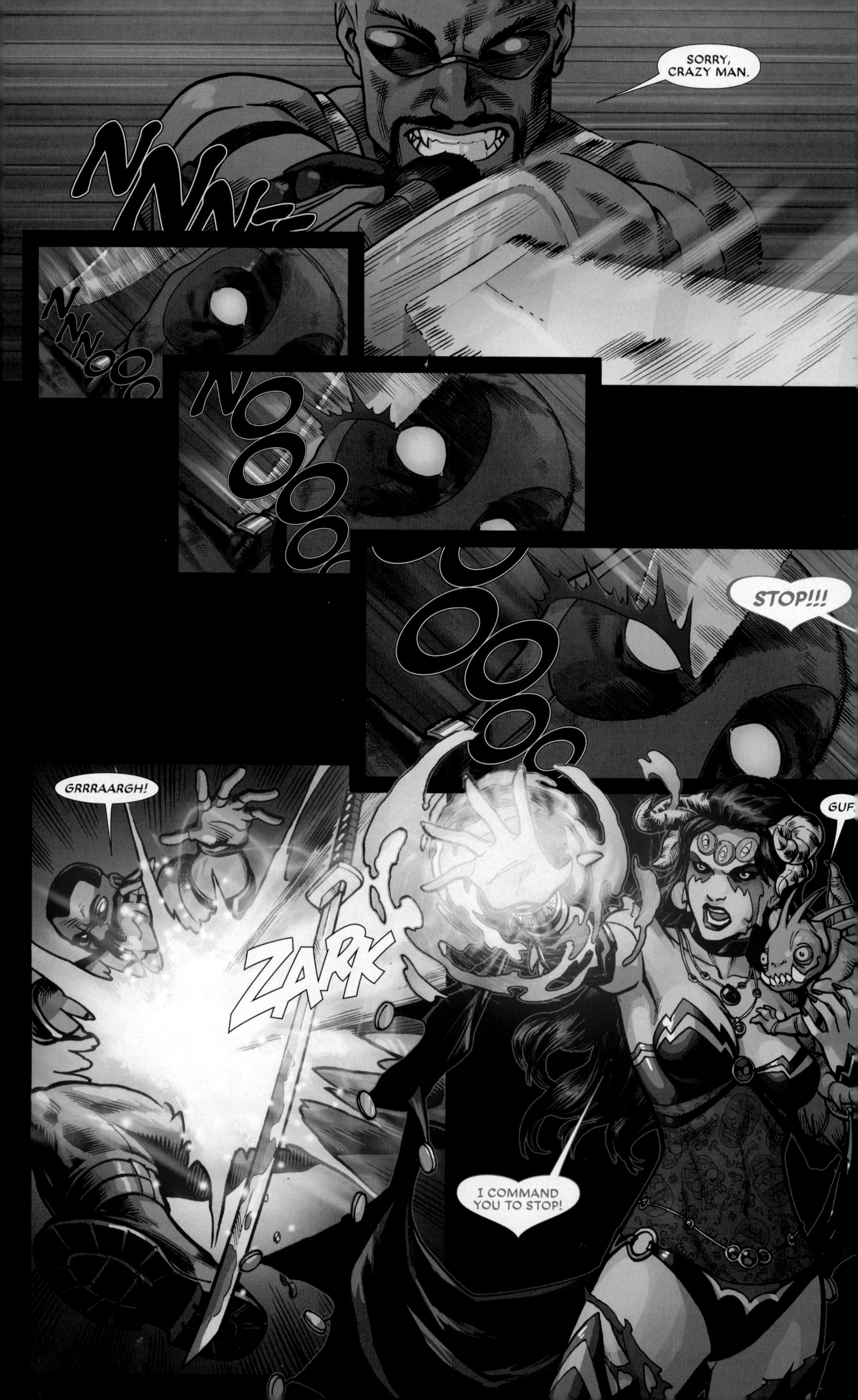
SORRY, CRAZY MAN.
NNNEE
NNNOOOO
NOOOOOO
OOOOOO
STOP!!!
GRRRAARGH!
GUF.
ZARK
I COMMAND YOU TO STOP!

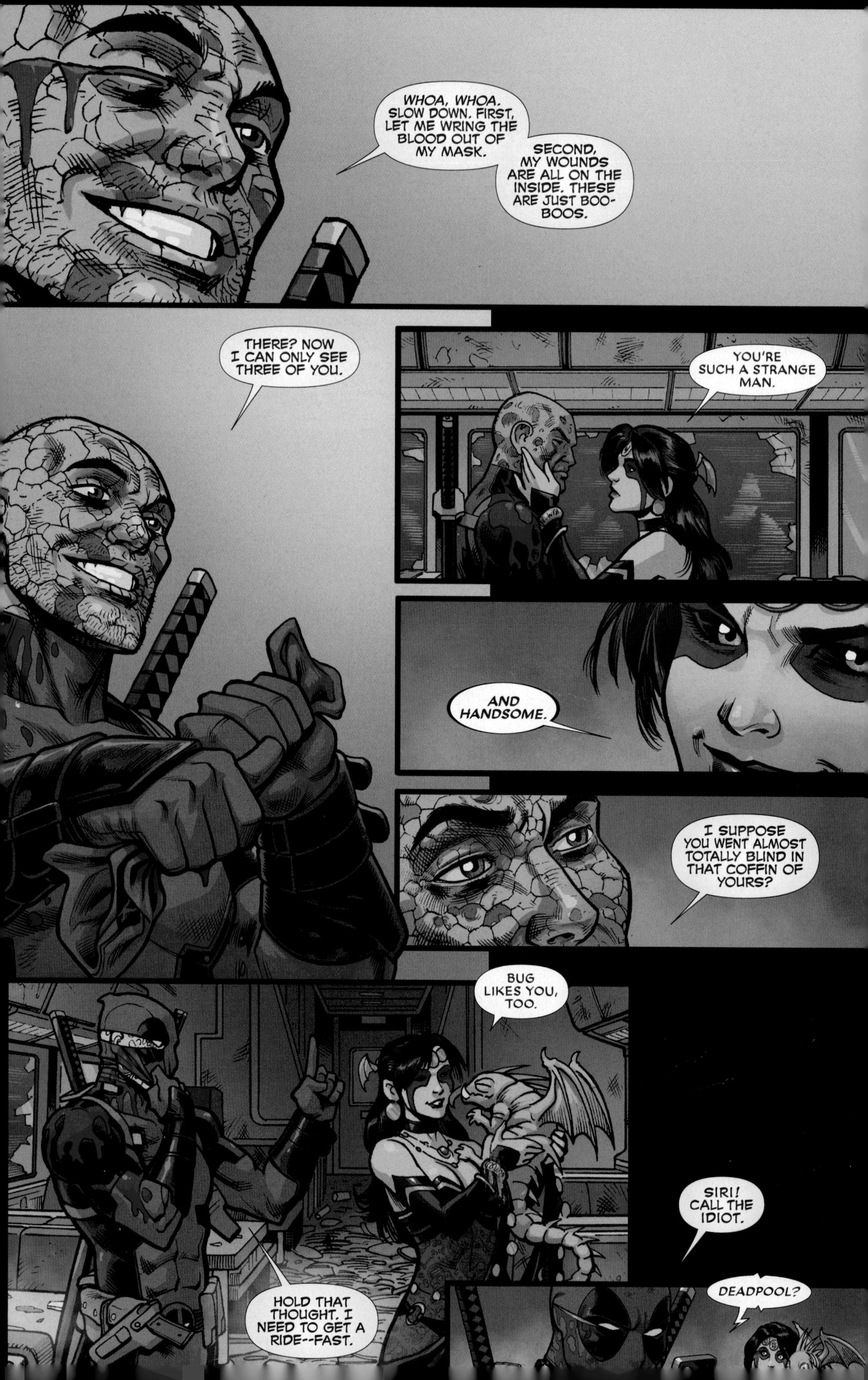
WHOA, WHOA. SLOW DOWN. FIRST, LET ME WRING THE BLOOD OUT OF MY MASK.
SECOND, MY WOUNDS ARE ALL ON THE INSIDE. THESE ARE JUST BOO-BOOS.
THERE? NOW I CAN ONLY SEE THREE OF YOU.
YOU'RE SUCH A STRANGE MAN.
AND HANDSOME.
I SUPPOSE YOU WENT ALMOST TOTALLY BLIND IN THAT COFFIN OF YOURS?
BUG LIKES YOU, TOO.
HOLD THAT THOUGHT. I NEED TO GET A RIDE--FAST.
SIRI! CALL THE IDIOT.
DEADPOOL?

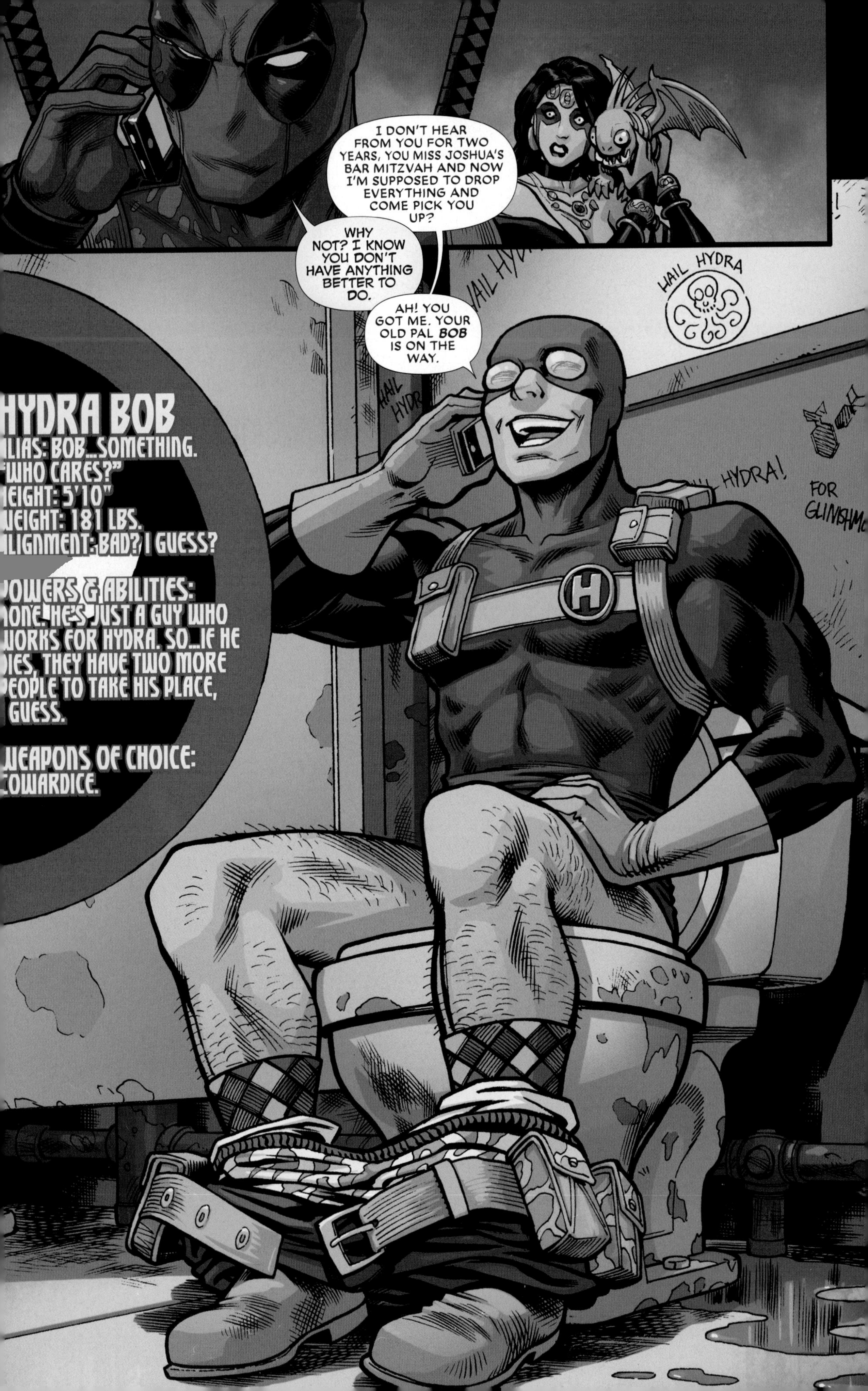

I DON'T HEAR FROM YOU FOR TWO YEARS, YOU MISS JOSHUA'S BAR MITZVAH AND NOW I'M SUPPOSED TO DROP EVERYTHING AND COME PICK YOU UP?
WHY NOT? I KNOW YOU DON'T HAVE ANYTHING BETTER TO DO.
AH! YOU GOT ME. YOUR OLD PAL BOB IS ON THE WAY.
HAIL HYDRA
HYDRA BOB
LIAS: BOB...SOMETHING.
"WHO CARES?"
EIGHT: 5'10"
EIGHT: 181 LBS.
LIGNMENT: BAD? I GUESS?
OWERS & ABILITIES:
ONE. HE'S JUST A GUY WHO
ORKS FOR HYDRA. SO...IF HE
IES, THEY HAVE TWO MORE
EOPLE TO TAKE HIS PLACE,
GUESS.
EAPONS OF CHOICE:
OWARDICE.
HYDRA!
FOR

DEADPOOL

THE GAUNTLET

SOMEWHERE OLD AND PLEASANT-LOOKING.

THE GAUNTLET

THOSE GUYS ARE PROBABLY ALL DEAD BY NOW.

CHAPTER SIX

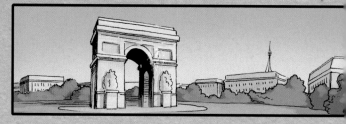

AN AMERICAN

MERCENARY

IF YOU WANT TO STAY IN THIS MUSEUM, YOU'RE GONNA WANT TO NOT LET THAT BUG OF YOURS GET SEXY ON ANYTHING IN HERE.

I'M SPEAKING FROM EXPERIENCE HERE.

MEANWHILE, AT THE DA VINCI CODE HALL OF JUSTICE...

ANCIENS SABRES JAPONAIS

ANCIENT JAPANESE SWORDS

THESE KATANAS AREN'T GOING TO SWING THEMSELVE INTO BODIES...BUT THAT WOULD BE PRETTY AWESOME IF THEY COULD.

IN PARIS

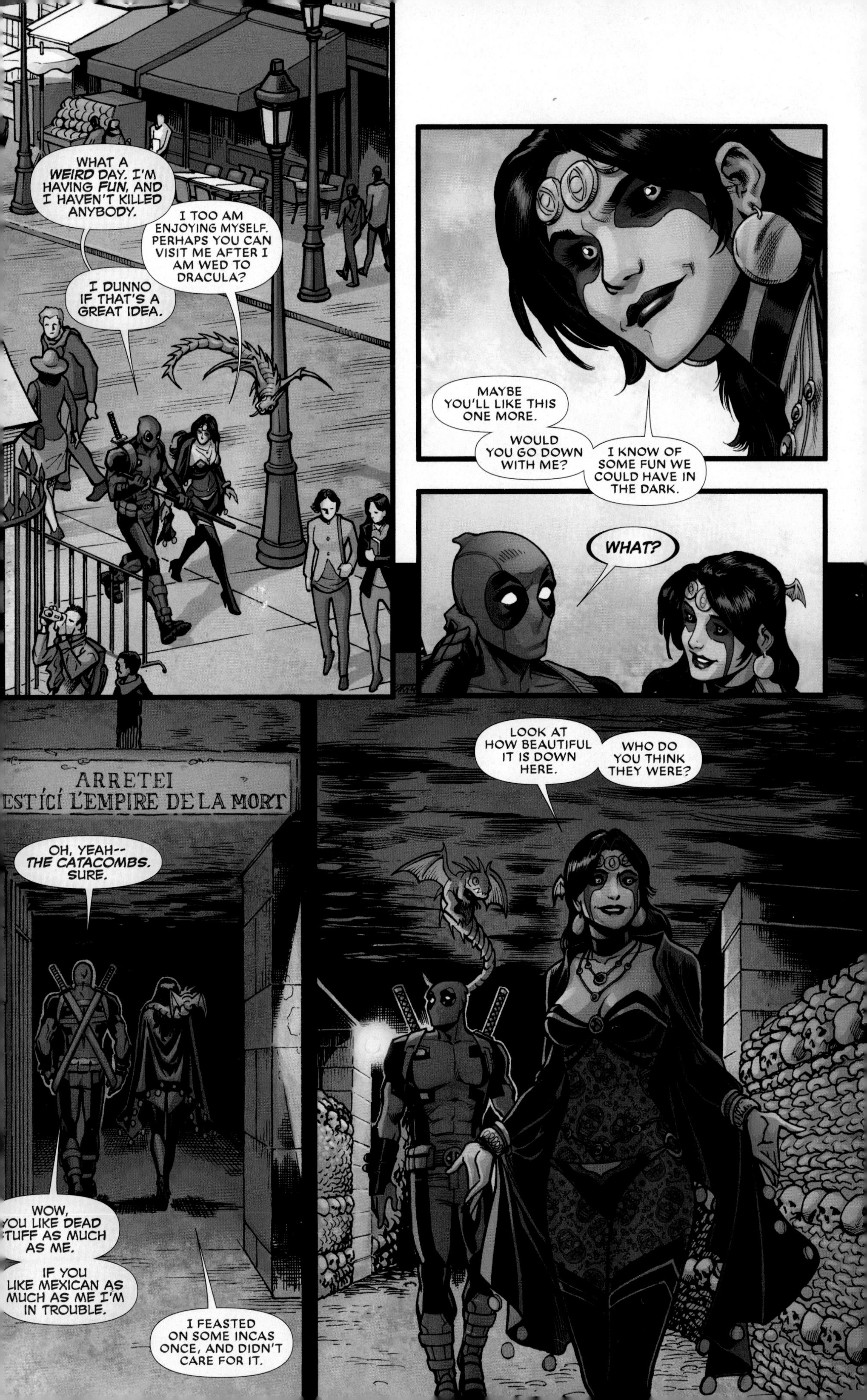
WHAT A WEIRD DAY. I'M HAVING FUN, AND I HAVEN'T KILLED ANYBODY.
I TOO AM ENJOYING MYSELF. PERHAPS YOU CAN VISIT ME AFTER I AM WED TO DRACULA?
I DUNNO IF THAT'S A GREAT IDEA.
MAYBE YOU'LL LIKE THIS ONE MORE.
I KNOW OF SOME FUN WE COULD HAVE IN THE DARK.
WOULD YOU GO DOWN WITH ME?
WHAT?
ARRETEI
ESTÍCÍ L'EMPIRE DE LA MORT
OH, YEAH-- THE CATACOMBS. SURE.
WOW, YOU LIKE DEAD STUFF AS MUCH AS ME.
IF YOU LIKE MEXICAN AS MUCH AS ME I'M IN TROUBLE.
I FEASTED ON SOME INCAS ONCE, AND DIDN'T CARE FOR IT.
LOOK AT HOW BEAUTIFUL IT IS DOWN HERE.
WHO DO YOU THINK THEY WERE?

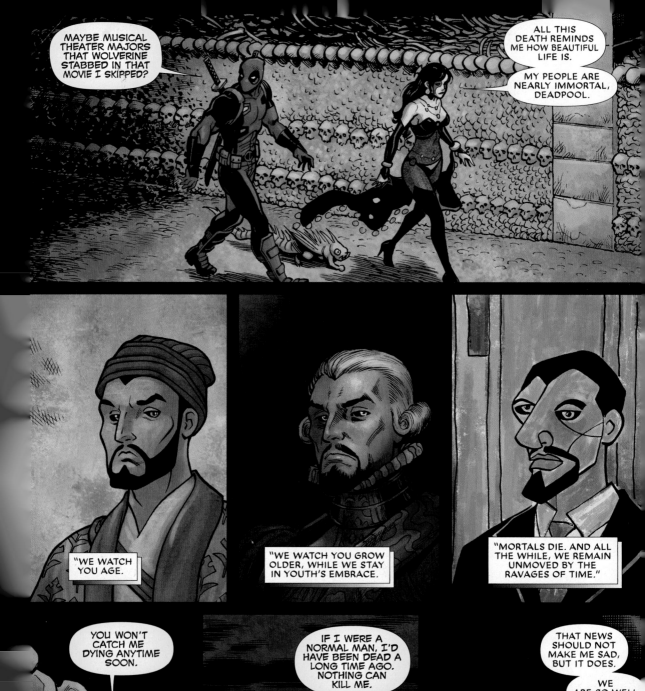

MAYBE MUSICAL THEATER MAJORS THAT WOLVERINE STABBED IN THAT MOVIE I SKIPPED?

ALL THIS DEATH REMINDS ME HOW BEAUTIFUL LIFE IS.

MY PEOPLE ARE NEARLY IMMORTAL, DEADPOOL.

"WE WATCH YOU AGE.

"WE WATCH YOU GROW OLDER, WHILE WE STAY IN YOUTH'S EMBRACE.

"MORTALS DIE. AND ALL THE WHILE, WE REMAIN UNMOVED BY THE RAVAGES OF TIME."

YOU WON'T CATCH ME DYING ANYTIME SOON.

IF I WERE A NORMAL MAN, I'D HAVE BEEN DEAD A LONG TIME AGO. NOTHING CAN KILL ME.

THAT NEWS SHOULD NOT MAKE ME SAD, BUT IT DOES.

WE ARE SO WELL MATCHED...

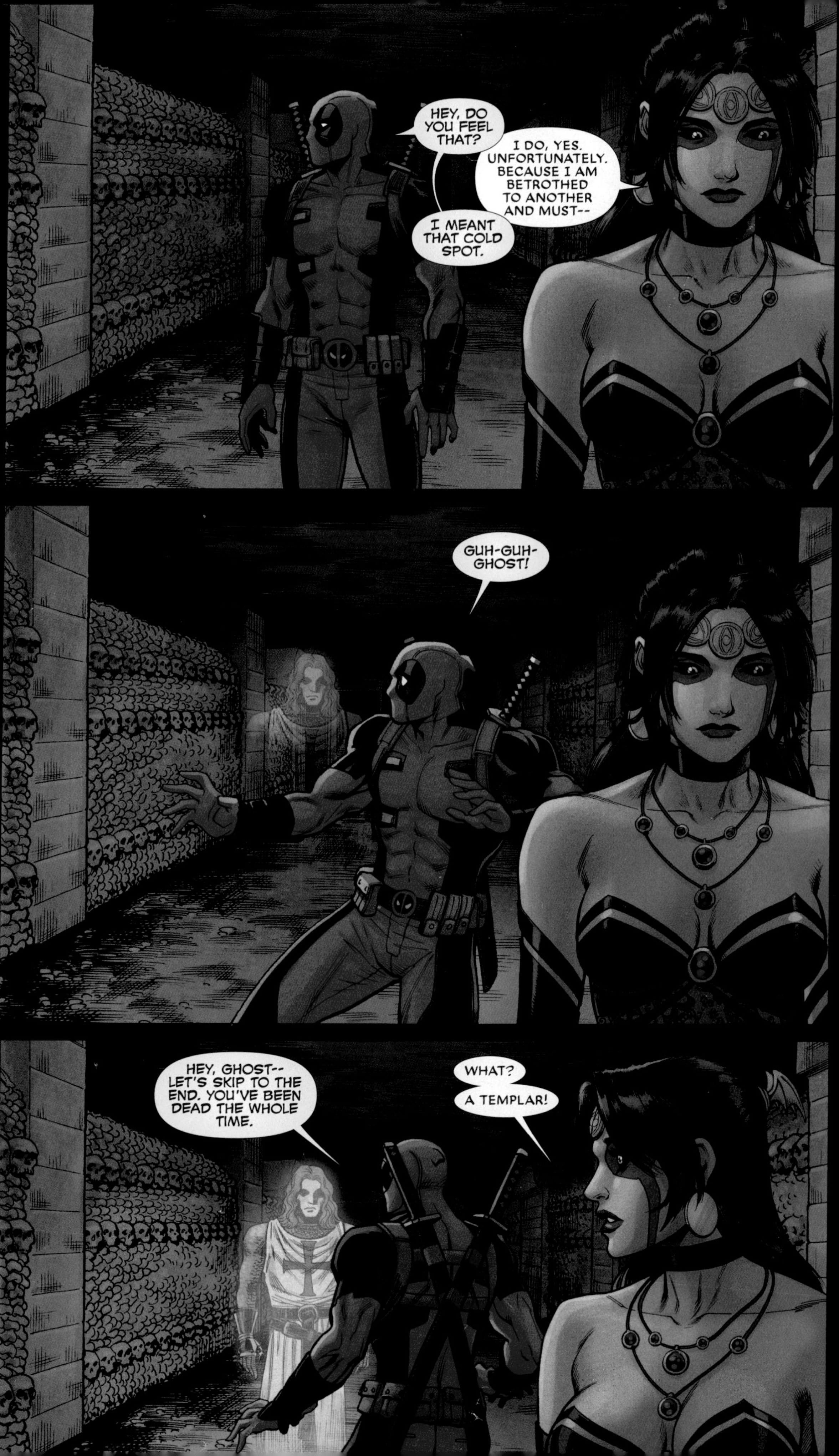
HEY, DO YOU FEEL THAT?
I DO, YES. UNFORTUNATELY. BECAUSE I AM BETROTHED TO ANOTHER AND MUST--
I MEANT THAT COLD SPOT.
GUH-GUH-GHOST!
HEY, GHOST--LET'S SKIP TO THE END. YOU'VE BEEN DEAD THE WHOLE TIME.
WHAT?
A TEMPLAR!

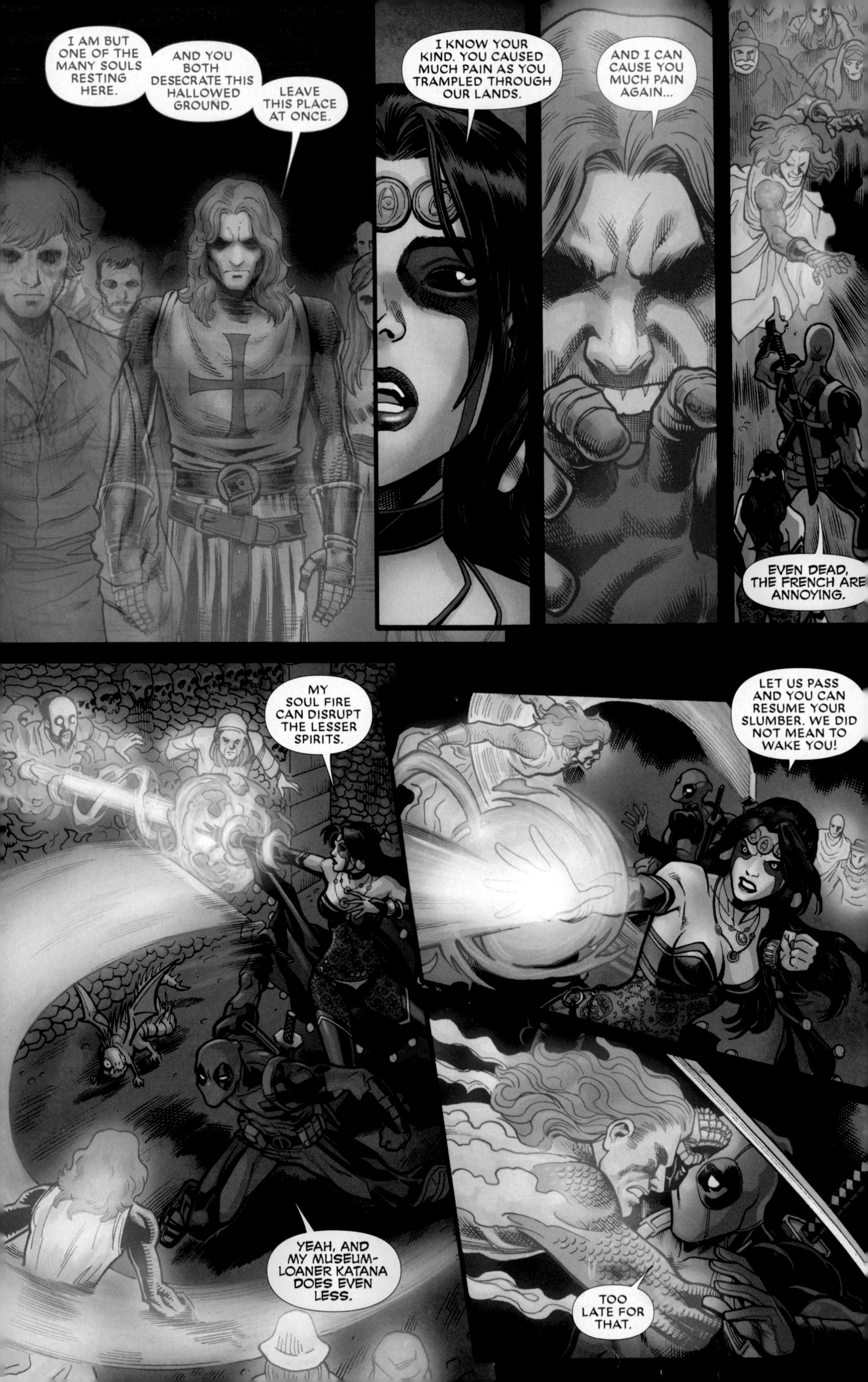
I AM BUT ONE OF THE MANY SOULS RESTING HERE.
AND YOU BOTH DESECRATE THIS HALLOWED GROUND.
LEAVE THIS PLACE AT ONCE.
I KNOW YOUR KIND. YOU CAUSED MUCH PAIN AS YOU TRAMPLED THROUGH OUR LANDS.
AND I CAN CAUSE YOU MUCH PAIN AGAIN...
EVEN DEAD, THE FRENCH ARE ANNOYING.
MY SOUL FIRE CAN DISRUPT THE LESSER SPIRITS.
YEAH, AND MY MUSEUM-LOANER KATANA DOES EVEN LESS.
LET US PASS AND YOU CAN RESUME YOUR SLUMBER. WE DID NOT MEAN TO WAKE YOU!
TOO LATE FOR THAT.

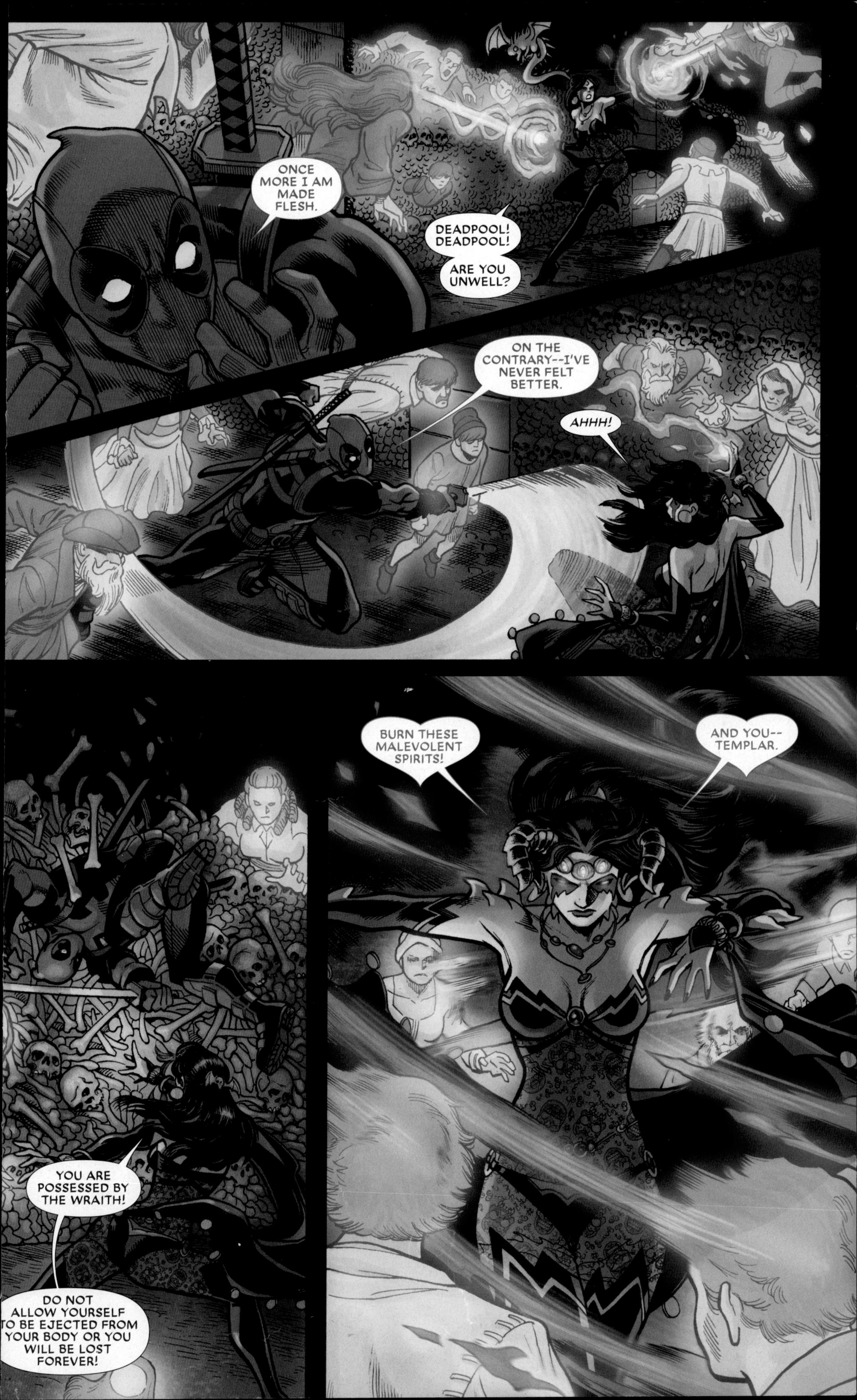
ONCE MORE I AM MADE FLESH.
DEADPOOL! DEADPOOL!
ARE YOU UNWELL?
ON THE CONTRARY--I'VE NEVER FELT BETTER.
AHHH!
YOU ARE POSSESSED BY THE WRAITH!
DO NOT ALLOW YOURSELF TO BE EJECTED FROM YOUR BODY OR YOU WILL BE LOST FOREVER!
BURN THESE MALEVOLENT SPIRITS!
AND YOU--TEMPLAR.

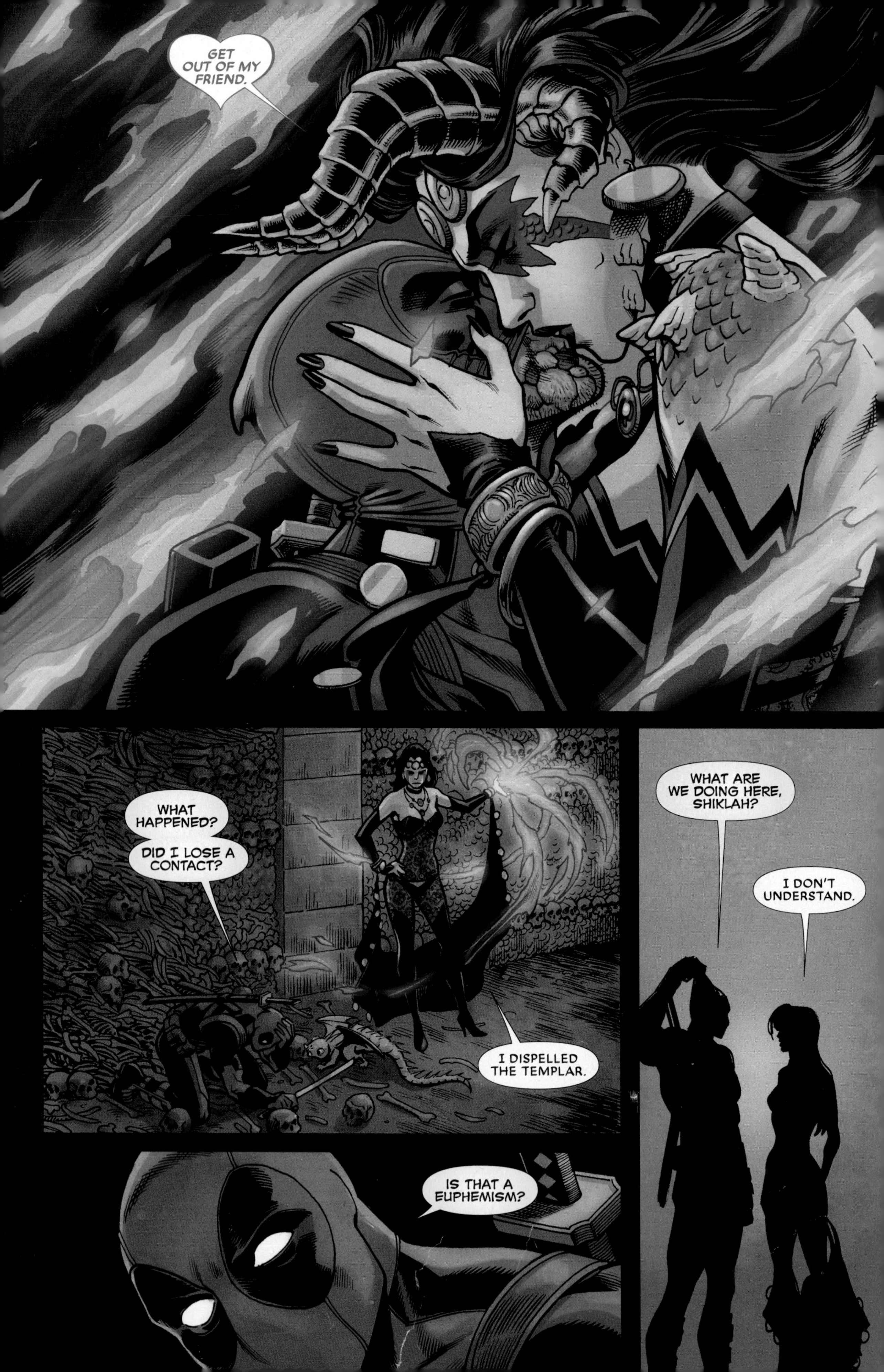
GET OUT OF MY FRIEND.
WHAT HAPPENED?
DID I LOSE A CONTACT?
I DISPELLED THE TEMPLAR.
IS THAT A EUPHEMISM?
WHAT ARE WE DOING HERE, SHIKLAH?
I DON'T UNDERSTAND.

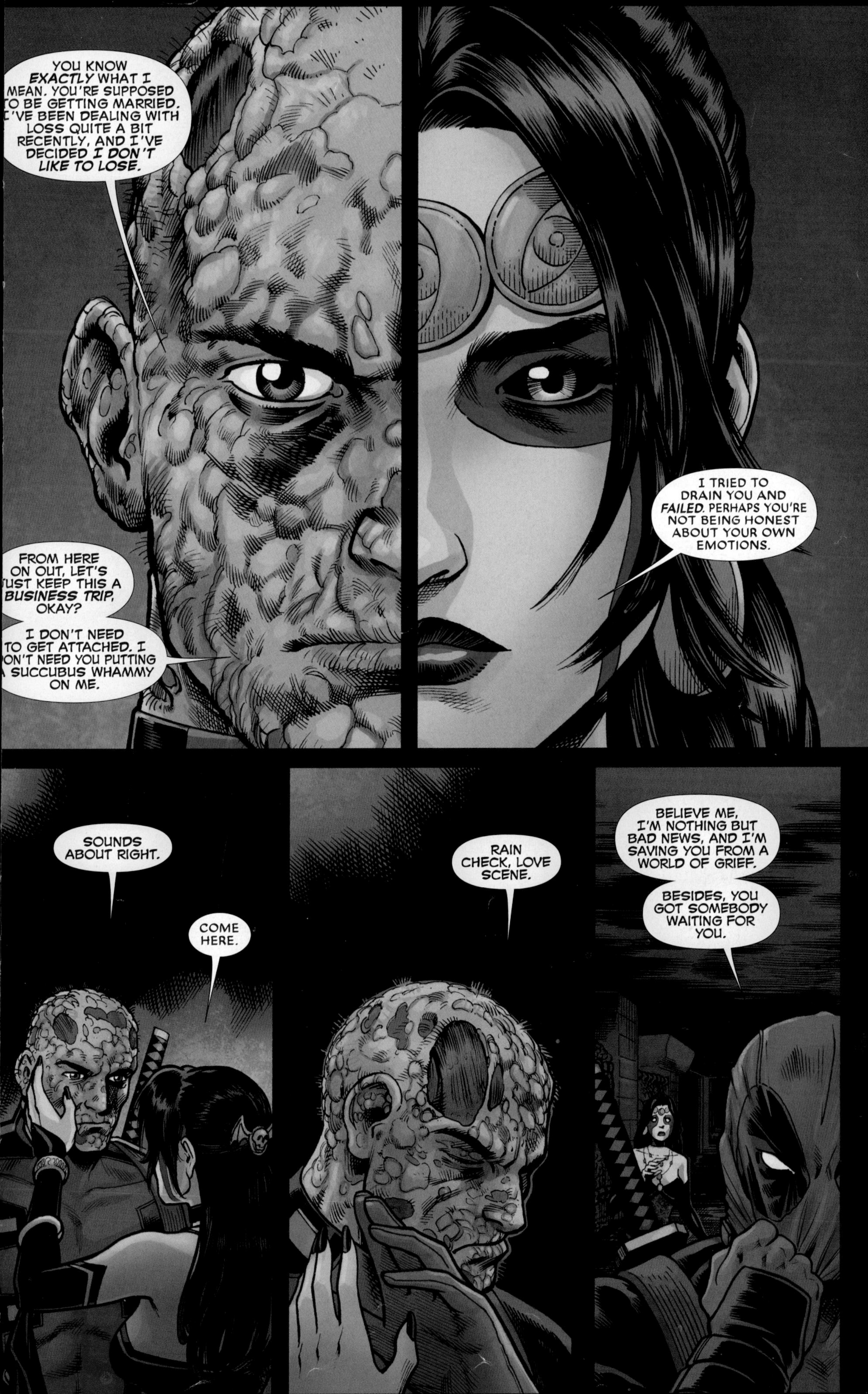

YOU KNOW *EXACTLY* WHAT I MEAN. YOU'RE SUPPOSED TO BE GETTING MARRIED. I'VE BEEN DEALING WITH LOSS QUITE A BIT RECENTLY, AND I'VE DECIDED *I DON'T LIKE TO LOSE.*
I TRIED TO DRAIN YOU AND *FAILED.* PERHAPS YOU'RE NOT BEING HONEST ABOUT YOUR OWN EMOTIONS.
FROM HERE ON OUT, LET'S JUST KEEP THIS A *BUSINESS TRIP,* OKAY?
I DON'T NEED TO GET ATTACHED. I DON'T NEED YOU PUTTING A SUCCUBUS WHAMMY ON ME.
SOUNDS ABOUT RIGHT.
COME HERE.
RAIN CHECK, LOVE SCENE.
BELIEVE ME, I'M NOTHING BUT BAD NEWS, AND I'M SAVING YOU FROM A WORLD OF GRIEF.
BESIDES, YOU GOT SOMEBODY WAITING FOR YOU.

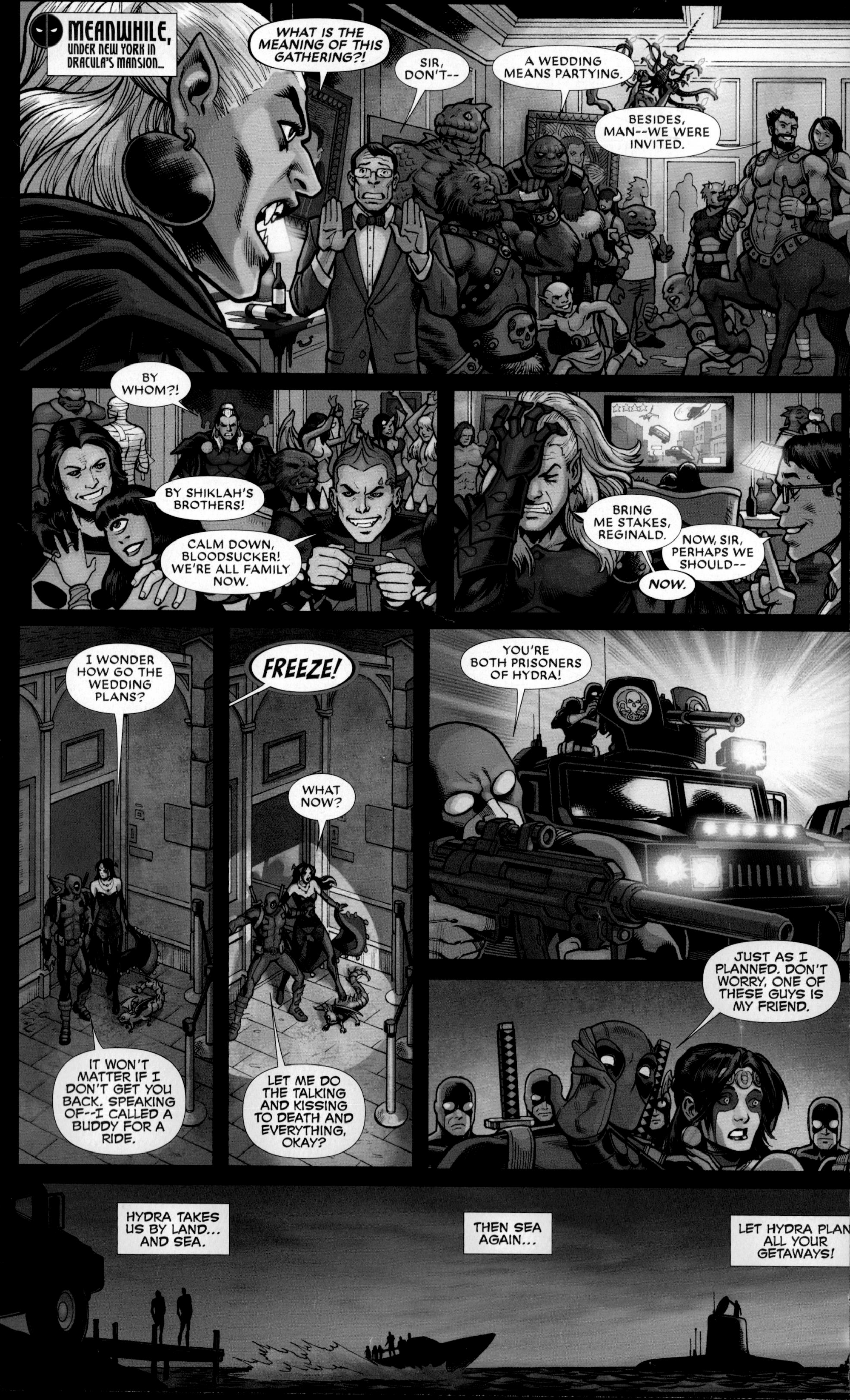
MEANWHILE, UNDER NEW YORK IN DRACULA'S MANSION...
WHAT IS THE MEANING OF THIS GATHERING?!
SIR, DON'T--
A WEDDING MEANS PARTYING.
BESIDES, MAN--WE WERE INVITED.
BY WHOM?!
BY SHIKLAH'S BROTHERS!
CALM DOWN, BLOODSUCKER! WE'RE ALL FAMILY NOW.
BRING ME STAKES, REGINALD.
NOW, SIR, PERHAPS WE SHOULD--
NOW.
I WONDER HOW GO THE WEDDING PLANS?
IT WON'T MATTER IF I DON'T GET YOU BACK. SPEAKING OF--I CALLED A BUDDY FOR A RIDE.
FREEZE!
WHAT NOW?
LET ME DO THE TALKING AND KISSING TO DEATH AND EVERYTHING, OKAY?
YOU'RE BOTH PRISONERS OF HYDRA!
JUST AS I PLANNED. DON'T WORRY, ONE OF THESE GUYS IS MY FRIEND.
HYDRA TAKES US BY LAND... AND SEA.
THEN SEA AGAIN...
LET HYDRA PLAN ALL YOUR GETAWAYS!

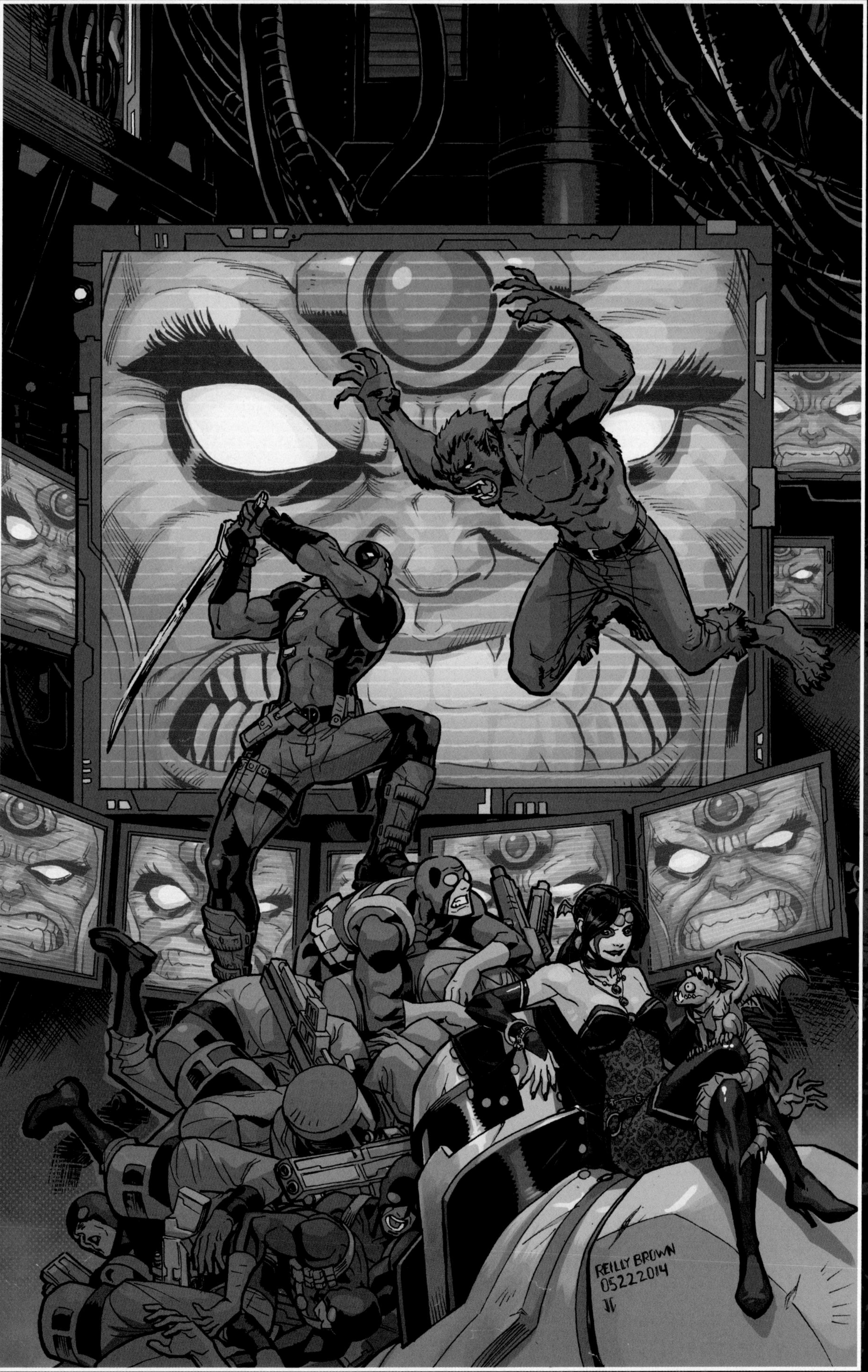
REILLY BROWN
05222014

"OH, MAN, THIS SUCKS!"

A.I.M. IS AFTER YOU!

WHY'D YOU SELL US OUT TO A.I.M., BOB?

I DIDN'T SELL YOU OUT! YOU GOTTA BELIEVE ME!

I KNOW! DID YOU THINK I WAS GOING TO BREAK YOUR NECK?

WHAT A BIG WEAPON YOU HAVE! WHY DON'T YOU PUT IT TO YOUR HEAD AND PULL THE--

NO QUICK MOVES. DROP YOUR WEAPONS.

LET ME HANDLE THIS.

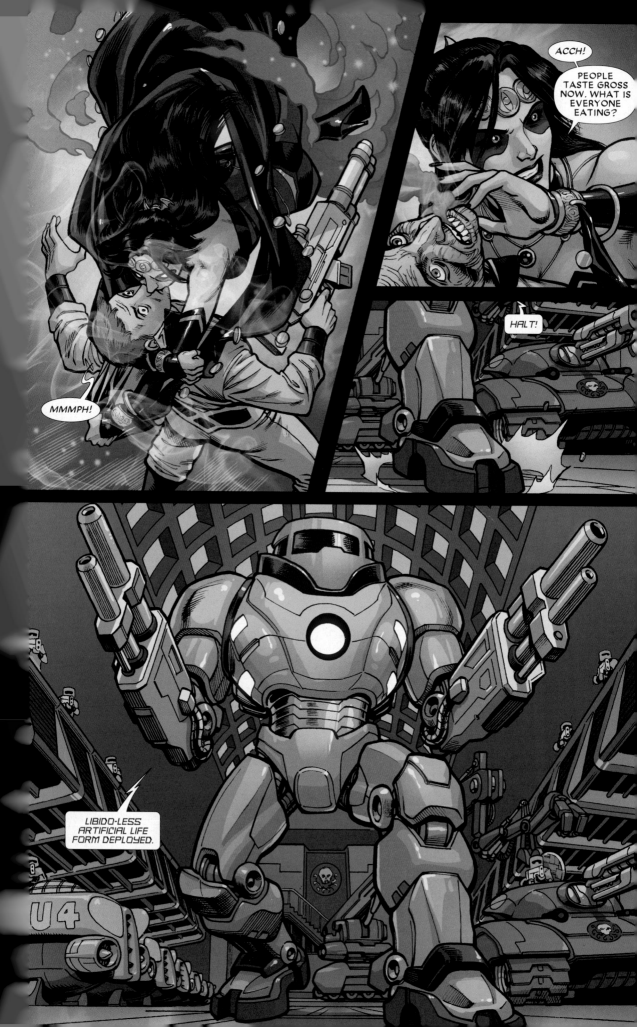

I CAN FEEL MY FULL POWER RETURN!

YES. YOUR POWER IS WHAT INTERESTS ME.

I AM M.O.D.O.K., A MENTAL ORGANISM DESIGNED ONLY FOR KILLING.

A TALENT YO[U] EXCEL AT.

M.O.D.O.K.
ALIAS: MENTAL ORGANISM DESIGNED ONLY FOR KILLING "THE BIG FACE GUY"
HEIGHT: 8'
WEIGHT: 750 LBS.
ALIGNMENT: BAD.

POWERS & ABILITIES:
BRAINY STUFF, YOU KNOW--BRAIN BLASTS, SUPER SMARTNESS, STUFF LIKE THAT. AND HE RUNS A.I.M., SOMETIMES. IT'S COMPLICATED.

WEAPONS OF CHOICE:
BRAIN BLASTS AND HENCHMEN.

CAN'T... MOVE.

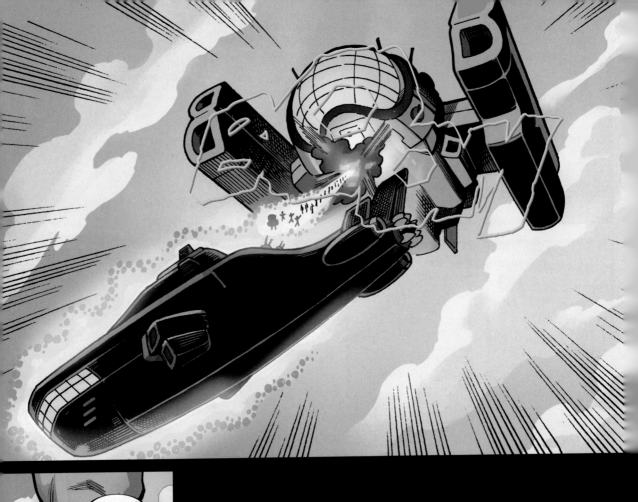

AHHH!

AEEIIII!

YOU FOOL!

M.O.D.O.K.'S CHAIR CAN FLY!

HOW WILL YOU SURVIVE?

FUNNY YOU SHOULD ASK.

THIS IS GREAT *FUN!* SO THE BOVINE MAN DIDN'T REQUIRE THIS ENCHANTED LITTER TO FLY?

OH, NO-- M.O.D.O.K. NEEDED THIS CHAIR TO FLY. R.I.P. M.O.D.O.K.

LAND THIS THING, DEADPOOL! I CAN'T HANG ON!

YEAAAAAaa

WALOOOF!

UGH.

DERP.

OF COURSE YOU CAN, BOB. YOU'RE A MEMBER OF A MAJOR TERRORIST ORGANIZATION. I'M SURE THERE ARE *FITNESS REQUIREMENTS.* YOUR MIND IS SAYING, "*NO*" BUT YOUR BODY CAN EASILY HANG ON.

AH AH AH AEEEEEIIIWOOOO

I'M SURE HE'S FINE.

POOR CREATURE. SHALL I HELP HIM?

I HAVE SOMETHING RIGHT HERE IN MY POUCH THAT WILL HELP YOU WITH THE PAIN.

COUNT BACKWARDS FROM 100...

OH GOD, DEADPOOL--PLEASE DON'T LET HER *EAT* MY SOUL, TOO.

SHH. SHE'S NOT GOING TO HURT YOU, AND I'M GOING TO HELP YOU.

THWAM

GAK!

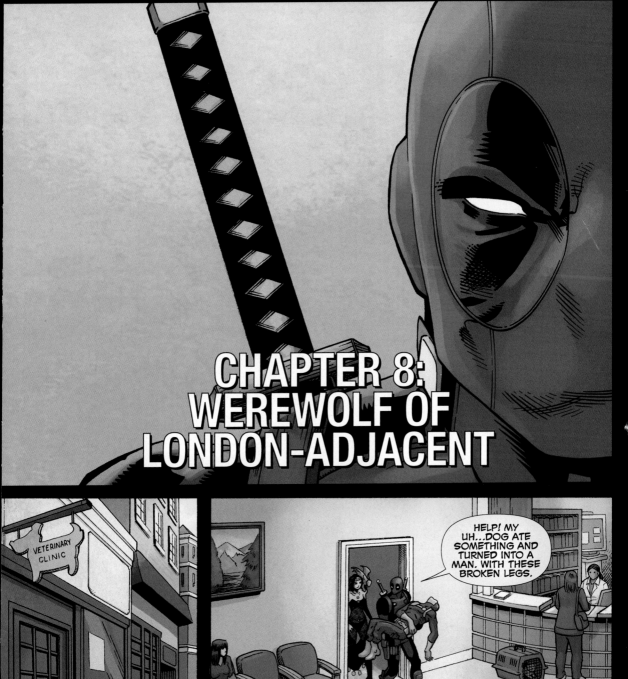

CHAPTER 8:
WEREWOLF OF LONDON-ADJACENT

HELP! MY UH...DOG ATE SOMETHING AND TURNED INTO A MAN. WITH THESE BROKEN LEGS.

EXCUSE ME, NURSE. WHILE YOU'RE LOOKING AT MR. FLUFFLE'S LEGS, HOW MUCH WOULD IT BE TO HAVE HIM FIXED?

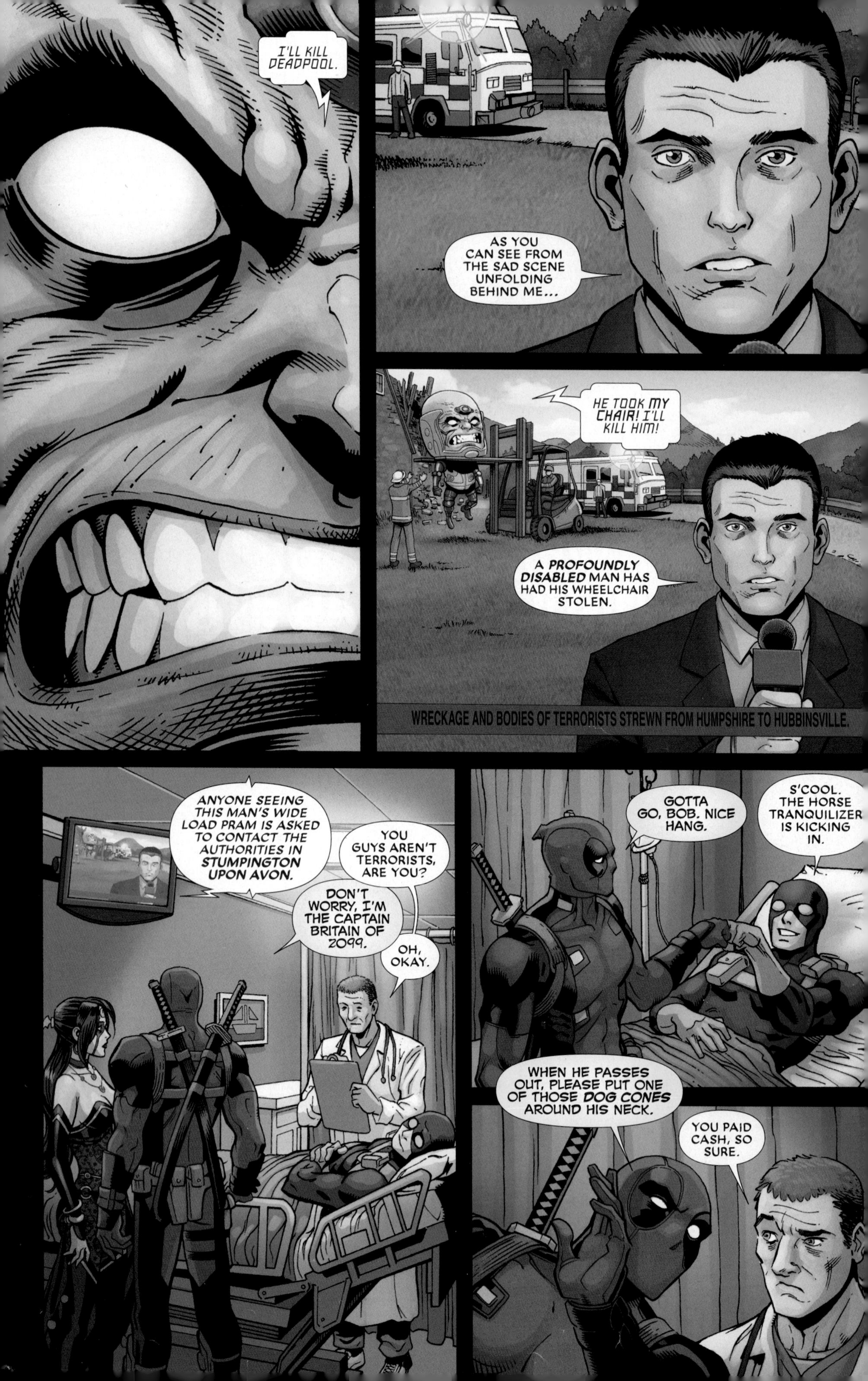
I'LL KILL DEADPOOL.
AS YOU CAN SEE FROM THE SAD SCENE UNFOLDING BEHIND ME...
HE TOOK MY CHAIR! I'LL KILL HIM!
A PROFOUNDLY DISABLED MAN HAS HAD HIS WHEELCHAIR STOLEN.
WRECKAGE AND BODIES OF TERRORISTS STREWN FROM HUMPSHIRE TO HUBBINSVILLE.
ANYONE SEEING THIS MAN'S WIDE LOAD PRAM IS ASKED TO CONTACT THE AUTHORITIES IN STUMPINGTON UPON AVON.
YOU GUYS AREN'T TERRORISTS, ARE YOU?
DON'T WORRY, I'M THE CAPTAIN BRITAIN OF 2099.
OH, OKAY.
GOTTA GO, BOB. NICE HANG.
S'COOL. THE HORSE TRANQUILIZER IS KICKING IN.
WHEN HE PASSES OUT, PLEASE PUT ONE OF THOSE DOG CONES AROUND HIS NECK.
YOU PAID CASH, SO SURE.

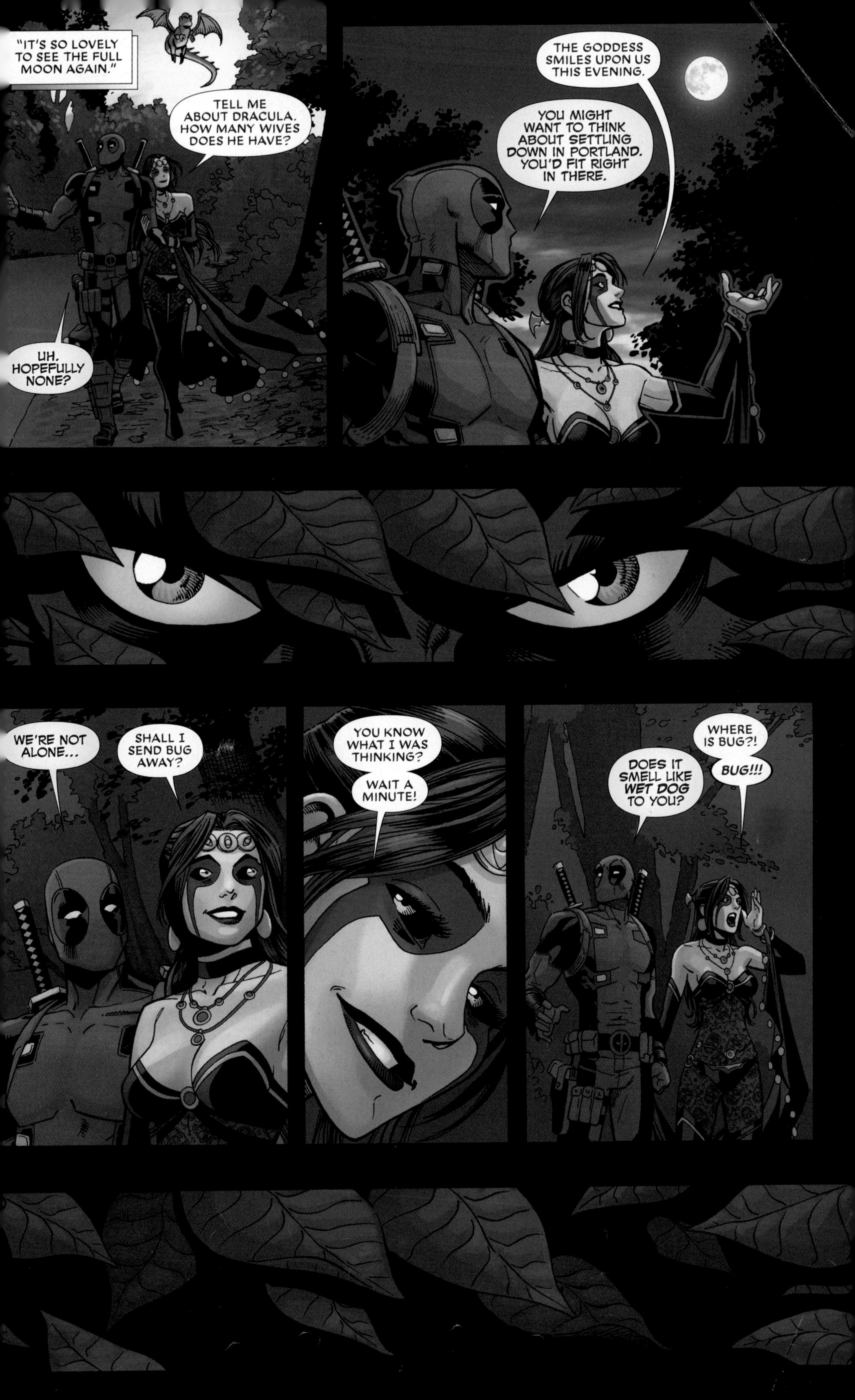
"IT'S SO LOVELY TO SEE THE FULL MOON AGAIN."
TELL ME ABOUT DRACULA. HOW MANY WIVES DOES HE HAVE?
UH. HOPEFULLY NONE?
THE GODDESS SMILES UPON US THIS EVENING.
YOU MIGHT WANT TO THINK ABOUT SETTLING DOWN IN PORTLAND. YOU'D FIT RIGHT IN THERE.
WE'RE NOT ALONE...
SHALL I SEND BUG AWAY?
YOU KNOW WHAT I WAS THINKING?
WAIT A MINUTE!
WHERE IS BUG?!
DOES IT SMELL LIKE WET DOG TO YOU?
BUG!!!

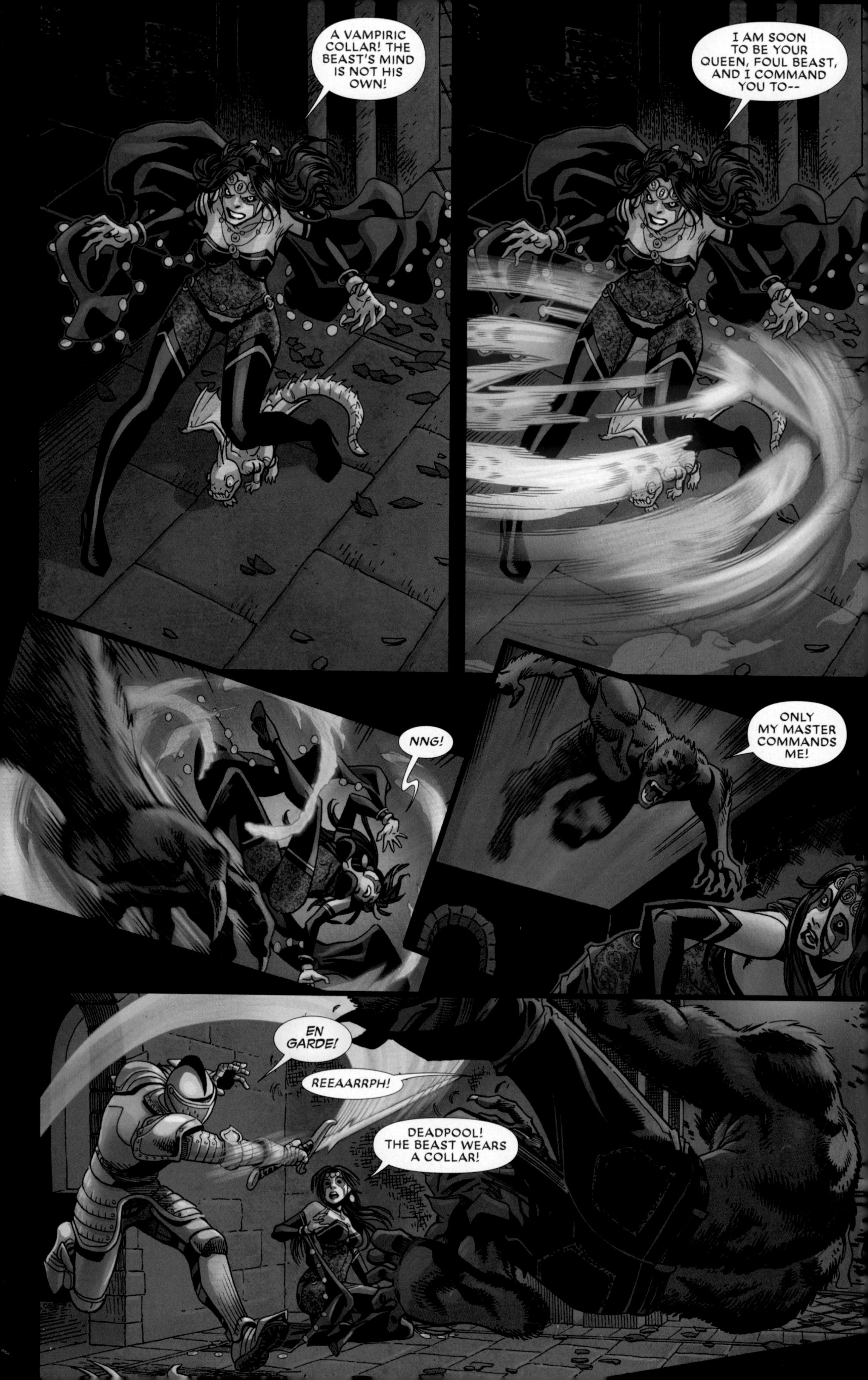
A VAMPIRIC COLLAR! THE BEAST'S MIND IS NOT HIS OWN!
I AM SOON TO BE YOUR QUEEN, FOUL BEAST, AND I COMMAND YOU TO--
NNG!
ONLY MY MASTER COMMANDS ME!
EN GARDE!
REEAARRPH!
DEADPOOL! THE BEAST WEARS A COLLAR!

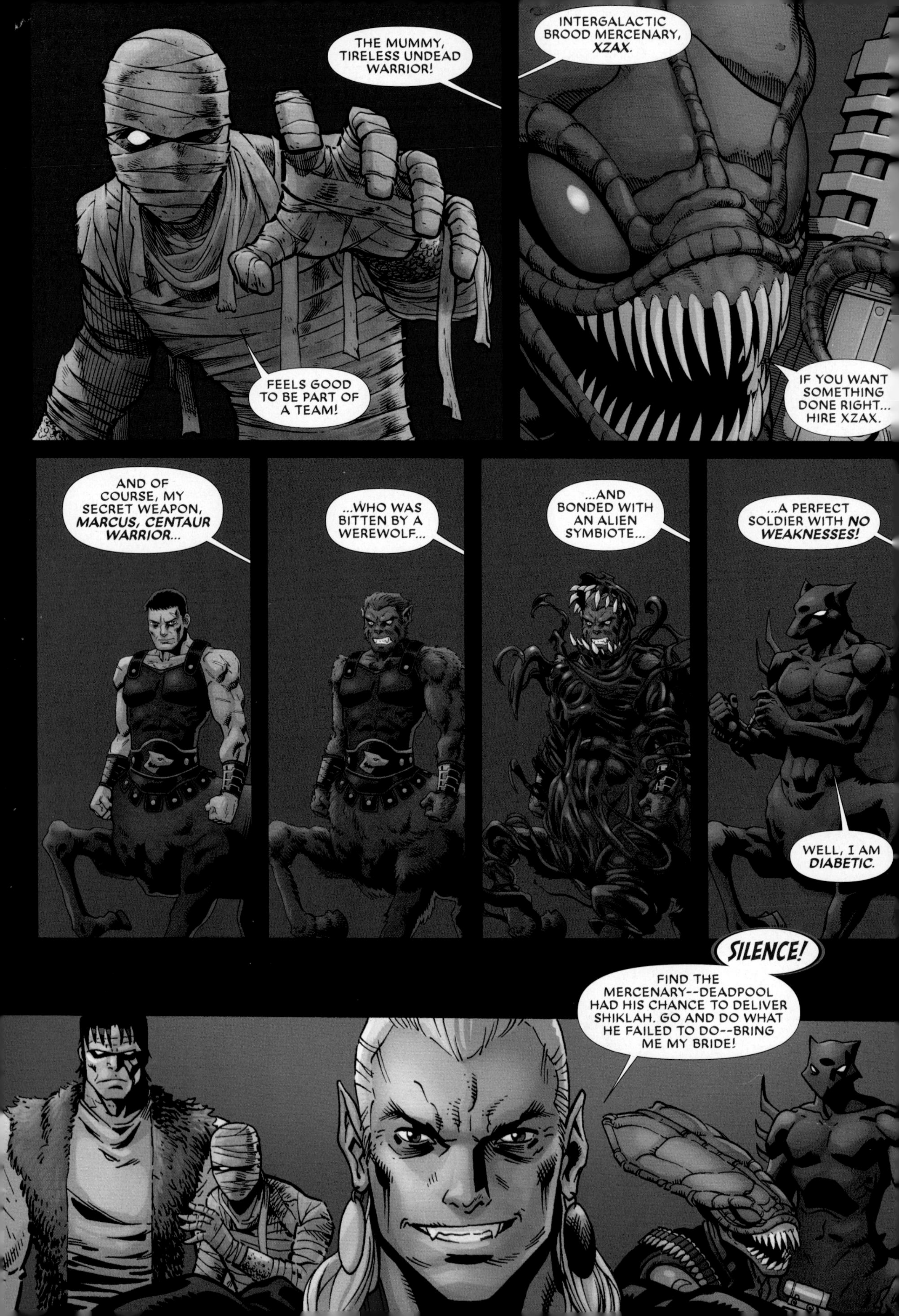

THE MUMMY, TIRELESS UNDEAD WARRIOR!
FEELS GOOD TO BE PART OF A TEAM!
INTERGALACTIC BROOD MERCENARY, ***XZAX***.
IF YOU WANT SOMETHING DONE RIGHT... HIRE XZAX.
AND OF COURSE, MY SECRET WEAPON, ***MARCUS, CENTAUR WARRIOR***...
...WHO WAS BITTEN BY A WEREWOLF...
...AND BONDED WITH AN ALIEN SYMBIOTE...
...A PERFECT SOLDIER WITH ***NO WEAKNESSES!***
WELL, I AM ***DIABETIC***.
SILENCE!
FIND THE MERCENARY--DEADPOOL HAD HIS CHANCE TO DELIVER SHIKLAH. GO AND DO WHAT HE FAILED TO DO--BRING ME MY BRIDE!

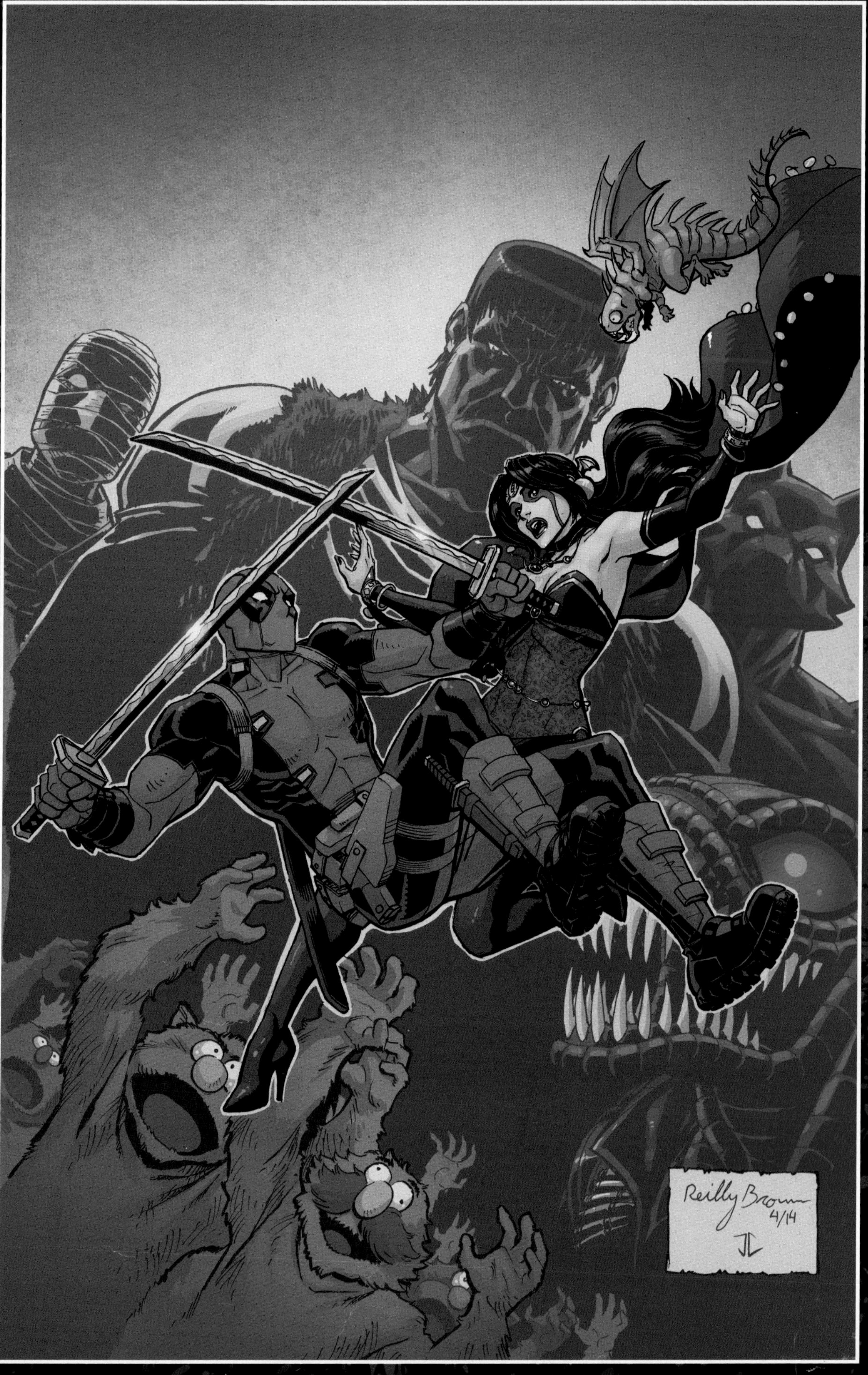
Reilly Brown
4/14
JC

DRACULA'S LAIR, MANHATTAN.

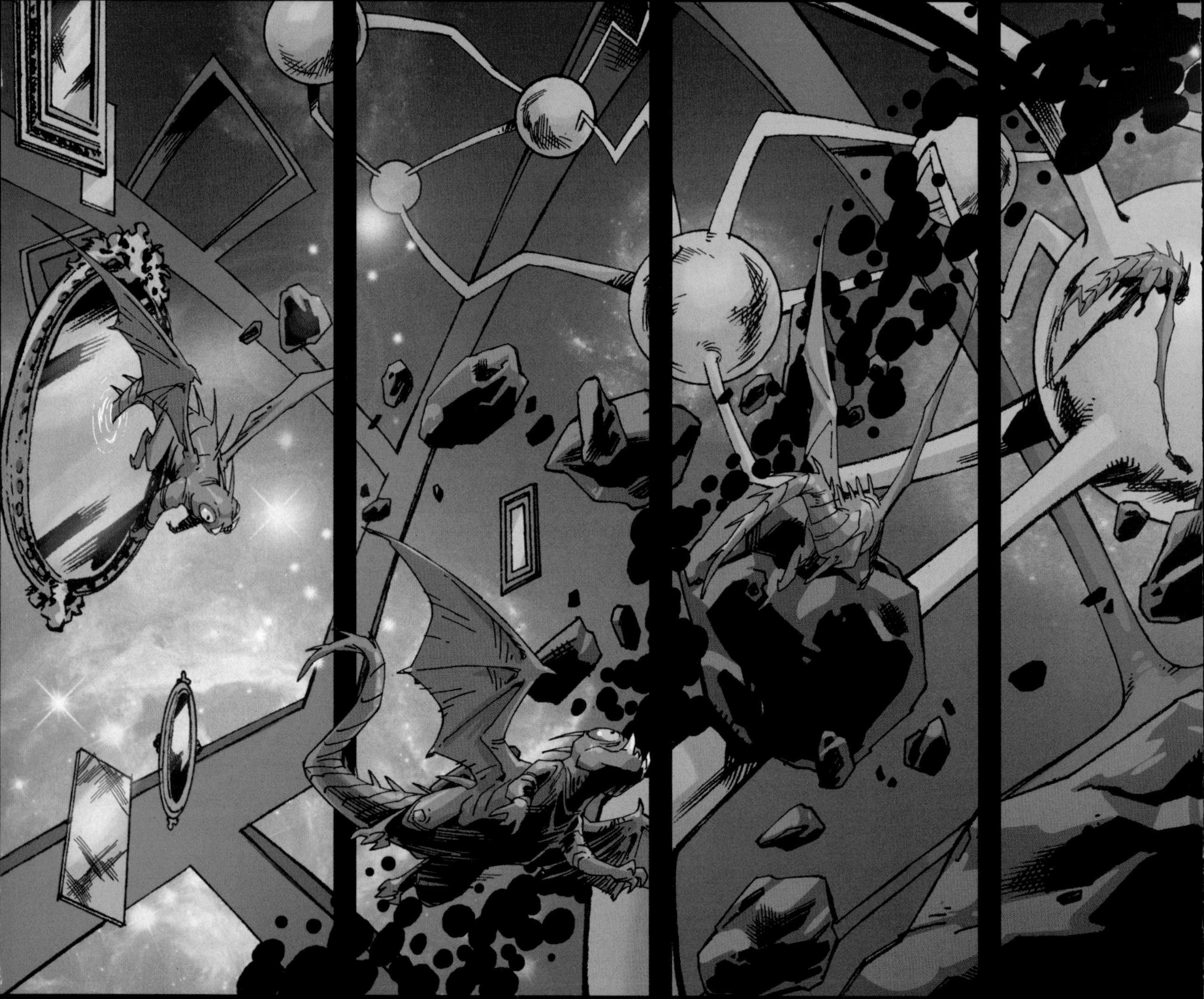

DEADPOOL
The Gauntlet
CHAPTER 9: GANGS OF NEW YORK

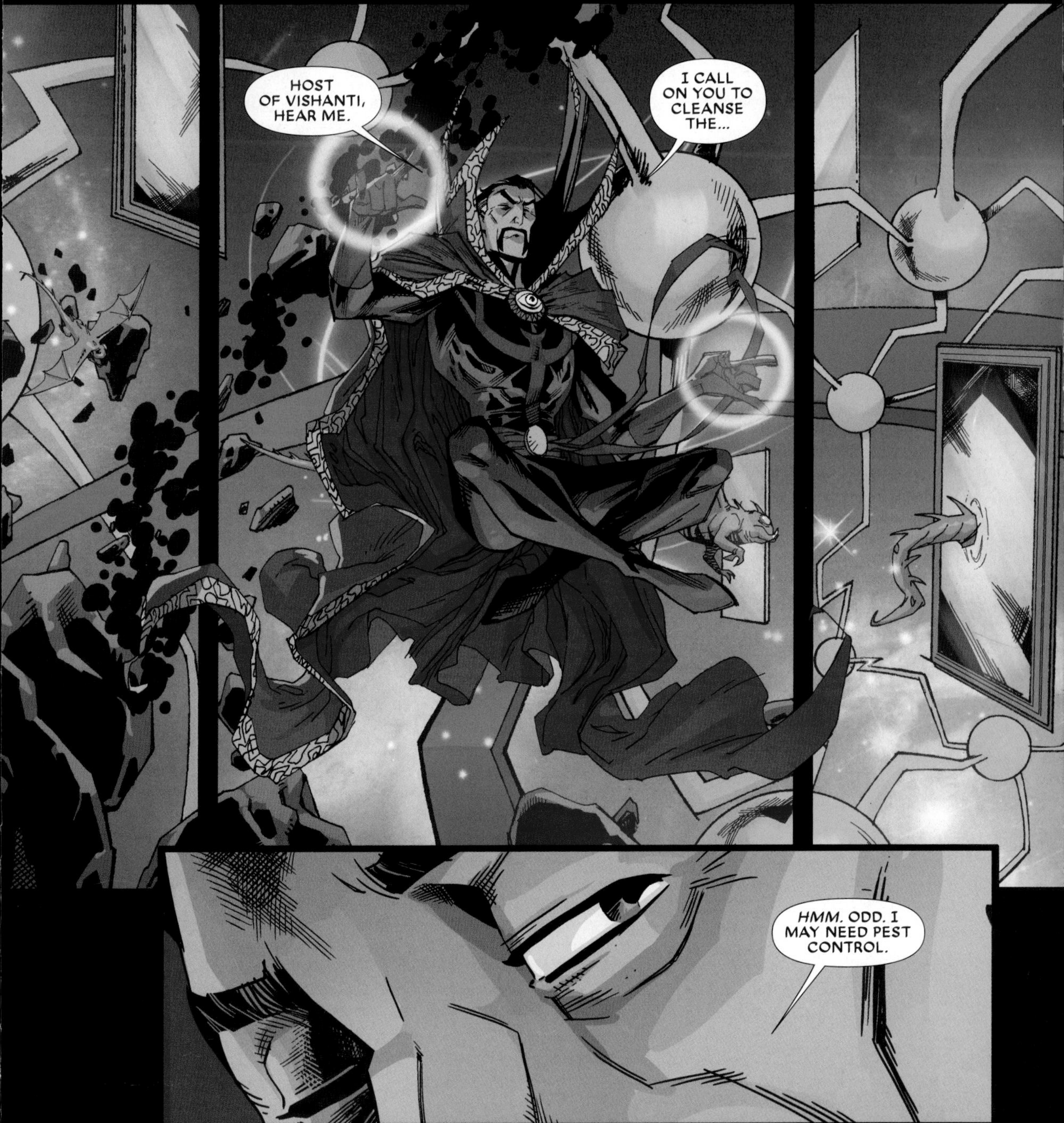
HOST OF VISHANTI, HEAR ME.
I CALL ON YOU TO CLEANSE THE...
HMM. ODD. I MAY NEED PEST CONTROL.

CAROUSEL CRUISES.

"THIS WILL BE THE MOST DANGEROUS PART OF OUR TRIP TO NEW YORK."

"SO THE ANCIENT MONSTERS OF THE DEEP STILL STALK THE EARTH, THEN?"

"NO, THERE ARE GERMS ON THIS SHIP THAT WILL MAKE YOUR BUTT PUKE. USE HAND SANITIZER AND OPEN DOORS WITH YOUR ELBOWS."

HEY!

BUG, YOU'RE BACK!

ZWIP

PLONK

UFF!

UH-- WE WERE JUST RESTING OUR EYES AND WRESTLING A LITTLE.

WHAT HAVE YOU SEEN ON YOUR TRAVELS?

DID YOU SEE DRACULA? MY BROTHERS?

THEY DON'T HAVE BUGS OF THEIR OWN, DO THEY? DID THEY JUST SEE OUR "NAP TIME"?

MY BROTHERS!!!

C'MERE.

OH, NO NO NO!!!

THEY'RE GONE. HE KILLED THEM...

I CAN SEE THROUGH MY BUG. HE...

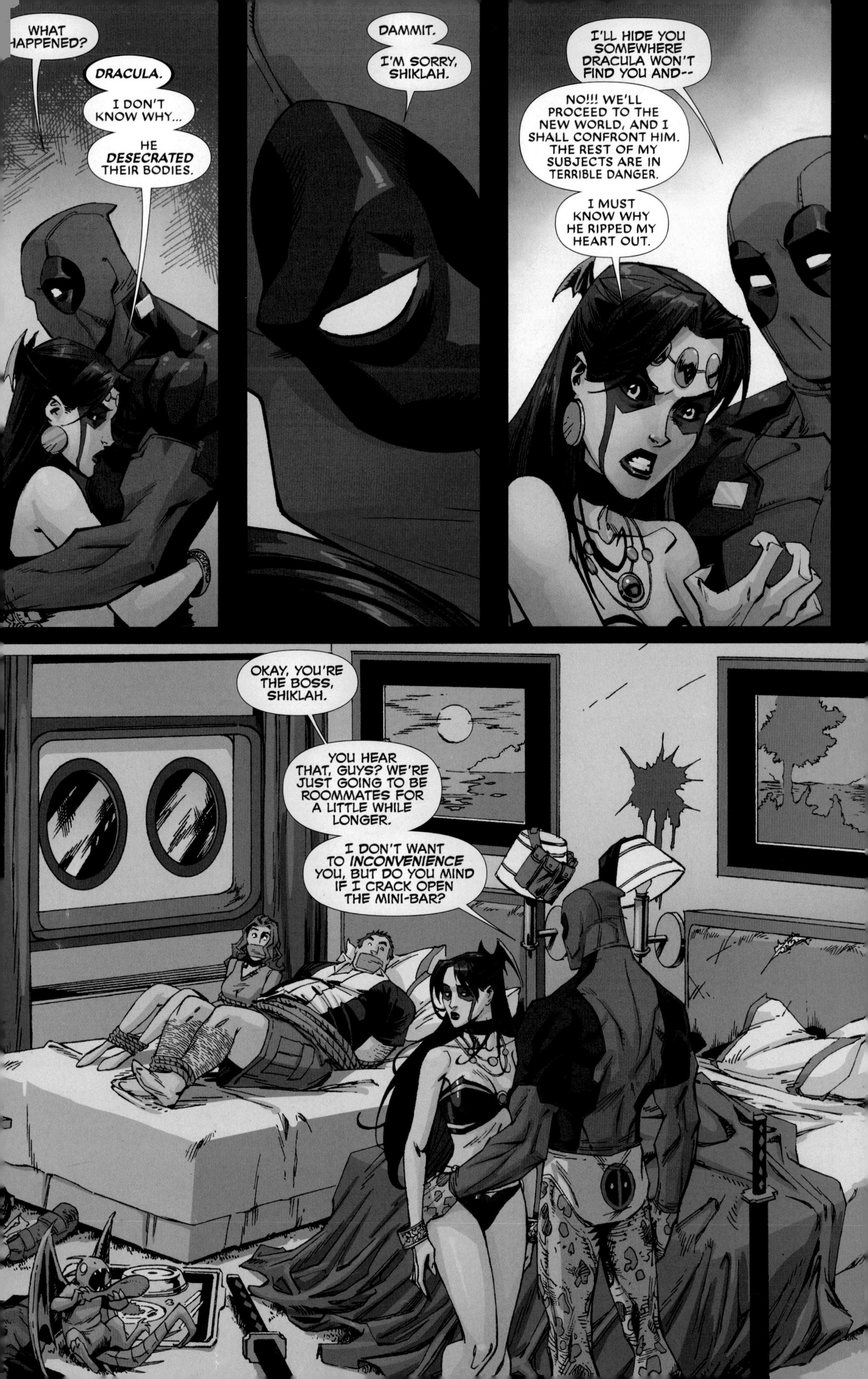
WHAT HAPPENED?
DRACULA.
I DON'T KNOW WHY...
HE DESECRATED THEIR BODIES.
DAMMIT.
I'M SORRY, SHIKLAH.
I'LL HIDE YOU SOMEWHERE DRACULA WON'T FIND YOU AND--
NO!!! WE'LL PROCEED TO THE NEW WORLD, AND I SHALL CONFRONT HIM. THE REST OF MY SUBJECTS ARE IN TERRIBLE DANGER.
I MUST KNOW WHY HE RIPPED MY HEART OUT.
OKAY, YOU'RE THE BOSS, SHIKLAH.
YOU HEAR THAT, GUYS? WE'RE JUST GOING TO BE ROOMMATES FOR A LITTLE WHILE LONGER.
I DON'T WANT TO INCONVENIENCE YOU, BUT DO YOU MIND IF I CRACK OPEN THE MINI-BAR?

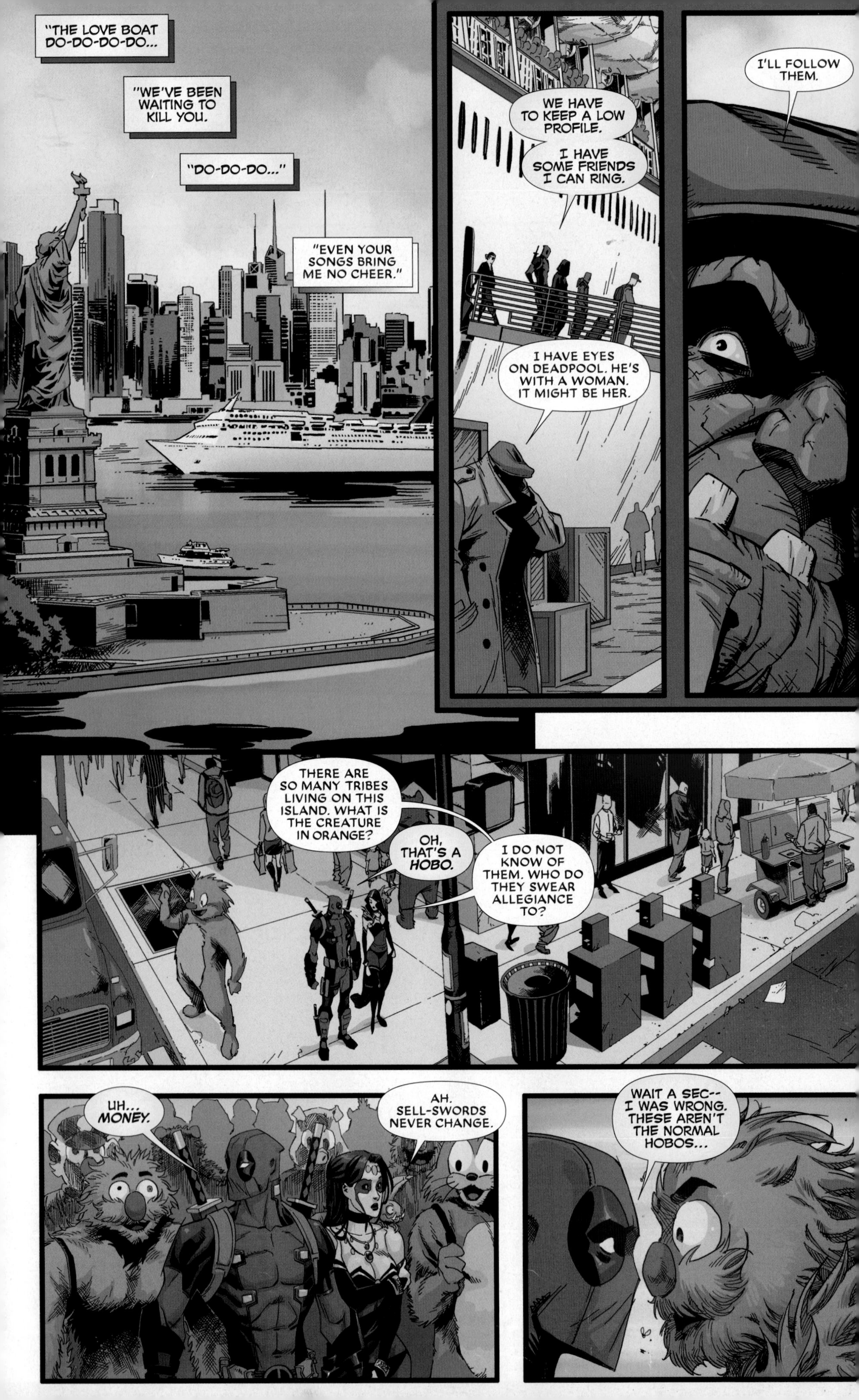
"THE LOVE BOAT DO-DO-DO-DO...
"WE'VE BEEN WAITING TO KILL YOU.
"DO-DO-DO..."
"EVEN YOUR SONGS BRING ME NO CHEER."
WE HAVE TO KEEP A LOW PROFILE.
I HAVE SOME FRIENDS I CAN RING.
I HAVE EYES ON DEADPOOL. HE'S WITH A WOMAN. IT MIGHT BE HER.
I'LL FOLLOW THEM.
THERE ARE SO MANY TRIBES LIVING ON THIS ISLAND. WHAT IS THE CREATURE IN ORANGE?
OH, THAT'S A *HOBO.*
I DO NOT KNOW OF THEM. WHO DO THEY SWEAR ALLEGIANCE TO?
UH... *MONEY.*
AH. SELL-SWORDS NEVER CHANGE.
WAIT A SEC-- I WAS WRONG. THESE AREN'T THE NORMAL HOBOS...

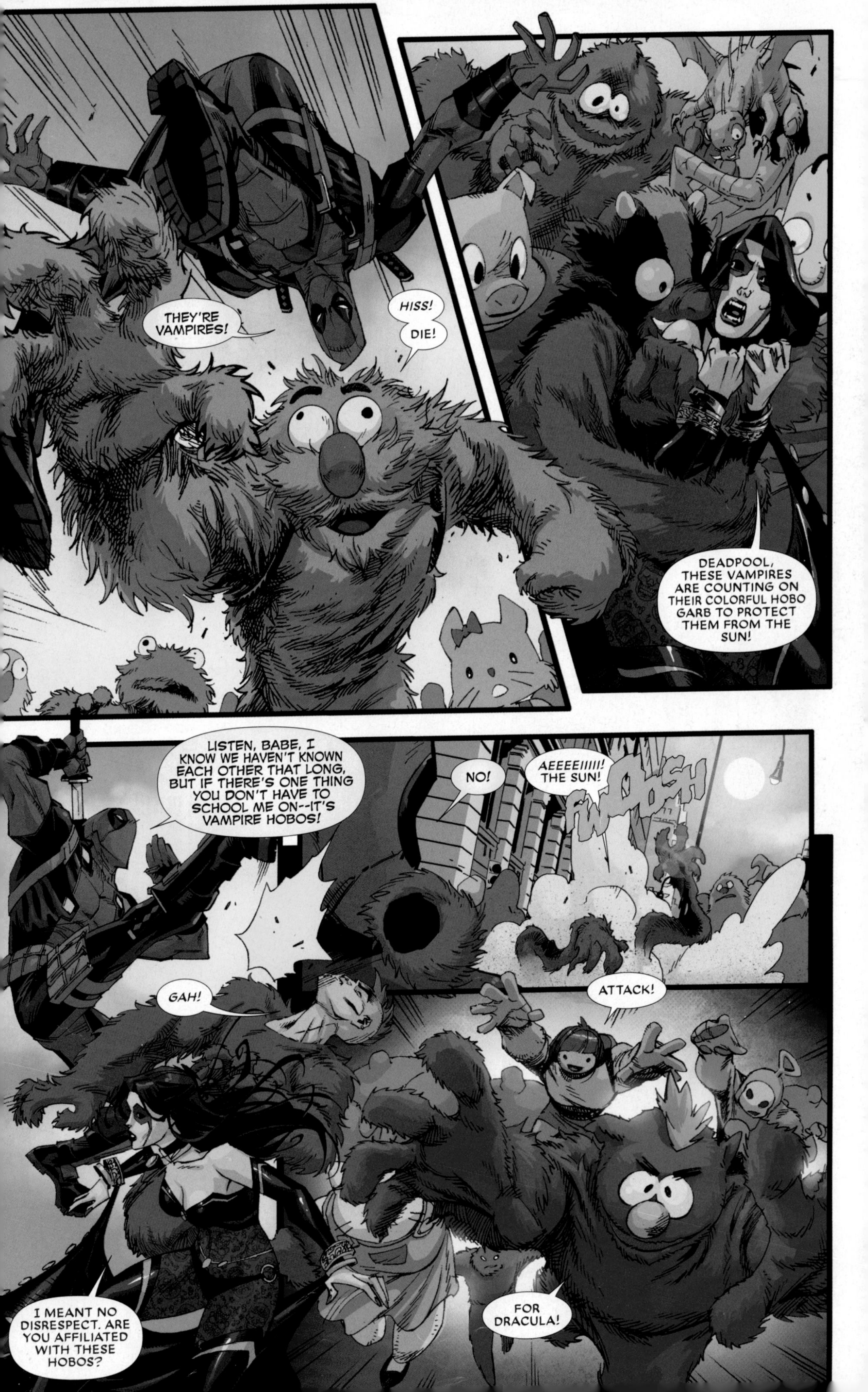
THEY'RE VAMPIRES!
HISS!
DIE!
DEADPOOL, THESE VAMPIRES ARE COUNTING ON THEIR COLORFUL HOBO GARB TO PROTECT THEM FROM THE SUN!
LISTEN, BABE, I KNOW WE HAVEN'T KNOWN EACH OTHER THAT LONG, BUT IF THERE'S ONE THING YOU DON'T HAVE TO SCHOOL ME ON--IT'S VAMPIRE HOBOS!
NO!
AEEEEIIIII! THE SUN!
FWOOSH
GAH!
ATTACK!
I MEANT NO DISRESPECT. ARE YOU AFFILIATED WITH THESE HOBOS?
FOR DRACULA!

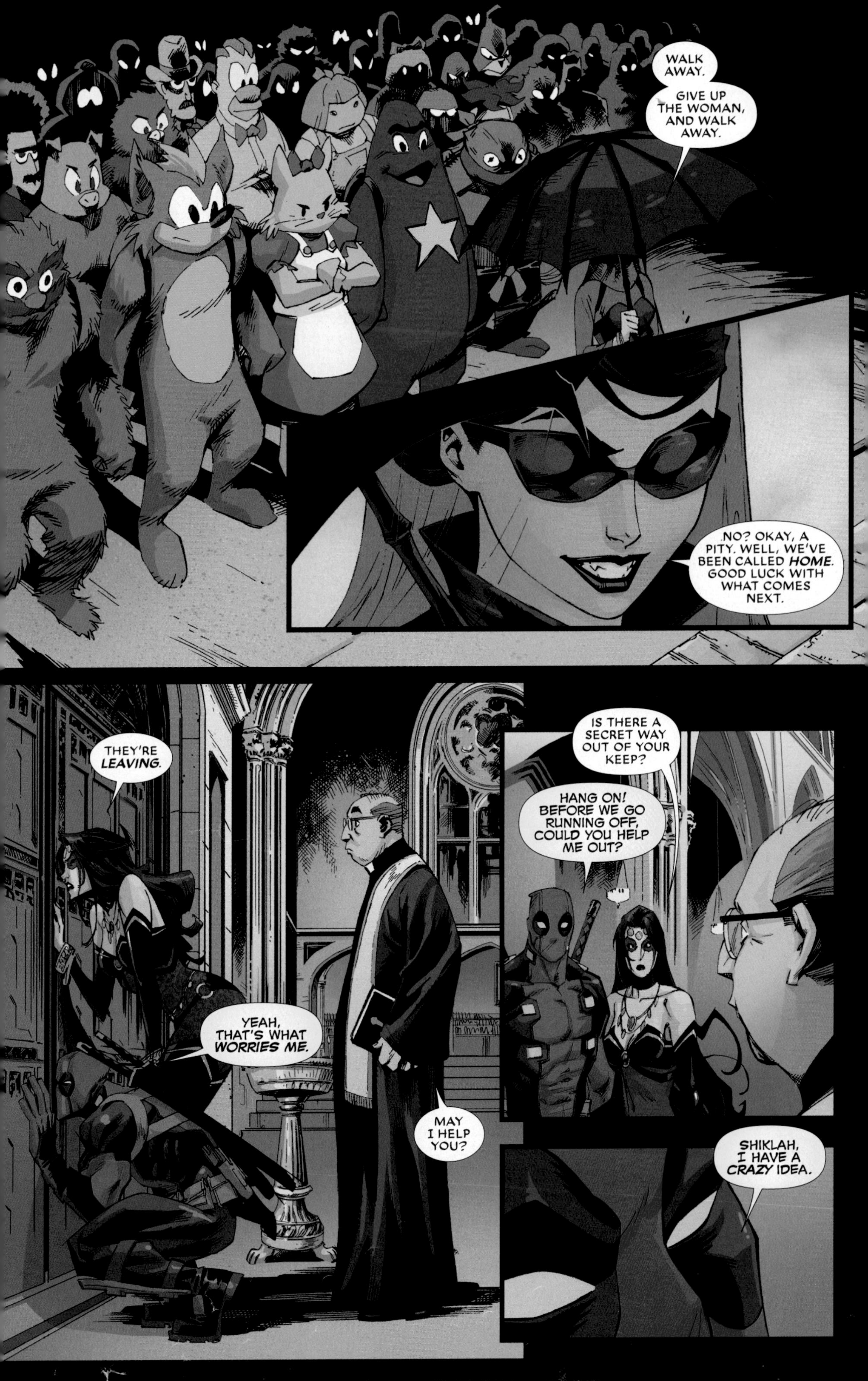
WALK AWAY.
GIVE UP THE WOMAN, AND WALK AWAY.
NO? OKAY, A PITY. WELL, WE'VE BEEN CALLED HOME. GOOD LUCK WITH WHAT COMES NEXT.
THEY'RE LEAVING.
YEAH, THAT'S WHAT WORRIES ME.
MAY I HELP YOU?
IS THERE A SECRET WAY OUT OF YOUR KEEP?
HANG ON! BEFORE WE GO RUNNING OFF, COULD YOU HELP ME OUT?
SHIKLAH, I HAVE A CRAZY IDEA.

DEADPOOL
The Gauntlet

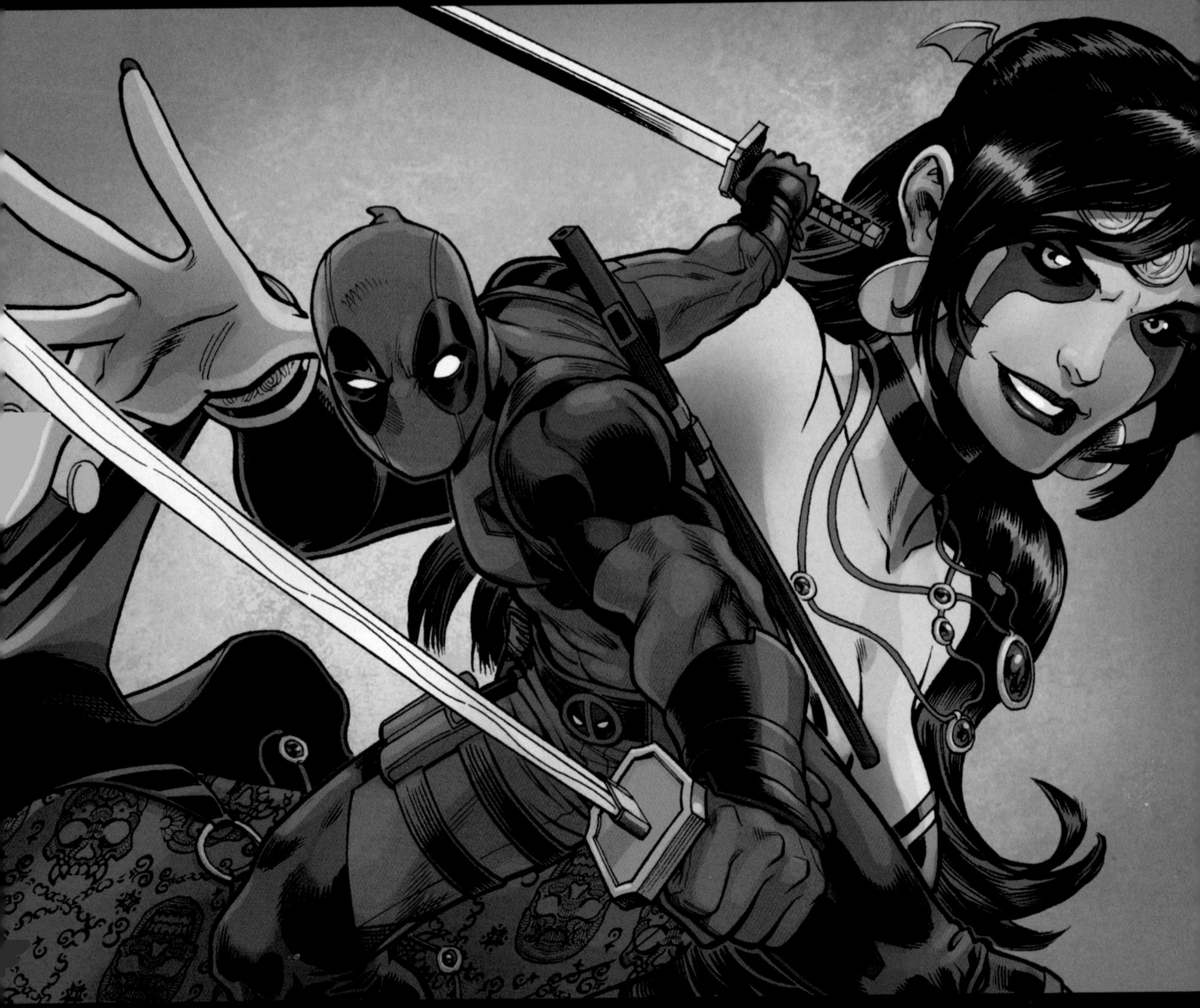

CHAPTER 10: WHEN COMETH THE FRIGHTFUL FOUR

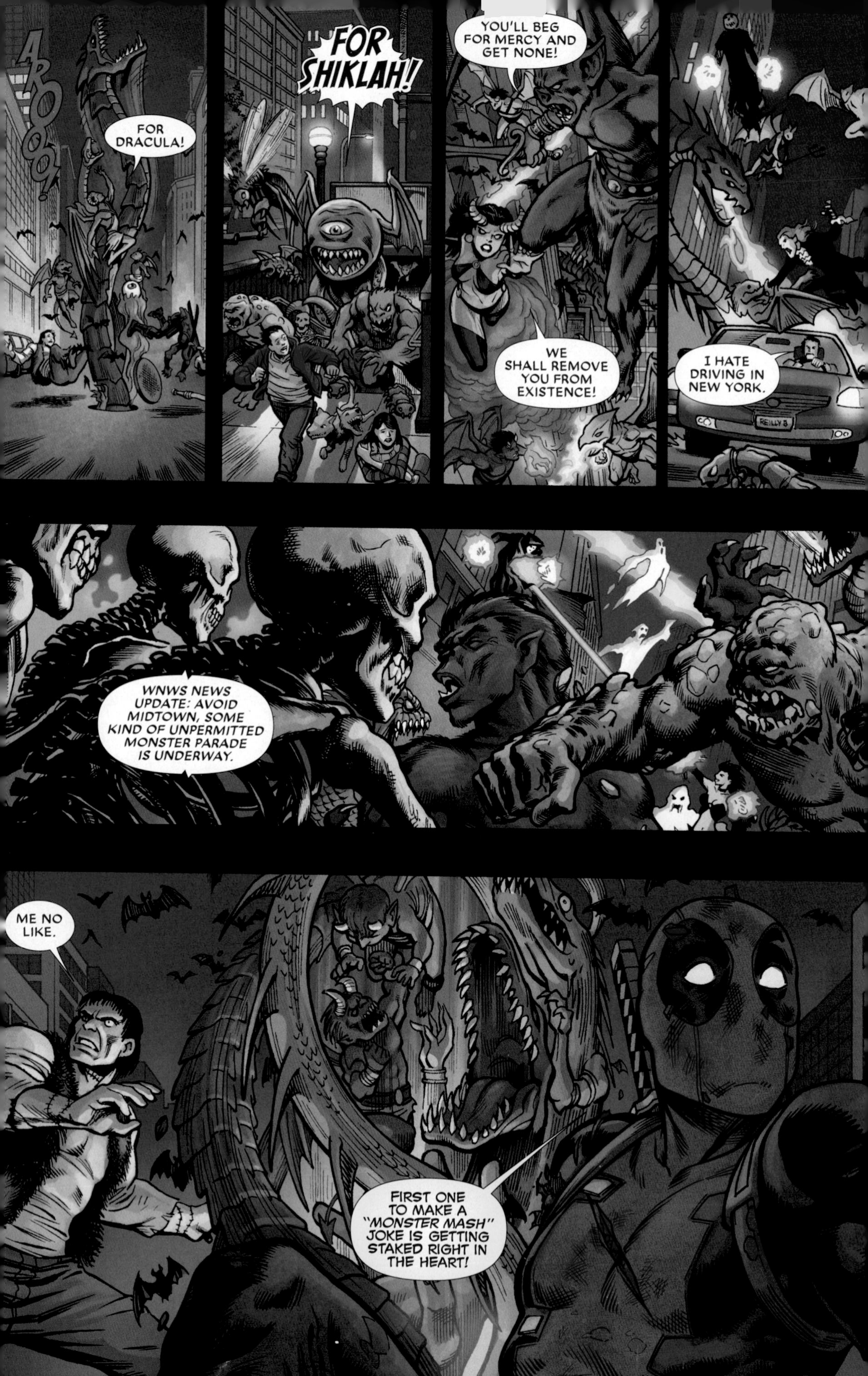
AROOO!
FOR DRACULA!
FOR SHIKLAH!
YOU'LL BEG FOR MERCY AND GET NONE!
WE SHALL REMOVE YOU FROM EXISTENCE!
I HATE DRIVING IN NEW YORK.
WNWS NEWS UPDATE: AVOID MIDTOWN, SOME KIND OF UNPERMITTED MONSTER PARADE IS UNDERWAY.
ME NO LIKE.
FIRST ONE TO MAKE A "MONSTER MASH" JOKE IS GETTING STAKED RIGHT IN THE HEART!

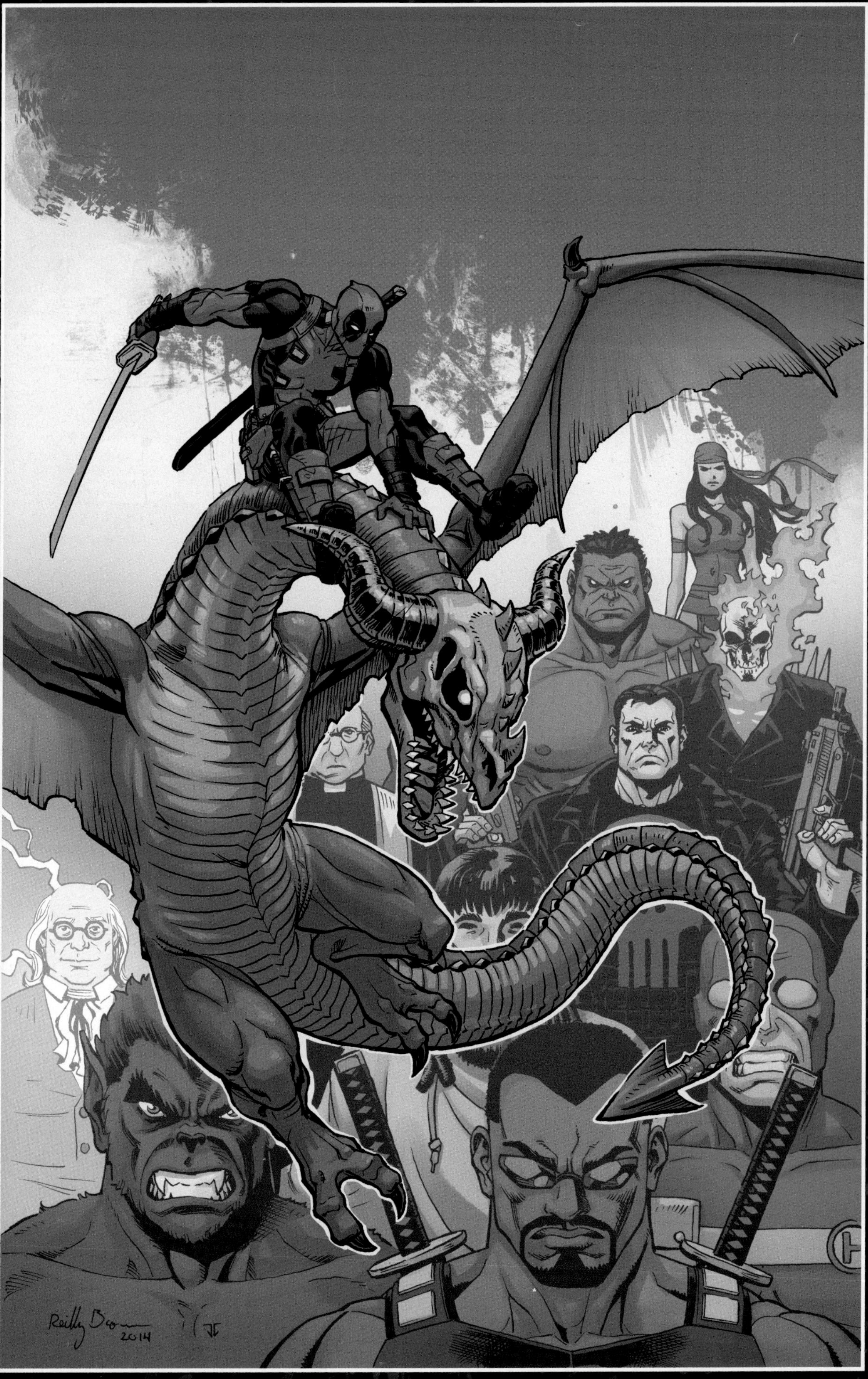

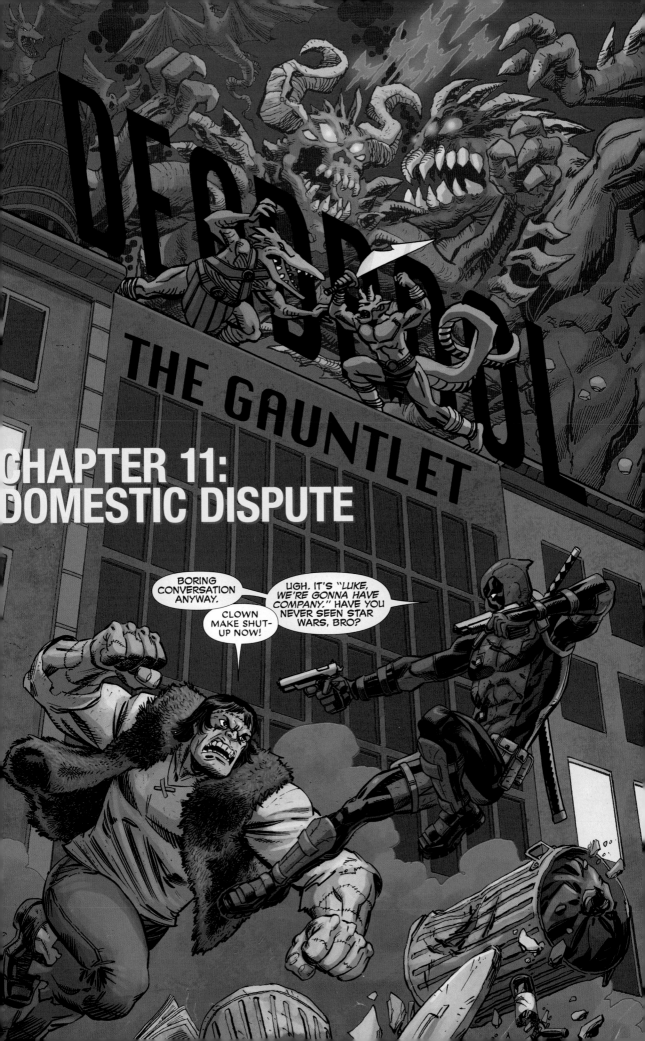

CHAPTER 11: DOMESTIC DISPUTE

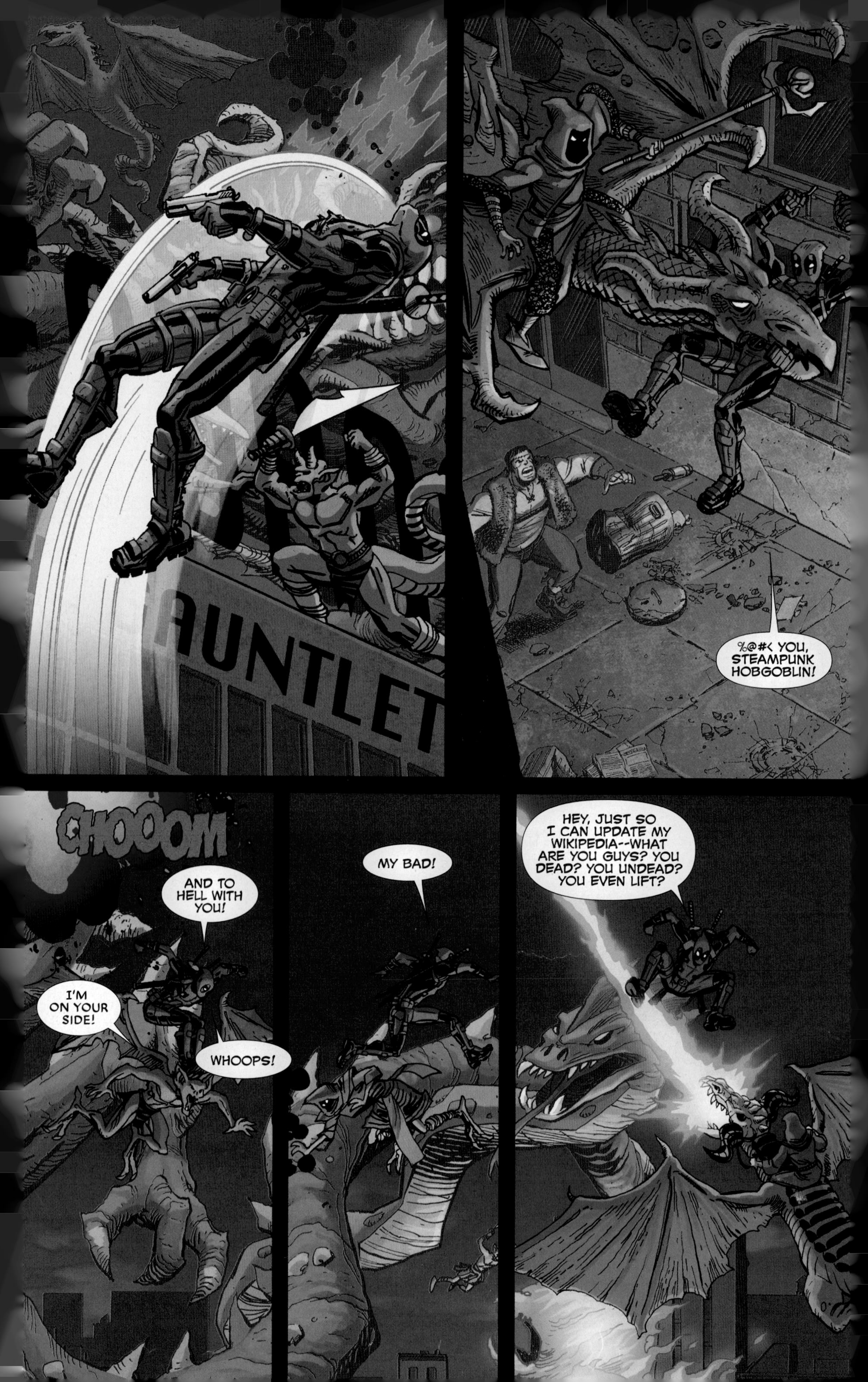
AUNTLET
%@#< YOU, STEAMPUNK HOBGOBLIN!
CHOOOM
AND TO HELL WITH YOU!
I'M ON YOUR SIDE!
WHOOPS!
MY BAD!
HEY, JUST SO I CAN UPDATE MY WIKIPEDIA--WHAT ARE YOU GUYS? YOU DEAD? YOU UNDEAD? YOU EVEN LIFT?

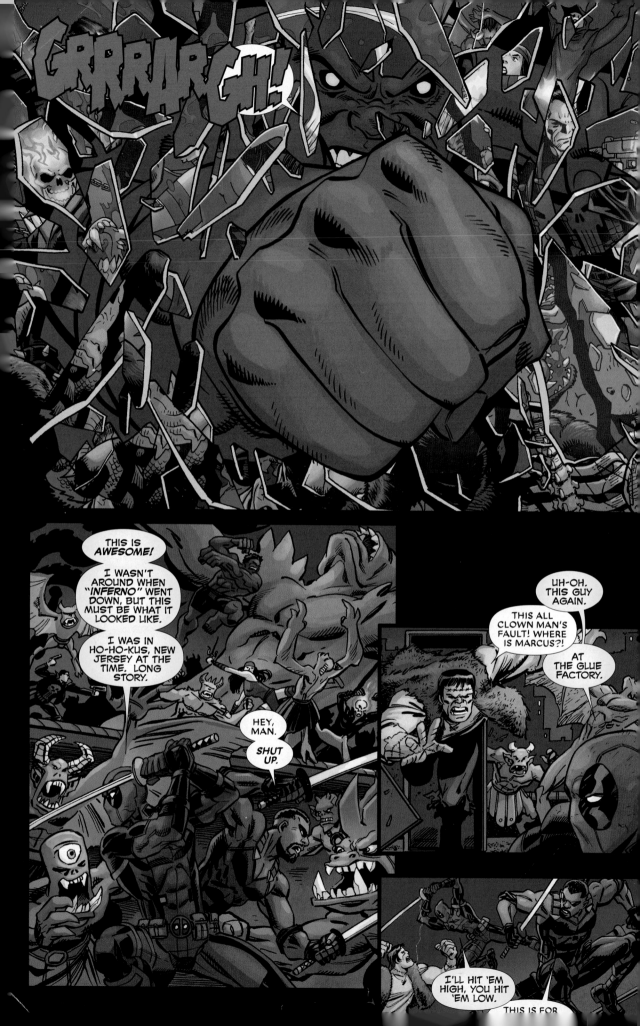

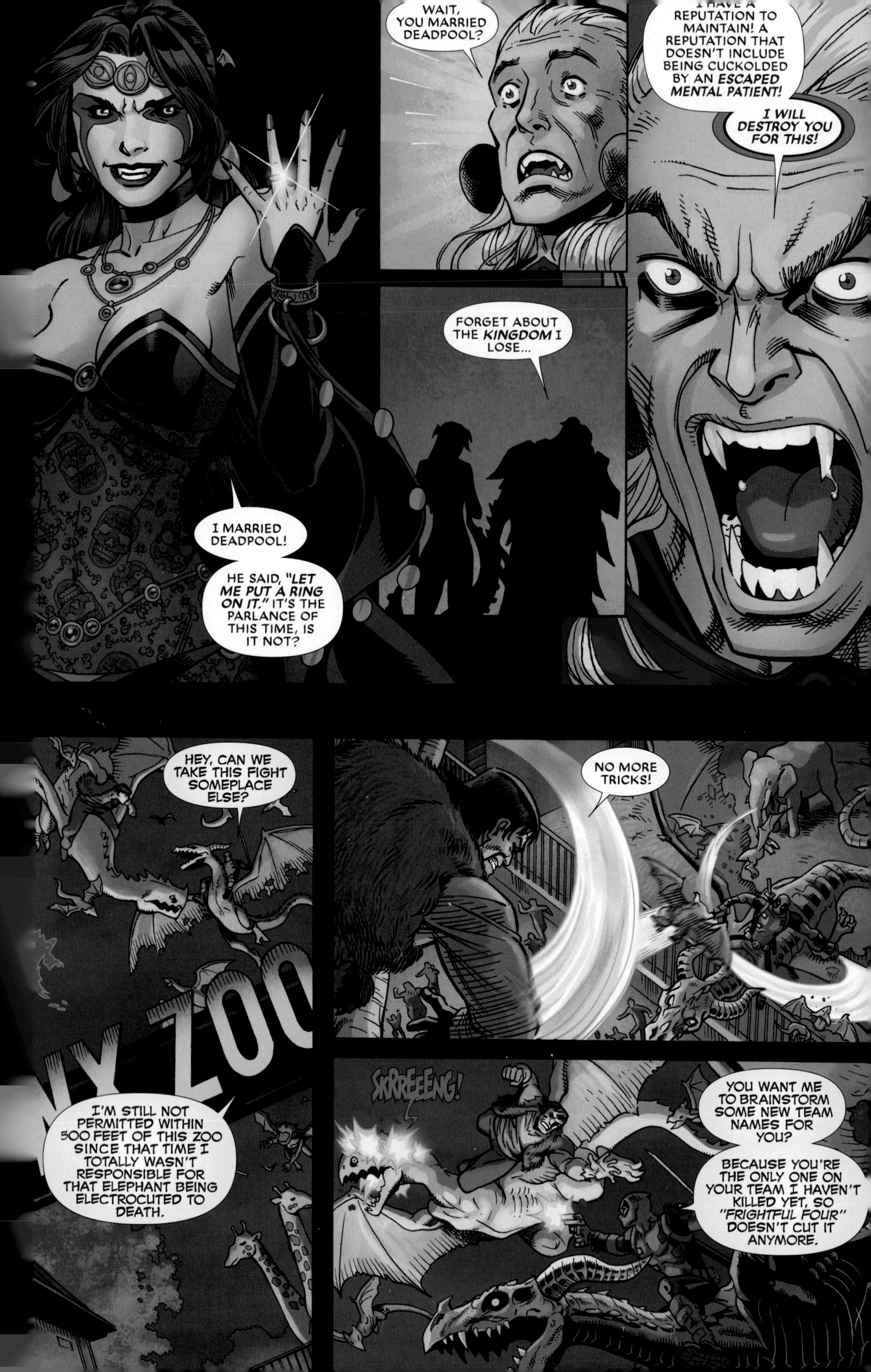
WAIT, YOU MARRIED DEADPOOL?
I HAVE A REPUTATION TO MAINTAIN! A REPUTATION THAT DOESN'T INCLUDE BEING CUCKOLDED BY AN *ESCAPED MENTAL PATIENT!*
I WILL DESTROY YOU FOR THIS!
FORGET ABOUT THE *KINGDOM* I LOSE...
I MARRIED DEADPOOL!
HE SAID, *"LET ME PUT A RING ON IT."* IT'S THE PARLANCE OF THIS TIME, IS IT NOT?
HEY, CAN WE TAKE THIS FIGHT SOMEPLACE ELSE?
NY ZOO
I'M STILL NOT PERMITTED WITHIN 500 FEET OF THIS ZOO SINCE THAT TIME I TOTALLY WASN'T RESPONSIBLE FOR THAT ELEPHANT BEING ELECTROCUTED TO DEATH.
NO MORE TRICKS!
SKRREEENG!
YOU WANT ME TO BRAINSTORM SOME NEW TEAM NAMES FOR YOU?
BECAUSE YOU'RE THE ONLY ONE ON YOUR TEAM I HAVEN'T KILLED YET, SO *"FRIGHTFUL FOUR"* DOESN'T CUT IT ANYMORE.

DEADPOOL
The Gauntlet

CHAPTER 12: DEADPOOL, DISARMED

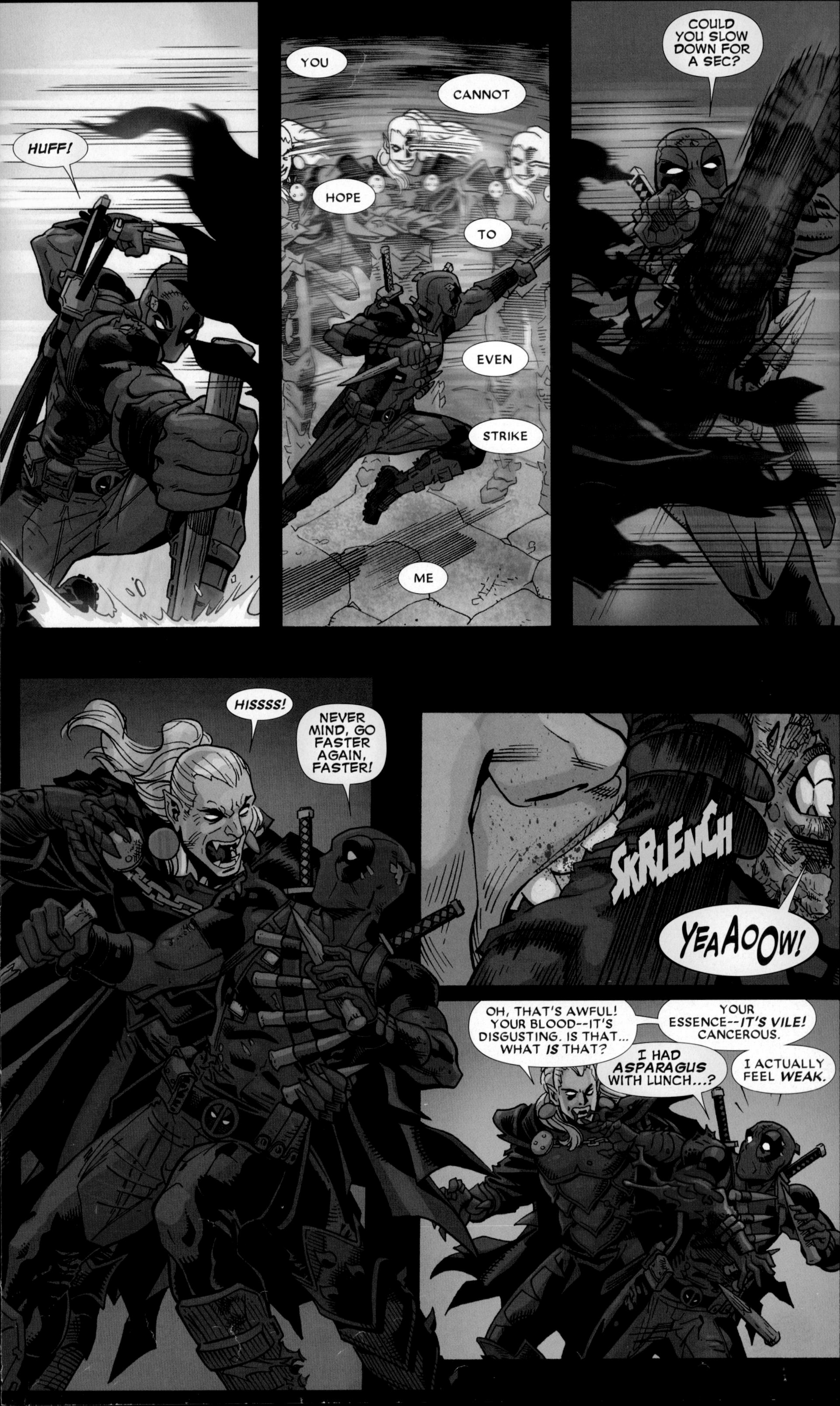

HUFF!
YOU
CANNOT
HOPE
TO
EVEN
STRIKE
ME
COULD YOU SLOW DOWN FOR A SEC?
HISSSS!
NEVER MIND, GO FASTER AGAIN, FASTER!
SKRLENCH
YEAAOOW!
OH, THAT'S AWFUL! YOUR BLOOD--IT'S DISGUSTING. IS THAT... WHAT IS THAT?
YOUR ESSENCE--IT'S VILE! CANCEROUS.
I HAD ASPARAGUS WITH LUNCH...?
I ACTUALLY FEEL WEAK.

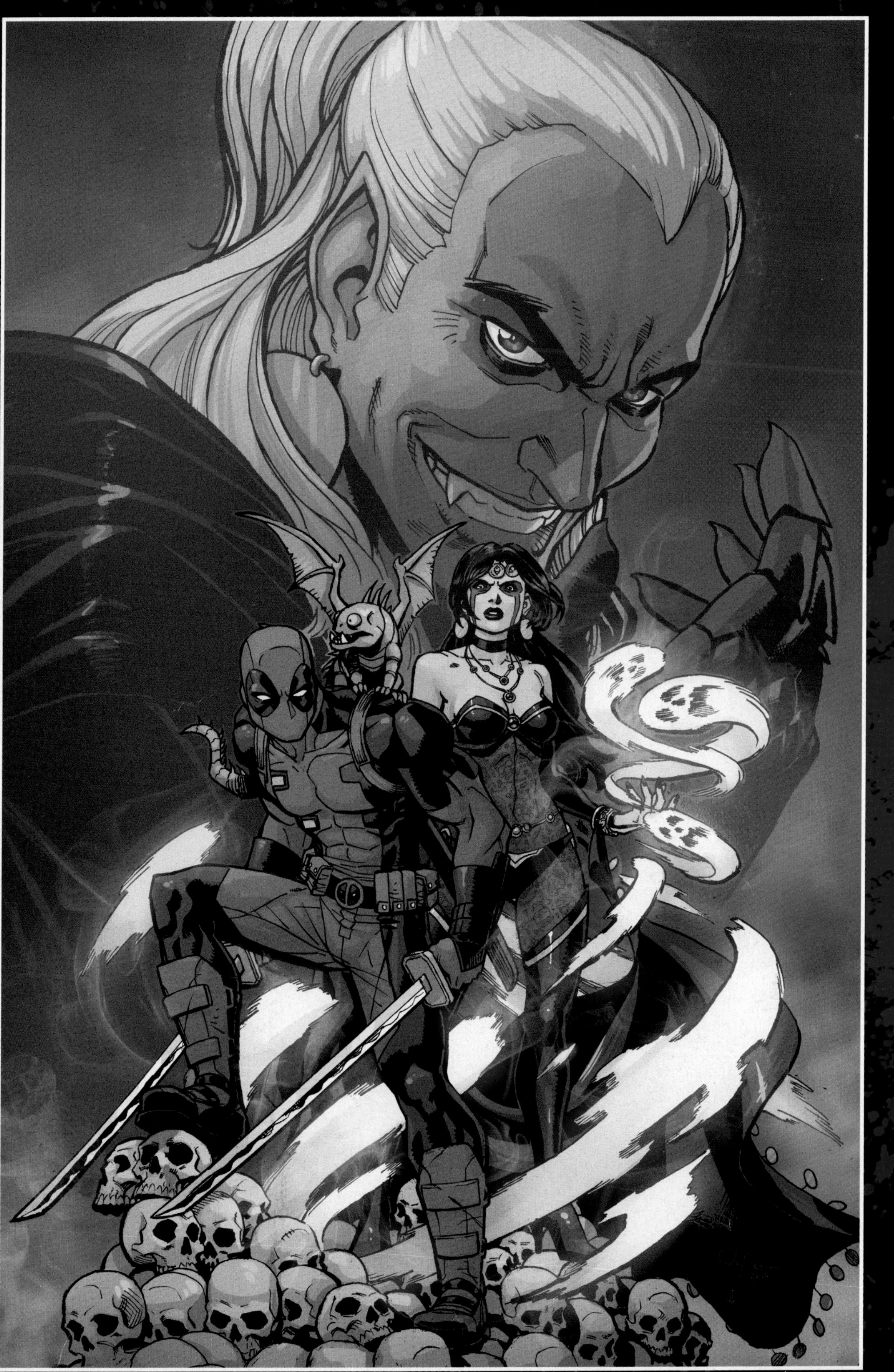

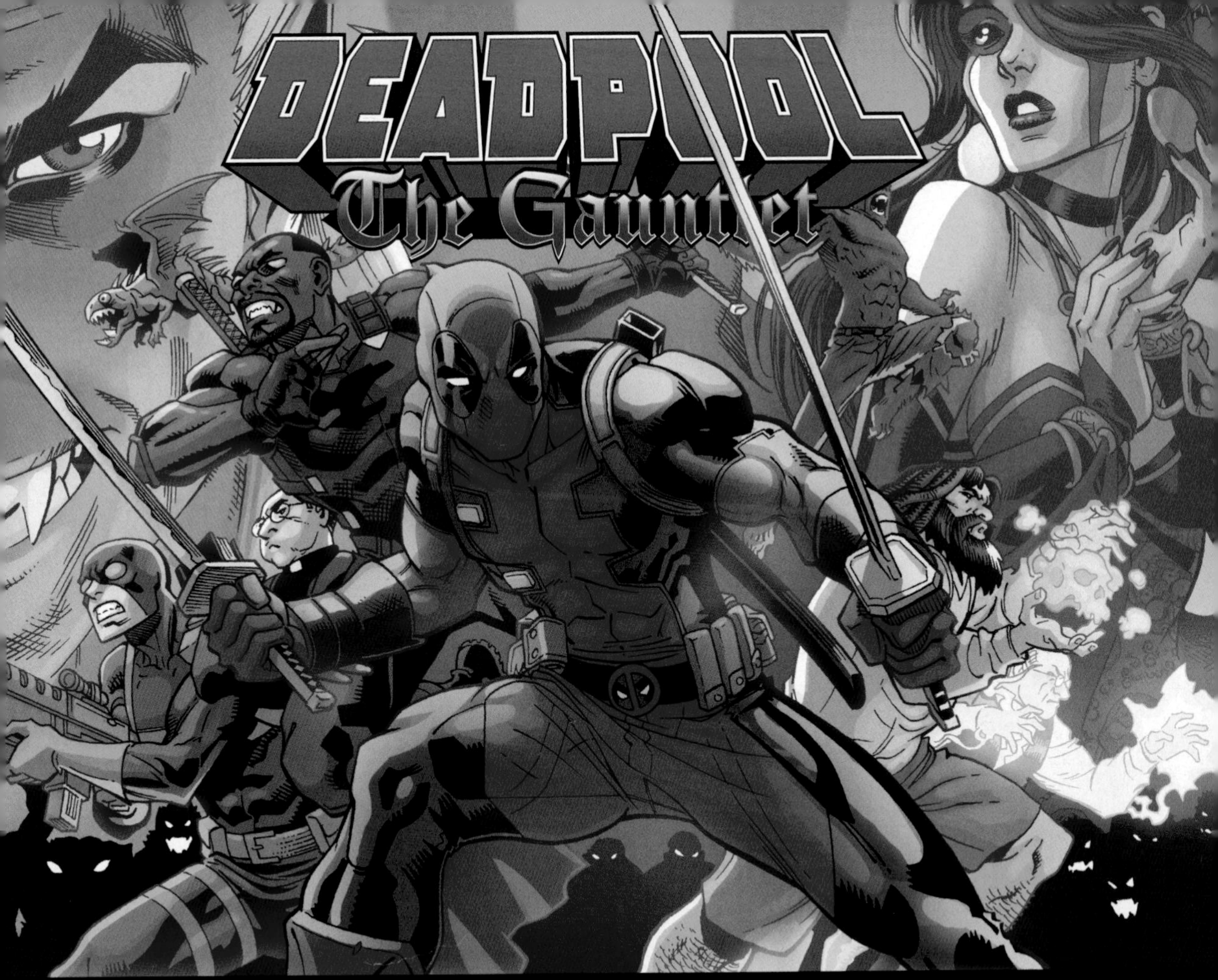
DEADPOOL
The Gauntlet

CHAPTER 13: GIVE LOVE A HAND

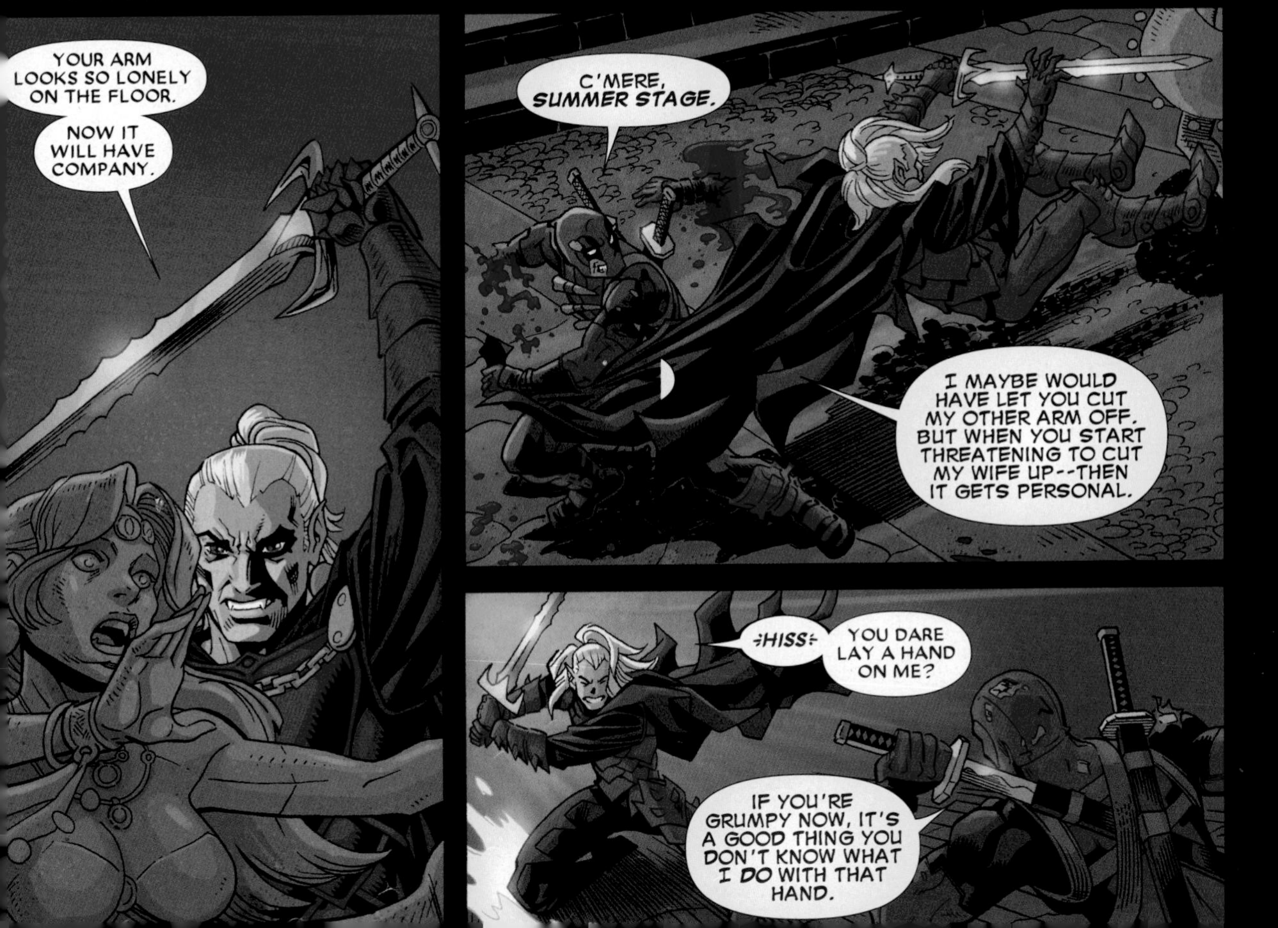
YOUR ARM LOOKS SO LONELY ON THE FLOOR.
NOW IT WILL HAVE COMPANY.
C'MERE, SUMMER STAGE.
I MAYBE WOULD HAVE LET YOU CUT MY OTHER ARM OFF. BUT WHEN YOU START THREATENING TO CUT MY WIFE UP--THEN IT GETS PERSONAL.
HISS
YOU DARE LAY A HAND ON ME?
IF YOU'RE GRUMPY NOW, IT'S A GOOD THING YOU DON'T KNOW WHAT I DO WITH THAT HAND.

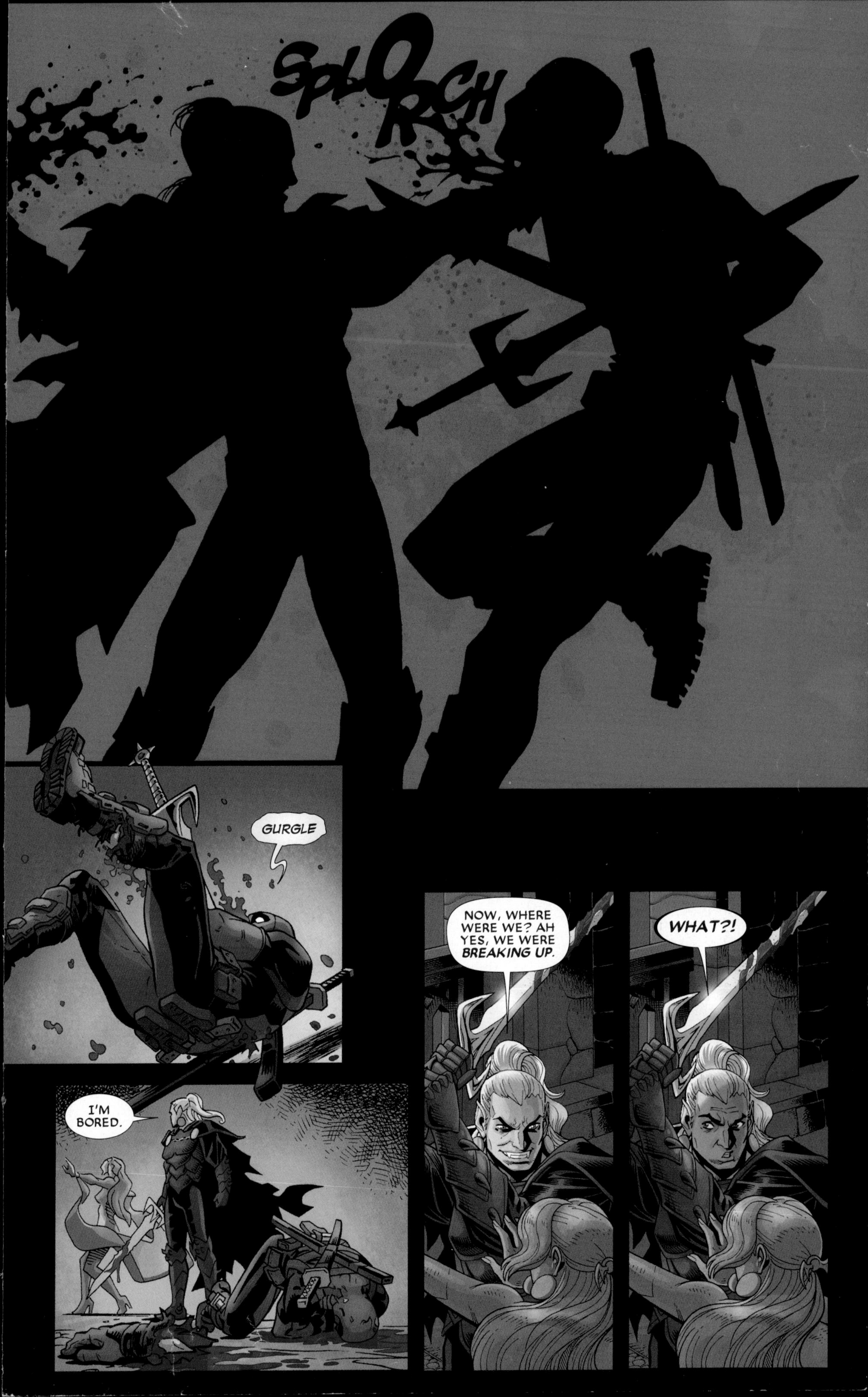
SPLORCH
GURGLE
I'M BORED.
NOW, WHERE WERE WE? AH YES, WE WERE *BREAKING UP*.
WHAT?!

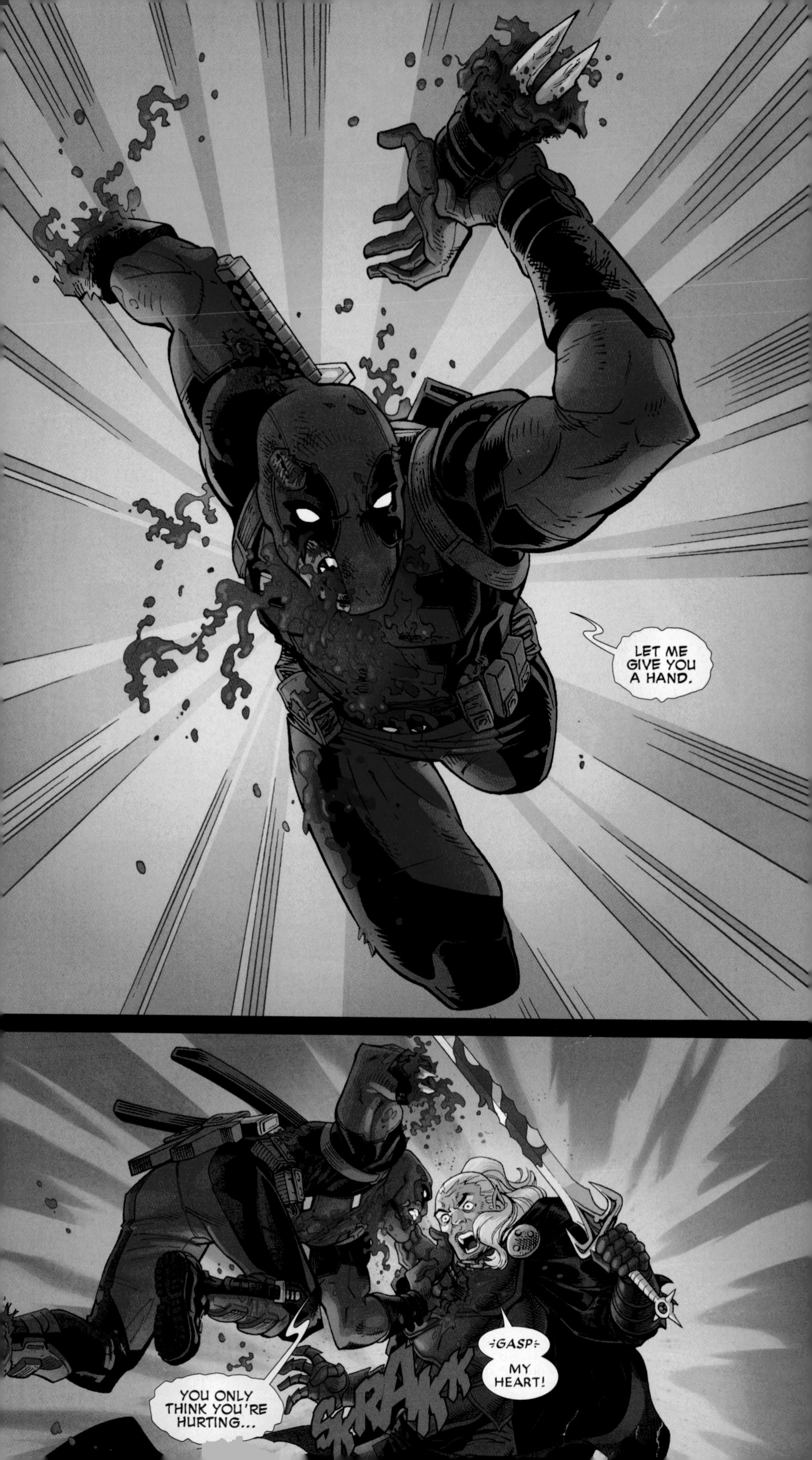
LET ME GIVE YOU A HAND.
YOU ONLY THINK YOU'RE HURTING...
SKRAKK
GASP
MY HEART!

OKAY, MEDUSA, YOU'RE GOING TO PUT A *REVERSE WHAMMY* ON MY WIFE SHIKLAH OVER THERE.

HANG ON, HONEY.

YOU FREE HER, AND I'LL HELP YOU GET A NEW BODY. IF YOU DON'T...WELL, IN THAT CASE I'LL JUST ∻WHISPER∻ ∻WHISPER∻

OH, I'M SO SCARED!

PFFT! PLEASE! YOU'RE NOT EVEN THE SCARIEST GUY THAT ROLLS WITH BATS.

ENOUGH! I WILL DO AS YOU ASK.

SAY CHEESE, HONEY.

WHY ISN'T IT WORKING?

IT IS-- BEHOLD!

YOU'RE BACK!

YOU SAVED ME.

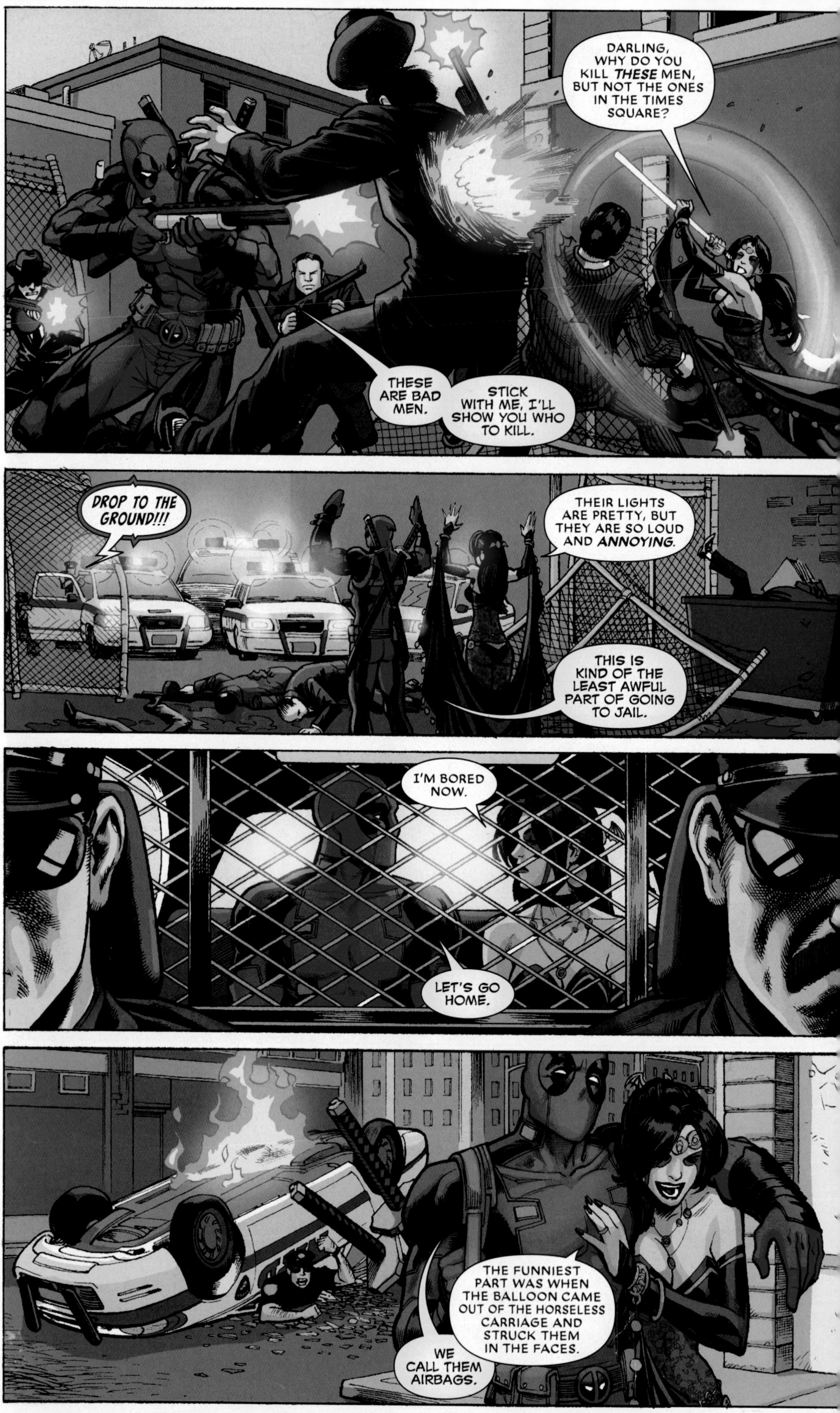
DARLING, WHY DO YOU KILL *THESE* MEN, BUT NOT THE ONES IN THE TIMES SQUARE?
THESE ARE BAD MEN.
STICK WITH ME, I'LL SHOW YOU WHO TO KILL.
DROP TO THE GROUND!!!
THEIR LIGHTS ARE PRETTY, BUT THEY ARE SO LOUD AND *ANNOYING*.
THIS IS KIND OF THE LEAST AWFUL PART OF GOING TO JAIL.
I'M BORED NOW.
LET'S GO HOME.
THE FUNNIEST PART WAS WHEN THE BALLOON CAME OUT OF THE HORSELESS CARRIAGE AND STRUCK THEM IN THE FACES.
WE CALL THEM AIRBAGS.

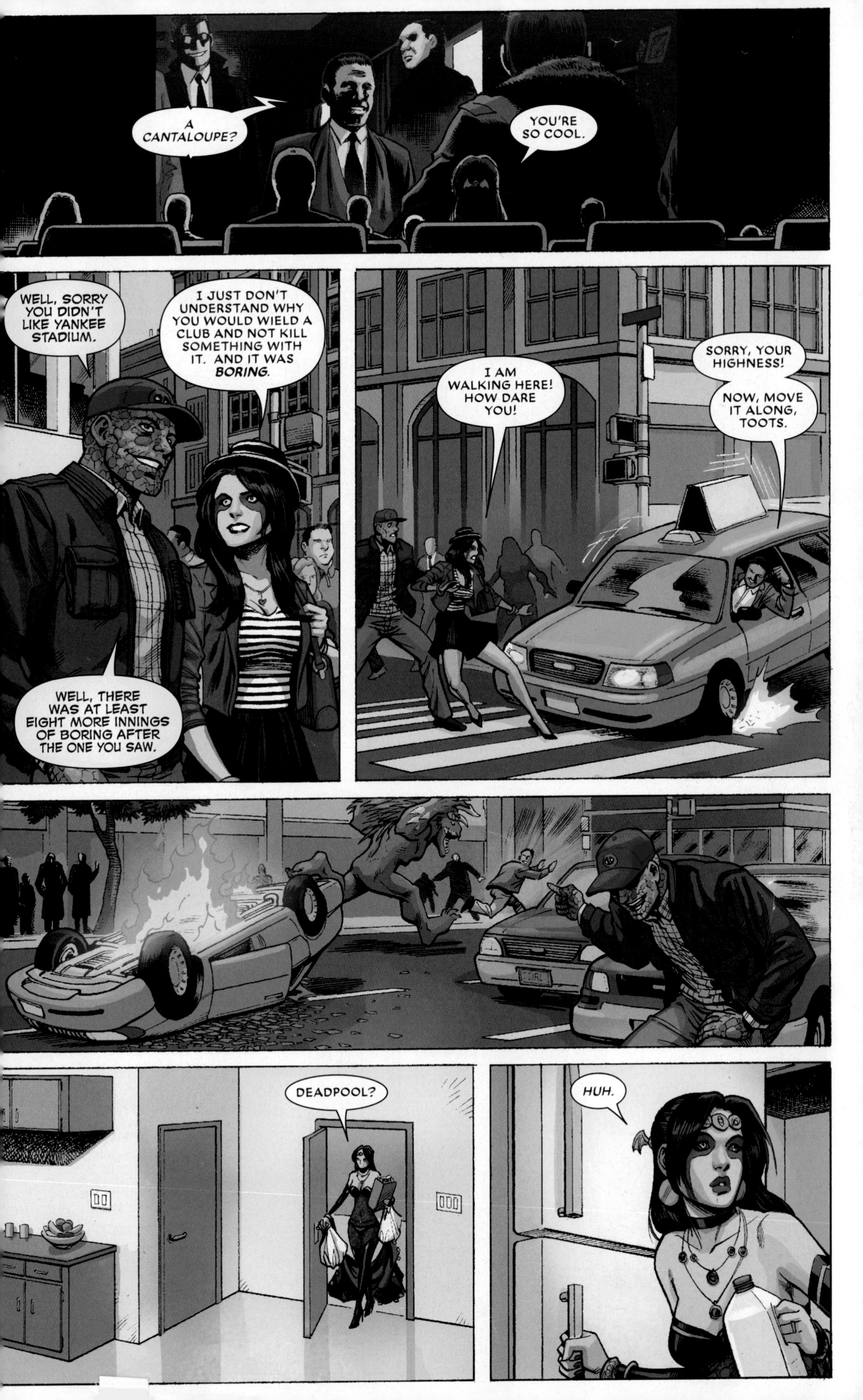
A CANTALOUPE?
YOU'RE SO COOL.
WELL, SORRY YOU DIDN'T LIKE YANKEE STADIUM.
I JUST DON'T UNDERSTAND WHY YOU WOULD WIELD A CLUB AND NOT KILL SOMETHING WITH IT. AND IT WAS BORING.
WELL, THERE WAS AT LEAST EIGHT MORE INNINGS OF BORING AFTER THE ONE YOU SAW.
I AM WALKING HERE! HOW DARE YOU!
SORRY, YOUR HIGHNESS!
NOW, MOVE IT ALONG, TOOTS.
DEADPOOL?
HUH.

IT'S CALLED *SCOTCH*?

YUP.

IT TASTES LIKE I'M KISSING A *CAMPFIRE*!

WHAT THE HELL?

I TOLD YOU.

DRACULA ALLOWED HIS PEOPLE TO BE MOCKED THUSLY?!

WAS THIS MADE BY A WIZARD?

YEAH, I GUESS KIND OF...

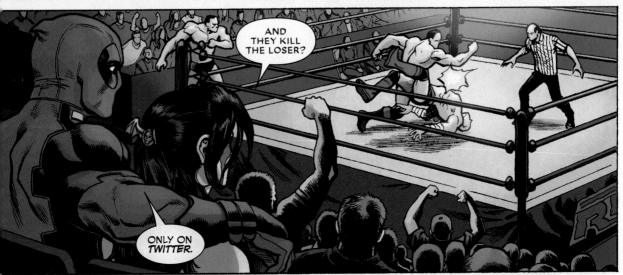

AND THEY KILL THE LOSER?

ONLY ON *TWITTER*.

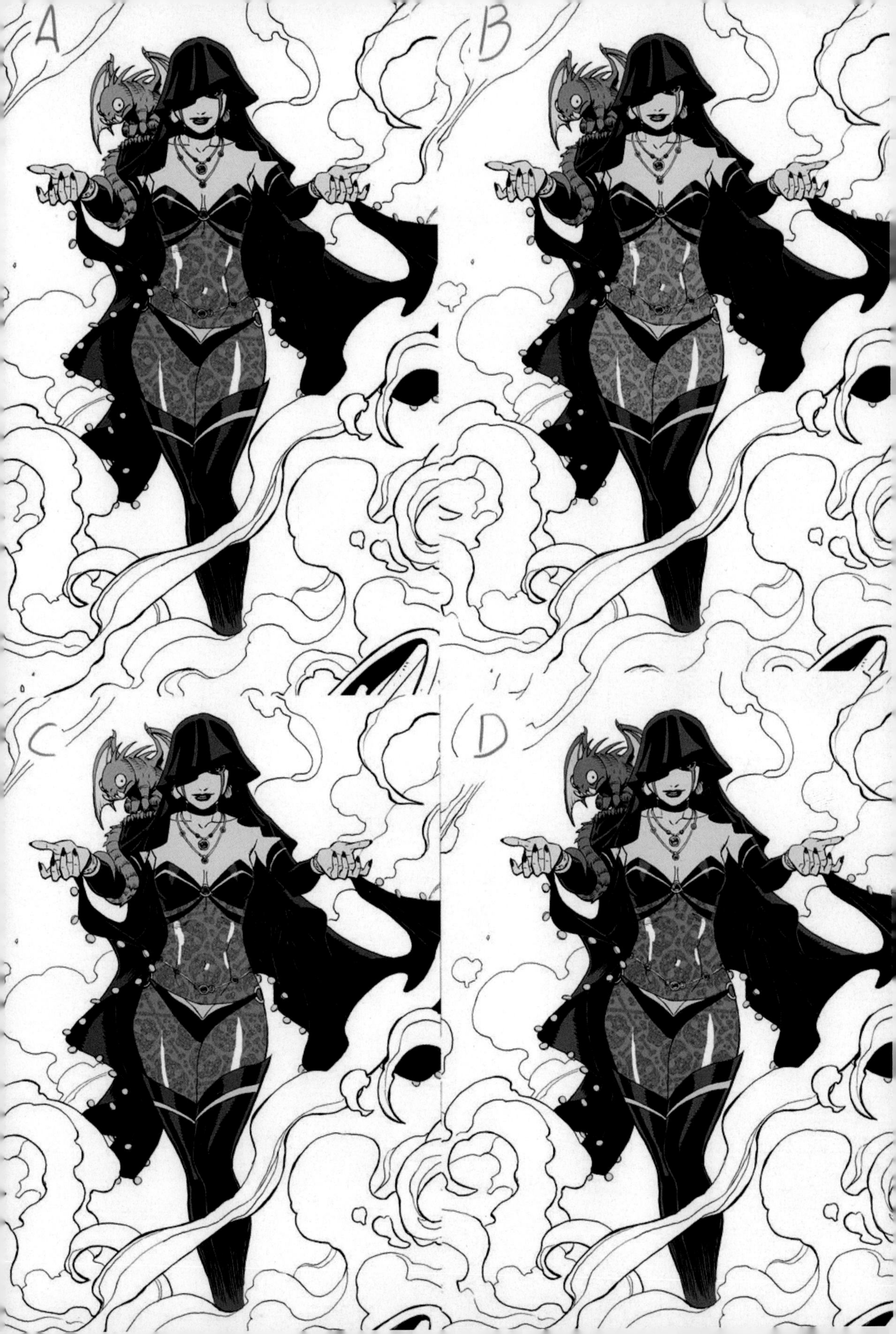
A
B
C
D

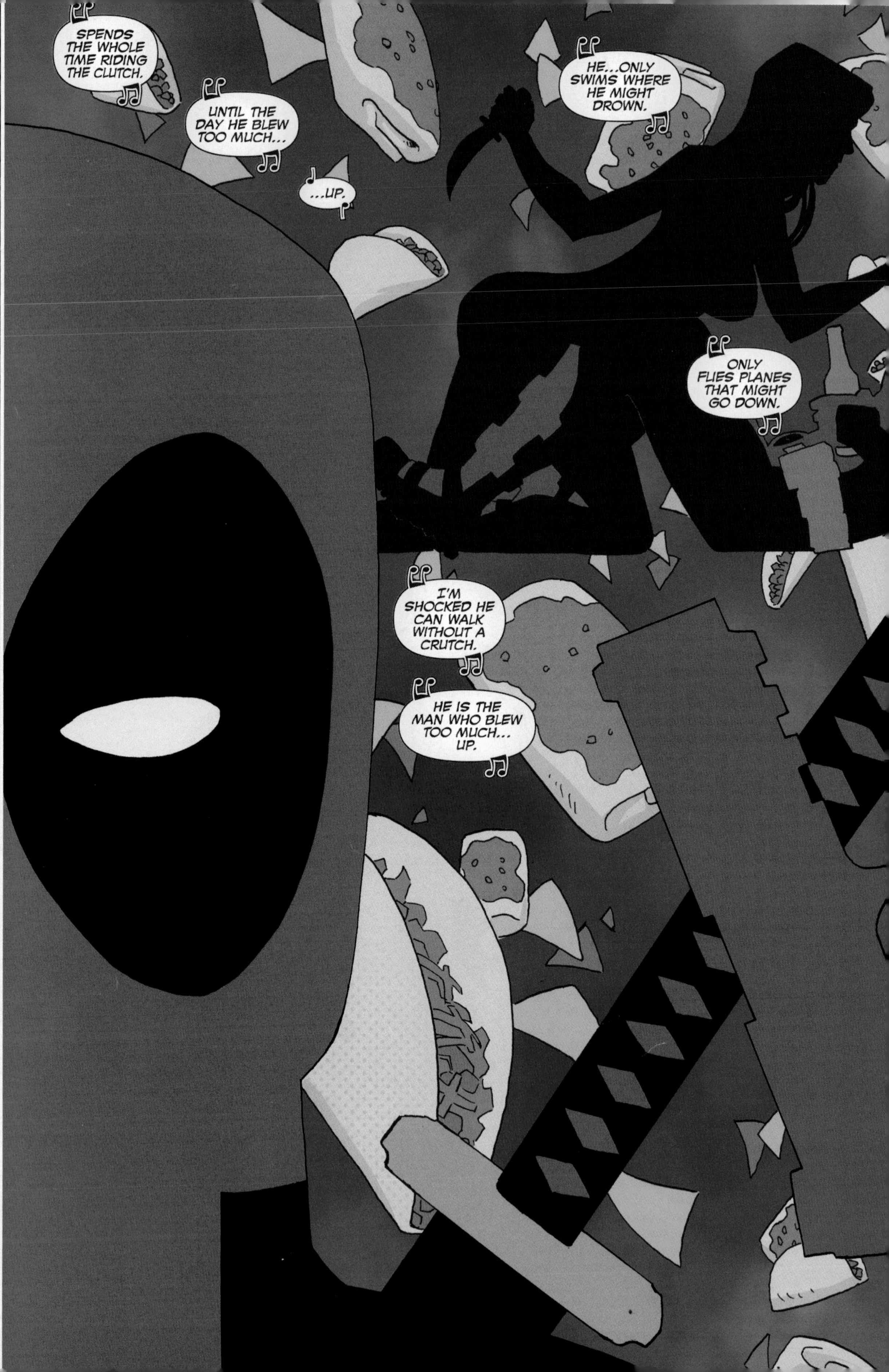
SPENDS THE WHOLE TIME RIDING THE CLUTCH.
UNTIL THE DAY HE BLEW TOO MUCH...
...UP.
HE...ONLY SWIMS WHERE HE MIGHT DROWN.
ONLY FLIES PLANES THAT MIGHT GO DOWN.
I'M SHOCKED HE CAN WALK WITHOUT A CRUTCH.
HE IS THE MAN WHO BLEW TOO MUCH... UP.

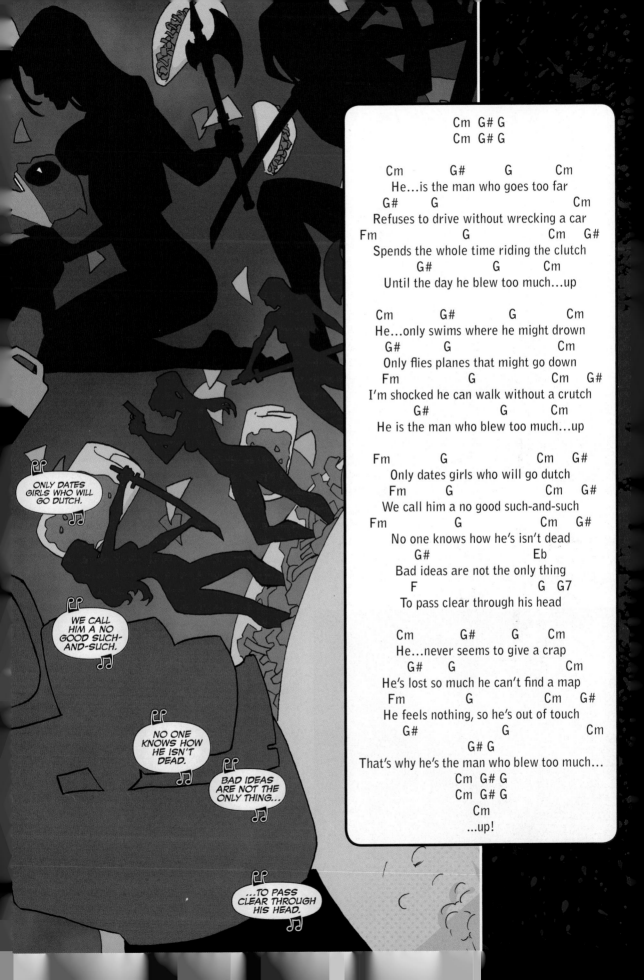

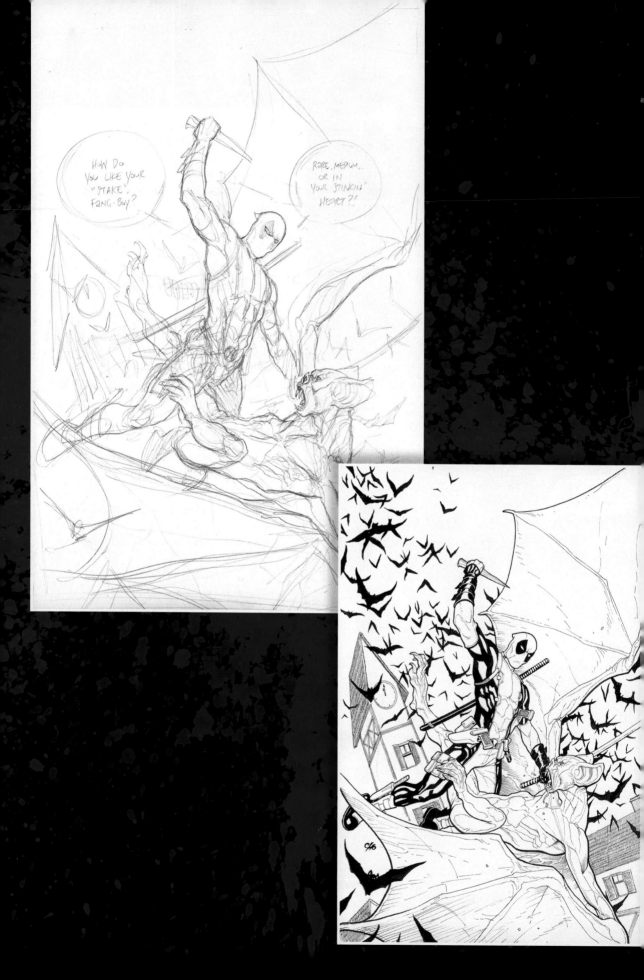

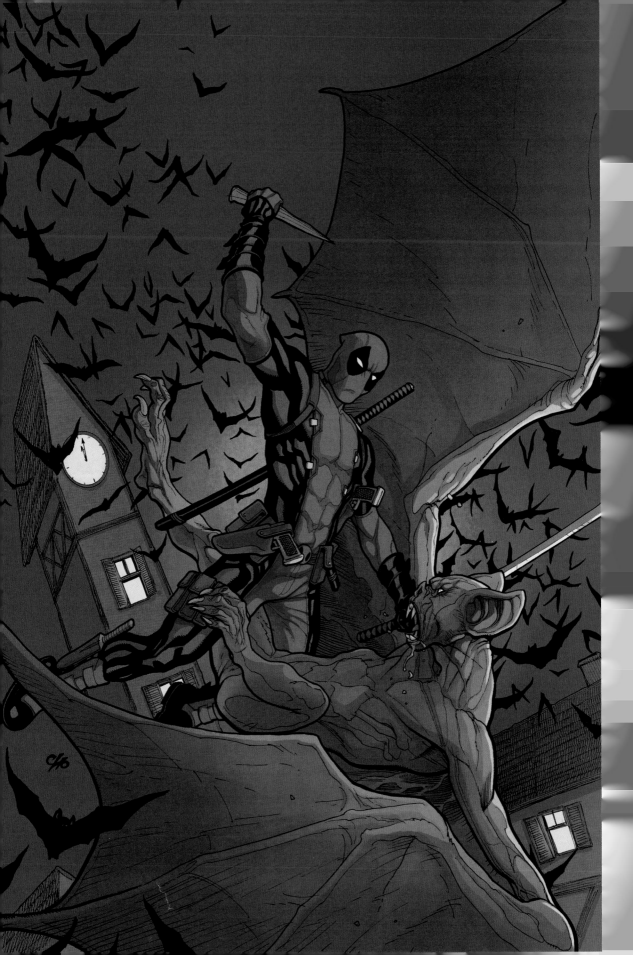

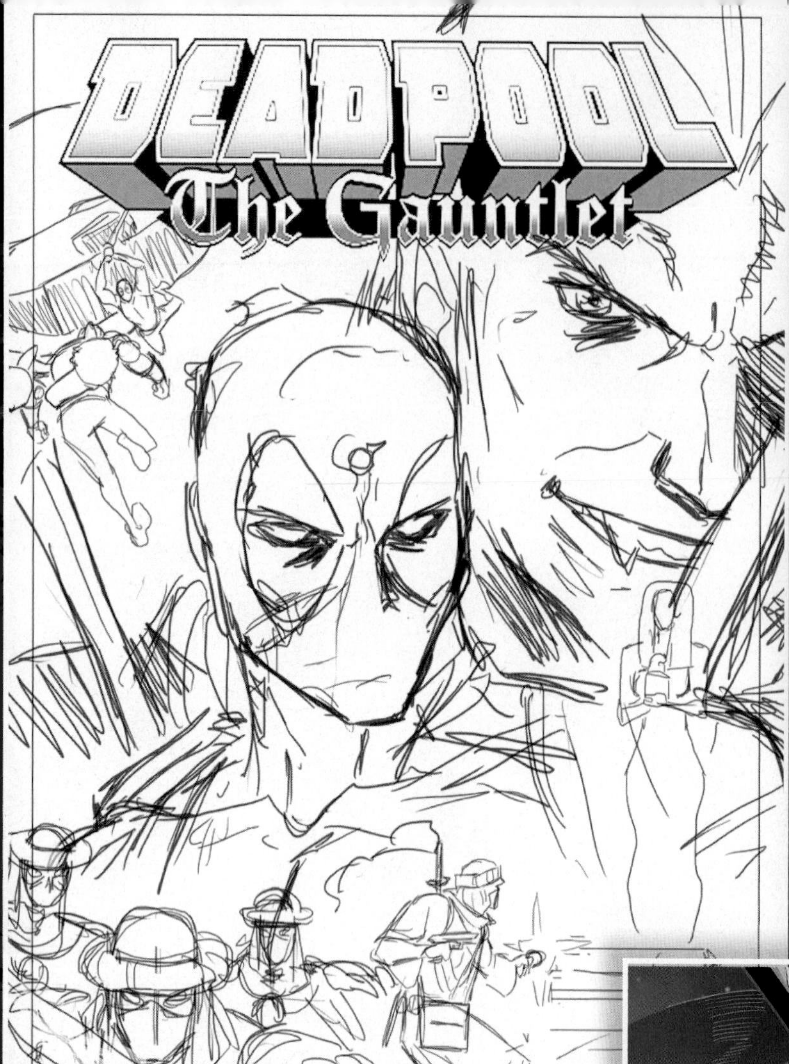
DEADPOOL
The Gauntlet

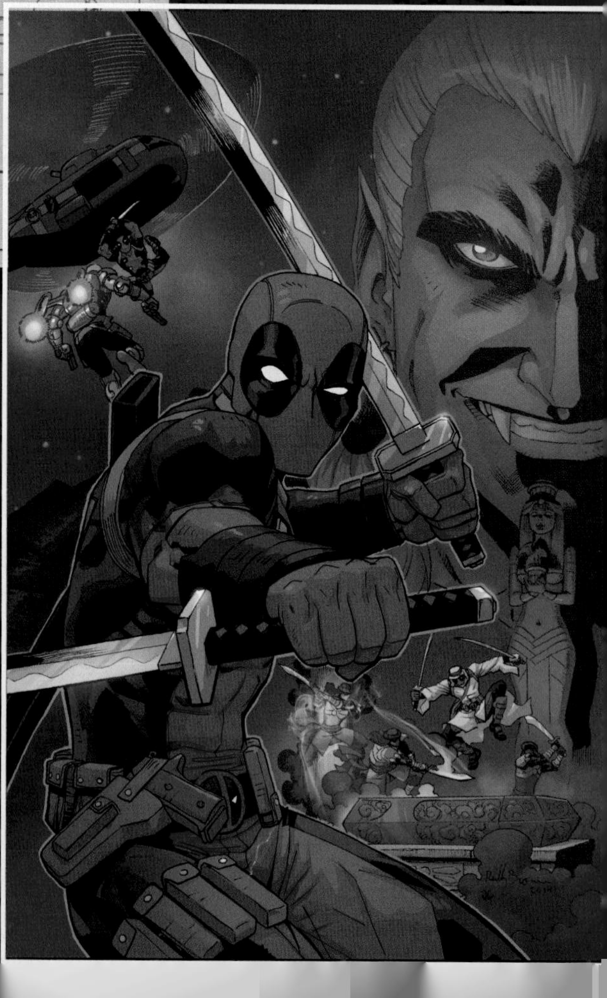

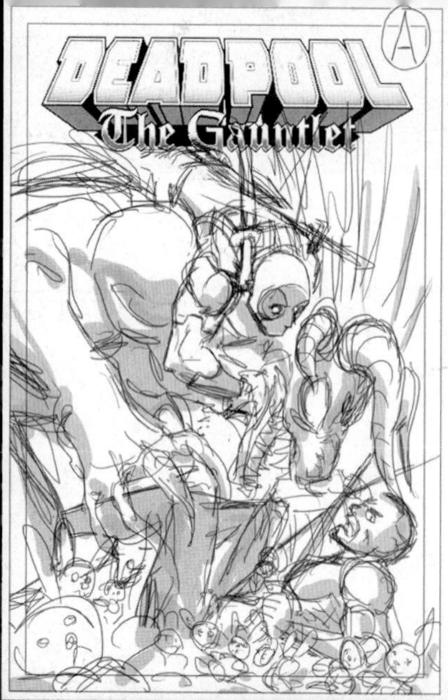
A
DEADPOOL
The Gauntlet
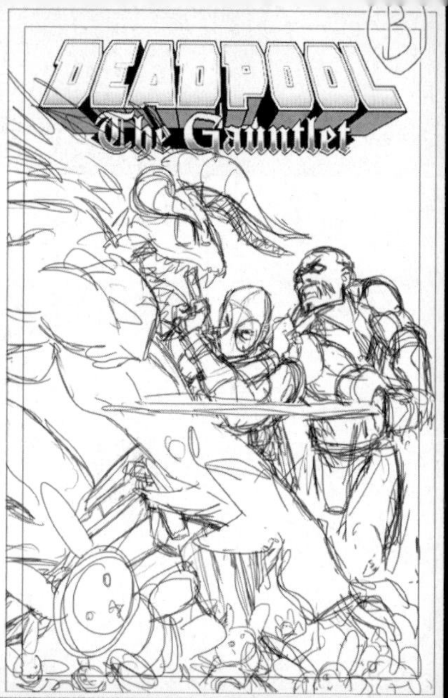
B
DEADPOOL
The Gauntlet
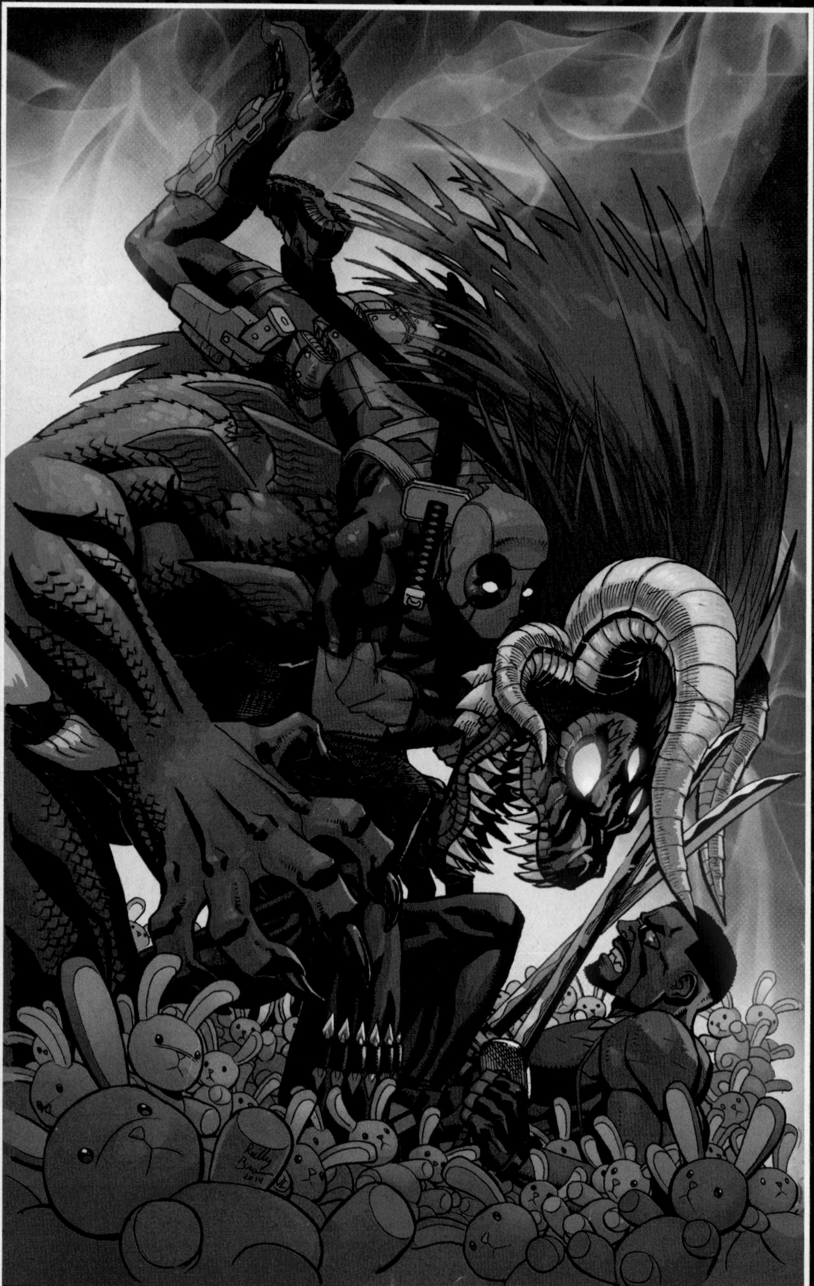

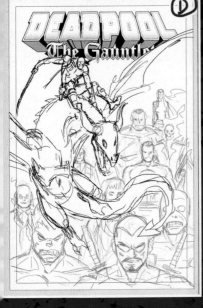

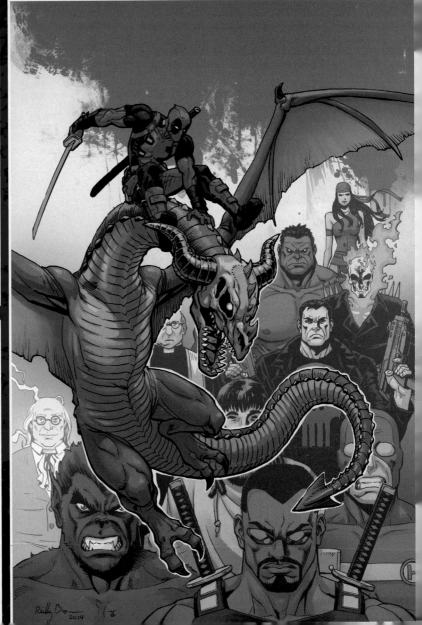

Infinite Comics are Marvel's newest and boldest jump into the world of digital comics. Crafted specifically to be read on the Marvel Comics App, Infinite Comics take advantage of new storytelling opportunities the digital realm makes possible. This story has been restructured into traditional print comics, but the original versions can be read on the Marvel Comics App to get the full effect.

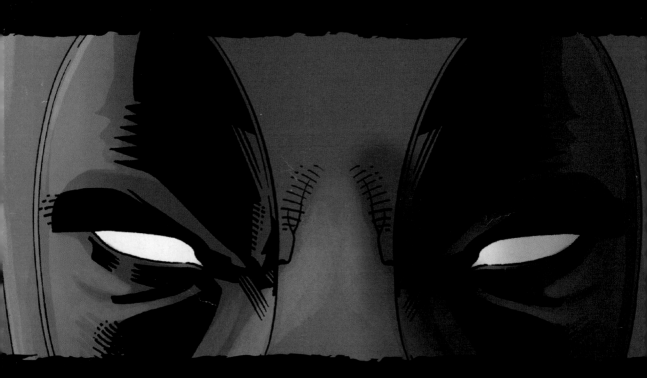